The Aftermath of Rape

Thomas W. McCahill
Linda C. Meyer
Arthur M. Fischman
Joseph J. Peters Institute

LexingtonBooks
D.C. Heath and Company
Lexington, Massachusetts
Toronto

Library of Congress Cataloging in Publication Data

McCahill, Thomas W
    The aftermath of rape.

    Includes index.
    1. Rape—Pennsylvania—Philadelphia—Case studies. 2. Victims of crimes—Pennsylvania—Philadelphia—Case studies. 3. Criminal justice, Administration of Pennsylvania—Philadelphia—Case studies. I. Meyer, Linda C., joint author. II. Fischman, Arthur M., joint author. III. Title.
    HV6568.P5M23   364.1'53   79–1952
    ISBN 0–669–03018–X

Second printing, April 1981.

Published simultaneously in Canada

Printed in the United States of America

International Standard Book Number: 0–669–03018–X

Library of Congress Catalog Card Number: 79–1952

This book is dedicated to the memory of Dr. Joseph J. Peters, whose pioneering work continues to provide impetus for the improved treatment of the victims of sexual assault.

Contents

List of Figures

List of Tables

Foreword

The history of the project reported here is nearly as fascinating as the results. Dr. Joseph Peters, the late director, the most humane psychiatrist researcher I have ever known, was the father of the concern for studying the victims of rape. His indefatigable energy, his abiding empathy and understanding of his patients and research subjects, led him to propose a project that involved following rape victims far beyond the immediate moment of the act of victimization. Joe Peters had already spent many years in the study and therapy of sex offenders, including those who had committed rape. But he became more and more interested in rape victims, and initiated one of the first and most elaborate research projects dealing with victims. Since then, coinciding with the rapid rise of women's groups of various kinds, many rape centers and clinics have appeared all over the country. Books and articles on rape and rape victims have emerged in such abundance that it is difficult for any of us to keep up with, or properly evaluate, these publications.

Between Menachem Amir's *Patterns of Forcible Rape* and Susan Brownmiller's *Against Our Will: Men, Women and Rape,* there have been many reports on rape. But I know of no publication that contains the quantity and quality of data on rape victims that appear in this volume. The researchers involved in this project have visited the police, the courts, the victims at different times, and have followed the criminal justice attrition of cases. There are facts never before collected on what happens to mind and body, and the dreams and the work habits of victims of rape.

If there are flaws in the methods of data collection or in the precision of some information, we should remember that all social science studies are vulnerable to rigorous scrutinizing. In general, however, even the most critical observer will have to concede that this volume covers new territory and must be considered a pioneer effort. I am pleased to have been involved in this project in a small way.

Rape is a trauma experienced primarily by women but also by men, mostly in prison, presumably. Rape is an act of violence, an unwanted invasion of one's corporeal privacy. The vicissitudes of culture, to a great extent, determine our response to this violent invasion. In some cultures both the victim and the victim's peers prefer death to living with the knowledge of the experience. In the United States and much of Western society, the responses of the victim and friends have been muted and the notion of helping to overcome the experience in order to live a normal life has taken hold. Such a reaction does not reduce the seriousness of the offense; it reduces the trauma of the episode to the victim. I see this change as desirable. For it promotes continued treatment of the crime as serious with severe sanctions while encouraging the victim's emotional health.

In this volume the reader will find entirely new data, carefully analyzed, clearly presented. I can well imagine that this study will be a prototype for the future.

July 1979   *Marvin E. Wolfgang*
                                                        University of Pennsylvania

Acknowledgments

The most important contributors to this project were the thousands of victims of sexual assault who shared their feelings, problems, and concerns with us. They opened themselves to our questions and gave us their confidence, because they hoped that their experiences would help others and that, perhaps, if they talked about what had happened, other victims who followed them would suffer less.

Whenever a project of this scope and duration is undertaken, the number of individuals whose efforts make it possible is enormous. Hundreds of individuals were involved in the collection and analysis of data and compilation of findings.

We are greatly indebted to the late Joseph J. Peters, M.D. It was in 1970, 15 years after beginning his work with sex offenders, that Joe Peters began this project. In his private psychiatric practice, he uncovered cases where childhood sexual abuse profoundly affected the lives of victims far into adulthood. And, while the feminist response to rape was just beginning to stir, Joe Peters wrote "The Lonely Plight of the Victim of Rape." As project director and founder of the Center for Rape Concern, he led us in our work. His death in 1976 was a professional and personal loss.

It is to Joseph J. Peters that we dedicate this book, and it is in his memory that the Center for Rape Concern has changed its name to the Joseph J. Peters Institute.

Special thanks must go to research assistant Nancy E. Carroll, whose careful attention to detail was critical in her supervision of coding and data preparation. Her untiring assistance was applied to many tasks, including analysis of findings and preparation of earlier reports.

Anne Lawrence, our court observer, made a major contribution to the manuscript. Her persistence in her task and thoughtful observations have provided us with added insight into the true workings of the courts and have given life to the impersonal data of the computers.

Kathleen Flanagan, chief social worker during the project period, was the first person hired for the project. She spoke with many victims to learn of their concerns and took from them information that led to the development of our research interviews. The task of using clinicians to collect data was a difficult one, requiring a balancing of clinical empathy and research objectivity. Kathy Flanagan was able to maintain this balance.

Special clinical consultants to this book were Maddi-Jane Stern, A.C.S.W., and Lance S. Wright, M.D. Their thoughtful comments and the in-depth analysis offered in their review of book drafts provided clinical insight and assisted greatly in development of part II of this book.

The staff and board of directors of the Joseph J. Peters Institute, funded by the Philadelphia County Office of Mental Health/Mental Retardation, have supported us throughout our task. Elaine Palusci Bencivengo, executive director, has aided in the editing process and has been a source of encouragement in the completion of this work. Board members provided useful comments and suggestions. Our thanks go especially to board members Marvin E. Wolfgang, Ph.D., and Robert Sadoff, M.D., who have offered their assistance in all stages of this project. Their input into part III of this book was critical to its development, as they offered constructive feedback as dissertation supervisor and committee member for two of the authors. The Office of the Court Administrator of the Philadelphia Court of Common Pleas and the Philadelphia Police Department provided much useful data and case materials to the Center. Particular thanks go to J. Dennis Moran, Esq., chief deputy court administrator; William Fischer, deputy court administrator for data processing; and Mary Picado, systems analyst.

In addition, computer analysis was completed by Gerard Mitchell and Sally Preston of the ECTA Corporation and William Lattimer, formerly of the Wharton Computer Center. Editing of the final manuscript was aided by Gerard Mitchell, research assistance was provided by Barbara Malett, Esq., and the arduous task of typing was completed by Linda Thorpe.

Finally, special thanks must go to our respective spouses Jane, Bruce, and Janet, for their support and patience during the two years devoted by the authors to the preparation of this book.

Thomas W. McCahill
Linda C. Meyer
Arthur M. Fischman

Part I
Background and Methodology

1

Introduction

Before the 1970s, attention was rarely focused on rape victims and their adjustment problems. Their invisibility served both to express and to reinforce a broad range of assumptions about male–female sexuality and roles, and about rape victims and their assailants in particular. Victims were assumed to be defiled by and responsible for the actions of rapists, who seemed to be exercising, in extremis, a male prerogative. Silence, then, was a socially endorsed form of contempt, since it could so easily be mistaken for an expression of protectiveness and pity for these now "fallen" women.

By the date of the American bicentennial, however, enough had been written on rape to fill a small bookshelf with books, reprints from magazines and professional journals, and copies of government-sponsored reports. Susan Brownmiller's *Against Our Will* appeared on the *New York Times's* bestseller list. *A Case of Rape,* starring Elizabeth Montgomery, captured the largest Neilsen ratings of any television movie up to that time. In some cities rape crisis centers celebrated their fifth birthday during a decade when most state legislatures changed their laws, many police departments altered their practices, and many judges and prosecutors reevaluated their response to rape cases. At least one judge lost his job because he stated in the courtroom that many victims deserved what they got.

This accelerated pace of change occurred in response to a series of specific charges raised in the early seventies, mostly by members of the newly emerging feminist movement. Feminists claimed that the sociosexual attitudes held by many Americans tend to discredit the accounts of rape victims and that this same attitude tends to excuse or even champion rape. In this context, friends and family members (particularly husbands) often were seen to blame rather than support the victim, thus making her postrape adjustment even more difficult. Charges were leveled against practices in emergency rooms that treated or refused to treat rape victims, against police handling of complaints, against laws that incorporated the logic of blaming rape victims, and against courtroom procedures, characterized as inquisitional, that placed on trial the victim and her sex life rather than the defendant.

This project was supported from 1972-1975 by a grant from the National Institute of Mental Health, Center for Studies in Crime and Delinquency, grant R01#21304. When funds from NIMH were exhausted, the project was continued to completion with support from the Philadelphia General Hospital Research Fund, private contributions, personal investment by the authors, and funds provided by the ECTA Corporation.

On the face of things, there was enough validity and sufficient victim testimony to make these charges undeniable. As one result, a new image of the rape victim began to take hold. The character portrayed by Elizabeth Montgomery serves as a paradigm. Her victimization only begins when she is raped twice by an assailant: her marriage deteriorates, the rapist is acquitted, and the entire medical–judicial system betrays her. It is in response to this paradigm that efforts have begun to aid victims of sexual assault.

In the past, however, no investigation has systematically explored the consequences of rape. Much of the available evidence has been retrospective and highly subjective in nature. Although some studies have made excellent use of such data, conclusions are often founded on the impressions of a small number of people.

In contrast, this book is based on the largest investigation of rape victims ever conducted. Persons surveyed include 1,401 women of all ages who reported a rape or sexual assault to authorities in Philadelphia. For the purposes of this study, rape and/or sexual assault is defined to include sexual intercourse, cunnilingus, fellatio, anal intercourse, and any intrusion of any part of another's body or any object manipulated by the other into the genital or anal opening of the victim's body, or the intentional touching of the victim's sexual parts by another when this was accomplished by force, by threat of force, or against the victim's will. Attempted rapes were included, as were cases of statutory rape (defined by Pennsylvania law, at the time of the study, as sexual intercourse with a person under the age of 16).

The Center for Rape Concern (CRC) in Philadelphia managed the collection of information and its analysis, supported by several funding sources over a 5–year period.

In addition to this large sample, this book utilizes information gathered from a variety of sources. Some victims had as many as four interviews conducted at their homes; most interviews lasted one or two hours, with the initial interview occurring within 48 hours after the rape. Many victims also agreed to an interview with a psychiatrist. This book details the problems victims encountered immediately after the rape and the adjustment patterns present then and 1 year later. Police provided information on each case, as did the emergency room staff and the court administrator. In addition, each case is detailed at every stage of the criminal justice process. Information was collected on whether police believed the victim, whether the case went to trial, the case's ultimate outcome, and so forth.

The findings are presented with several specific audiences in mind. For social workers, crisis center staff, psychiatrists, and other professionals who interact with rape victims, the findings will aid in estimating the problems they are likely to encounter.

In addition, the rape victim can see that her reactions are not abnormal—that they are a natural consequence of crisis. Other victims have experienced—and overcome—problems similar to hers. This book, then, can provide the victim with some of the reassurance often gained from what is called "crisis intervention."

The findings are presented in such a way that a rape victim, her family members, and friends can better understand exactly what is happening. By examining closely the lives of the victims in this book, a careful reader may be able to arrive at a clearer self-understanding.

Part III deals with the criminal justice response to rape, presenting a variety of findings of special interest to police, prosecutors, and judges who handle rape complaints. Very few studies in the field of criminology specify what occurs in cases of a particular crime from the moment police are notified through ultimate disposition in court, if the case gets that far. This book details not only the processing of rape complaints in the criminal justice system but also the types of cases eliminated at each stage.

Nor is this presentation entirely descriptive. National surveys are drawn on to aid in the interpretation of findings, and prescriptive statements are frequently made. That is, the text goes beyond a description of what is to suggest what could and should be.

The following is a brief description of the organization of this book. The second chapter details how the information was obtained and how it was analyzed. Much of the technical information can be found in the notes following that chapter. However, it is important for all readers to understand the basic technique used to present the findings.

The four chapters in part II examine the adjustment patterns that victims have developed and explore factors associated with the development of each pattern.

One set of postrape adjustment patterns considered involves changes in eating and sleeping habits and in frequency of nightmares. Many victims eat less, sleep less, and experience nightmares they did not have before the rape.

Other parts of the analysis deal with fear and altered behavior. Most victims of rape report an increase in fear when they are out on the street alone or when they are home alone. Many victims make changes in their social activities; typically, they go out less.

Many of the findings in part II cover the subject of the victim's relationship with the opposite sex after the rape. Often victims begin to harbor feelings of fear or hatred toward men who are strangers; others have an increase in negative feelings toward men they know. These feelings may play a role in a number of possible changes in the lives of rape victims. For example, a victim may stumble over her words when she talks to the butcher or awkwardly cut short meetings with a male coworker. A relationship with a husband or boyfriend may deteriorate, and sexual relations may be adversely affected. A victim may suspect that she has become less attractive sexually because of the rape.

Additional findings focus on the impact rape has on the victim's life at home and on her relations with her family and, especially, with her husband. Part II includes a summary of the most important findings that result from an analysis of adjustment problems.

Part III of the book deals with the criminal justice response to rape. A large number of women who report that they have been raped are not believed by the police. A lengthy chapter examines how these victims were turned away by police and suggests why other victims are more likely to be believed.

Another group of victims is believed, but their cases are not labeled rape. They might be called "corrupting the morals of a minor" or "simple assault" and, therefore, do not count as rape complaints for the record.

Police activities aimed at apprehending the offender are carefully studied, as is police performance in court. Findings about police are then summarized, and the court system is introduced.

Victim complaints of rape are followed throughout the entire adult justice system. Some cases only make it as far as the preliminary hearing: disheartened by numerous continuances or frightened after witnessing other victims on the stand, the victim may withdraw cooperation and no longer show up.

In some cases the defendant pleads guilty; these cases are described. Experiences in jury trials are compared with experiences in nonjury trials, and cases that result in a guilty verdict are compared with those that end in acquittal. Cases that result in a prison sentence are contrasted with those which result in other dispositions. Finally, possible effects of the courtroom experience on the victim are discussed.

Following a criminal justice wrap-up, there is a summary of the entire book. Major findings are reiterated. There is discussion of both the myths refuted and the ideas supported by these findings, as well as a discussion on ways in which these findings can be used as a diagnostic tool by professionals who provide counseling to rape victims.

A special problem plagues studies like this one. Whereas reports based on a small sample can involve the reader in each victim's life, in a large sample study it is difficult to convey vividly the real costs of particular rapes. When presenting findings derived from hundreds of cases in which the victim was brutally beaten or intimidated with a knife or gun, the individual horror is lost. In the section on victim adjustment, therefore, several cases are presented in greater detail to concretize the findings. Although we are still not satisfied in this respect, we are confident that the present study will serve not only to document but also to combat the ugly consequences of sexual assault.

2

The Philadelphia Sexual Assault Victim Study

The basic source of information for this book, the Philadelphia Sexual Assault Victim Study, includes women of all ages who reported rape and who were examined at Philadelphia General Hospital between April 1, 1973 and June 30, 1974. Child victims (that is, those aged 12 and younger) were included up to June 30, 1975. During the study period there were 1,401 reports of rape made to Philadelphia General Hospital. The total number of victims, however, is less than 1,401, because twenty-five individuals made more than one report of rape during the course of the research. Following is a brief description of the characteristics of rape victims in the Philadelphia Sexual Assault Victim Study.

Characteristics of Rape Victims and Incidents

Victim age: Among all victims, 16.6% were children (0–11 years old), 23% were young adolescents (12–15 years old), 24.7% were young adults (16–20 years old), and 35.8% were adults (21 or more years old). For clients who were interviewed by a social worker, approximately two-thirds were under 21. Using census figures for comparison, victims who report rape to the authorities are disproportionately likely to be 20 to 24 years old and much less likely to be 45 or more years old.

Victim race: Three-fourths (75.4%) of the victims studied were black or hispanic. Among interviewed victims, the figure approaches 80%. Although black females make up 73.4% of the rape study sample, black females are only 34.3% of the female population in Philadelphia. Consequently, a black female is nearly six times as likely (5.7 to 1) to be a victim in a reported rape in Philadelphia as is a white female.

Victim marital status: The overwhelming majority (78.2%) of all victims were single at the time of rape, a finding which may be related to the high likelihood of victims to be under 21 years of age. Of the remainder, women formerly married (separated, widowed, or divorced) were slightly more than half as numerous as those who were currently married (13.2% of the total as compared to 8.7%).

Victim median income: Based on residence at time of rape and 1970 Bureau of Census data, a large majority (70.2%) of the victims in this study were determined to have a median income of less than $9,000 per year, and virtually all (95.4%) placed below an annual figure of $12,000. Women in lower-income groups, then, are much more likely to report rape than those in more affluent brackets.

Victim behavior problems prior to rape: Of victims for whom this information is available (here, and in subsequent victim characteristics, figures are derived from information collected at first home interviews, $N = 790$), almost one-fifth (19%) reported incidents of truancy and fighting, and a smaller number (12.2%) were runaways during childhood or adolescence. A similar proportion (15.1%) had had some previous trouble with police at the time of rape, either as adolescents or adults.

Victim prior psychiatric assistance: Over one-quarter (26.8%) of the victims interviewed had previously had some kind of private or publicly funded mental health counseling, including psychiatric, psychological, or other psychotherapy.

Victim source of income: Public assistance was a source of income for almost one-half (45.6%) of the victims interviewed; approximately one-fifth (18.6%) of the victims were themselves employed, and the remainder were dependent on employed family members.

Victim prior sexual assaults: Slightly more than one-fifth (20.1%) of the victims in this study had been sexually assaulted by the same or another offender at least once before the present rape.

Victim-offender relationship: A large percentage (45.6%) of the rapes for which this information is available involved an offender who was a total stranger to the victim. A relative stranger (that is, a person whom the victim had seen before but had never spoken to) was associated with a much smaller percentage of cases (13%). A casual acquaintance and/or friend figured in over one-third of all rapes (36.4%), and nuclear and/or extended family members were involved in proportionately the smallest group (10.3%). Most of the rapes (85.7%) were intraracial.

Physical force: A majority of victims (64.4%) reported being pushed or held in the course of the rape incident. Victims were often slapped (16.9%), beaten brutally (22%), and/or choked (19.7%).

Nonphysical force: In most of the cases under review (84.3%), some kind of nonphysical force was exerted on the victim. Coercion, or the threatening of bodily harm, was present in over one-half of the rapes (55.7%). Many incidents involved intimidation of the victim; that is, the offender made threatening statements or gestures, either with an object or weapon (36.2% of the cases) or without one (19.6%). Tempting (that is, verbal or nonverbal attempts by the offender to gain access to the victim) was a feature in over one-quarter of the incidents (28.1%).

Sexual acts perpetrated: Although penile-vaginal intercourse occurred during most of these rapes (83.4%), other sexual acts were also perpetrated by the offenders, including fondling/caressing (18.8% of the cases), fellatio

(10%), and other undefined sexual activity (11.9%). Some cases involved more than one kind of sexual act, and repeated intercourse by the same offender occurred in almost one-fourth of the cases (23.4%). Cunnilingus, rectal intercourse, and acts of penile-labial contact without penetration were rarely present (6.1%, 5.3%, and 5.6% respectively).

When rape occurred: More than half of these rapes took place when it was dark (59.1%), and weekends were slightly more likely to be times of assault than were weekdays.

Place of rape: Whereas a majority of rapes took place elsewhere, in a significant number (42%) the setting was either the victim's or the rapist's home.

Duration of assault incident: A majority (62.8%) of the rape incidents occurred in less than an hour, with most of these, in fact, lasting less than one-half hour. In a significant number of assaults (24.7% of the total), however, the duration of the incident was between one and three hours.

What victims think should be done to offender: For cases in which this information is available, a majority (58.8%) believed that the offender ought to be jailed after capture, whereas a very small group (3.6%) thought that the offender should be set free. Victims who endorse severe punishment—execution, castration, or beating—outnumber those who feel that professional help for the offender is in order (16.2% versus 13%).

Primary reason for reporting rape to police: A desire for help or comfort was most frequently listed as the primary reason for calling police (in 38% of the cases), followed by a wish to have the rapist punished (23.3%), a fear that the offender would rape the victim or someone else again (18.4%), a feeling of social responsibility (12.3%), and other reasons (7.9%).

Study Goals

Because so little was known about rape and the social and psychological effects of rape on victims, the Center for Rape Concern began a preliminary investigation in 1970. Research staff developed data collection forms that were loosely structured to permit a social worker or psychiatric resident to inquire into as many areas of the victims' reactions to their assaults as seemed productive. Between 1970 and 1972 victims who had reported rape to Philadelphia General Hospital were interviewed in regard to significant problem areas.

The information was analyzed, and the interviewers and research staff developed increasingly detailed and refined questionnaires oriented toward the major concerns expressed by the interviewed victims. In this respect, then, it was the victims' concerns and responses that helped to develop the research questionnaire. When several victims raised similar questions or problems, the item was considered appropriate for systematic study and was included in the data collection instrument eventually used in the Philadelphia Assault Victim Study.

The formal research study, begun in April 1973, had as primary goals: (1) the articulation of adjustment patterns to sexual assault based on problems and concerns uncovered in the preliminary 3–year investigation; and (2) the specification of techniques of long–term counseling of victims of sexual assault. Later, it became apparent that interactions with the criminal justice system were extremely important to rape adjustment. As a consequence, another goal was added: (3) the detailed description of the criminal justice response to rape. A discussion of how these goals were attained follows.

Methodology

A female rape victim became a subject of this research when she came to Philadelphia General Hospital Emergency Room alleging rape. In Philadelphia, according to police directive 107, all victims who reported a rape to the police were taken to the Philadelphia General Hospital Emergency Room for medical treatment and collection of legal evidence. In the event of serious injury requiring immediate medical or surgical attention, the victim was taken to the closest emergency room and later transferred to Philadelphia General Hospital (PGH) for gynecological services and collection of evidence. Because the police policy was known to other hospitals in Philadelphia, when a victim reported to any other hospital emergency room she was transferred to Philadelphia General Hospital.

Since police were on duty at Philadelphia General Hospital, they became aware of almost all victims who came to the emergency room. Therefore, the study subjects include few unreported cases. Occasionally, the police would interview a victim who came directly to the hospital, and, if she expressed the desire not to make an official police report, they would oblige. In the years during which the Center for Rape Concern conducted this research (1972 through 1975), 3,971 victims were seen at PGH.

When a victim was seen at PGH, a notification form was completed by the obstetrics and gynecology (OB–GYN) resident and forwarded, within 24 hours, to the Center for Rape Concern (CRC). Medical records were also provided to ensure the Center's awareness of all victims who reported, in the event that a resident neglected to submit a report.

On receipt of the reports by the Center, the cases were randomly assigned to the staff social workers. It was CRC policy that the social worker attempt to contact the victim within 48 hours of assignment or as soon as possible thereafter. The social worker tried to reach the victim first by telephone, if a number was available. The social worker used the telephone contact to explore any immediate major concerns the victim might have had and to arrange a home visit at a time convenient to both parties. At least one successful home visit was completed for 790 of the 1,401 victims.

The acceptable criteria for labeling a case unsuccessful were a victim's refusal, her absence for two or more home visit appointments, her failure to respond to a letter to call the social worker, or it the victim had moved or had given an incorrect address at the hospital and could not be located. A small number of cases were considered unsuccessful because informed consent to participate in the project could not be obtained.

Any victim or her guardian had the right to refuse to participate in the research. Eighty victims refused. Of this small percentage of refusals, the reasons for refusal were primarily related to the victim's or guardian's desire to refrain from discussing the incident because of the perceived upset the interview could possibly generate. Some victims also stated that everything was okay and that they did not want to discuss the incident with anyone.

Pediatric victims are overrepresented among the refusals when compared to the general sample. This is apparently a result of the concerns frequently voiced by parents, who often had difficulty coping with the incident, particularly when the offender was known to the family. Not discussing the incident with the child seemed to be the most common solution in the minds of these adults. When this reason was offered, the social worker indicated that she would be happy to interview the parent alone. Frequently this too was refused.

The representativeness of the sample of victims interviewed, when compared to all victims reporting to PGH, is difficult to assess, because of the unavailability of detailed information on those cases that were unsuccessful or refused to participate. The most transient of the victims were most often those who were not contacted. Those who did not want to be available for follow-up or who gave false or nonexistent addresses may have been attempting to ward off further abuse by the medical and criminal justice systems. The motivations of both victims and social workers may have played a part in the sample selection. The degree to which this selection process influences the external validity of the study is unknown. The large size of the sample may minimize some of this concern.

Few significant differences appear when the two samples—successful and unsuccessful—are compared on the basis of available demographic information.

Using standard statistical tests, the investigations found that there was no significant relationship between participation in the research and marital status of the victim, age of the victim, socioeconomic status of the victim, victim–offender relationship, degree of trauma, and presence of spermatozoa. It was found, however, that race was significantly related to participation in the interview. Whereas 75.4% of the total number of victims reporting were nonwhite, 79.1% of the interviewed sample were nonwhite. Conversely, whereas 24.6% of the total were white, only 20.9% of the interviewed sample was white. However, the strength of this relationship is not great.

In summary, it was found that the victims who participated in the research were representative of the total sample on the basis of age, victim-offender relationship, marital status, and medical findings. On the other hand, white victims were less likely to participate than blacks. The relationship is not strong, however, and should not raise significant questions of ability to generalize the findings based on the research group (790) to the total sample (1,401).

Interviews conducted by social workers during the research focused on the particulars of the rape incident, the victim's interaction with the medical and the criminal justice systems, the victim's social relationships, and the victim's adjustment in terms of behavioral, social, and psychological indicators. The research interview focused on the victim's psychosexual development and her psychological response to the rape. Both the psychiatric and social interviews attempted to assess the victim's prerape adjustment particularly as it related to subsequent reactions to the rape.

The interviews administered by female social workers were conducted at four time intervals: immediately following the report of the incident (usually within 5 days), at 3, 7, and 11 months after the report of the rape. Social workers were selected to interview victims because it was thought that their sensitivity, training, and experience would enable them to elicit valid information about the problems the victim might be experiencing. The psychiatric interview was usually conducted within 2 weeks of the first social worker interview. Furthermore, during the course of the study separate forms were developed to record details of the victim's court experiences, focusing on treatment of the victim by various criminal justice system personnel and the victim's reaction to the preliminary hearing and trial.

Home visiting by the social workers was selected as the preferred mode of interviewing for two reasons. First, a home visit enabled the social worker to observe the victim in her own environment where she would be most comfortable. This allowed some observation of family interactions and gave the social worker a less sterile view of the victim. Second, the number of successfully completed interviews would be increased if the social worker travelled to meet the victim rather than requesting her to return to PGH. It was thought that these benefits outweighed the negative features of home visiting, including the expense of travel time and transportation, the danger to the worker when entering areas of the city where the crime rate is high or when entering a household where the offender might still be present, and the lack of privacy in some homes.

At the time of the first home visit the research program was fully explained to the victim, and her informed consent was obtained. The social worker then asked the victim to accept an appointment with one of the psychiatrists at PGH. Although many of the victims agreed to this interview, many victims did not report for this scheduled appointment. They were recontacted in an attempt to schedule a second, third, or fourth appointment. Whereas travel to PGH was an inconvenience (bus fare was provided), it is thought that most victims who did not keep their appointment did not understand the purpose of the interview and/or feared contact with the psychiatrist. Of the 790 victims who had a first home visit, 331 (41.9%) were interviewed by a psychiatrist for research purposes.

In all cases in which a successful first home visit had been accomplished, a follow-up home visit was attempted. The social workers utilized the same methods for contacting victims at follow-up as were used for the initial visit, generally a telephone call or a letter. Whether or not the attempted 3-month follow-up home visit was successful, another visit was attempted at 7 months and so on unless the victim had moved and could not be located or had refused any further contact with the Center. Whereas it was difficult to locate many of the victims for follow-up visits, few victims refused the visit outright. In addition, the caseload of each social worker increased drastically as the research progressed, and the number of victims reporting to PGH increased. Therefore, the amount of effort each social worker could expend in attempting to reach each case became more limited over time.

The total number of successful follow-up home visits were as follows: 3-month follow-up: 307, 7-month follow-up: 217, and 11-month follow-up: 213. By collecting information at four discrete time intervals, the researchers intended to plot adjustment patterns as they changed over time. In this book, the first and fourth home visits are used exclusively. First home-visit patterns are designated as patterns "immediately after the rape," and fourth home-visit patterns are listed as patterns "1 year after the rape." The second and third home-visit findings were not utilized here. Our initial theoretical orientation is toward examining the reaction to the rape as measured by the long-term adjustment patterns (1-year later). A comparison of persons with a fourth home visit to those who did not have a fourth home visit reveals that persons who had a fourth home visit were more likely to be adolescents, less likely to be children, more likely to be employed, more likely to have been coerced, subjected to penile-vaginal intercourse, fondling and caressing, and repeated intercourse, and more likely to have been raped by a relative stranger. The differences were not great, however, and on over forty independent variables there were no significant differences. The authors conclude that findings drawn from the fourth home visit can be generalized to the total sample.

In summary, the analysis typically uses one of three groups as the basis for generating observations: the total sample of 1,401 victims; the sample of 790 victims who were interviewed by a social worker soon after the rape; and the sample of 213 victims who were interviewed by a social worker 11 months after the rape. Preliminary analysis indicates that findings derived from the smaller samples can be generalized to the larger sample. Later analyses introduce several new samples, but most of the research focuses on the groups listed.

The difficulties raised in the data analysis were numerous. The sample size and the detailed information collected resulted in a wealth of data, which could not be easily comprehended or synthesized without quantification. The responses of the victim to the areas of inquiry ranged from dichotomous (yes–no) responses to open–ended responses copied verbatim by the social worker. A review of the completed interview schedules could provide general knowledge, but these schedules required quantification to go beyond purely clinical impressions.

The coding was developed by the research staff after they had gained considerable familiarity with the questionnaires and the clinical responses of victims. The researchers eliminated from the coding the items that could not be translated into quantifiable form without considerable strain and without raising questions of validity and reliability. In addition, items that were deemed useless or redundant to the research were also eliminated.

The next part of this book concerns victim adjustment. Thirteen variables were selected for analysis, each focusing on a particular adjustment problem:

Increased fear of being out on the street alone

Increased fear of being home alone

Decreased social activities

Change in eating habits

Change in sleeping patterns

Increased nightmares

Worsened heterosexual relationships

Increased negative feelings toward known men

Increased negative feelings toward unknown men

Worsened relations with husband or boyfriend

Worsened sexual relations with partner

Increased insecurities concerning sexual attractiveness

Worsened relations with family

For each problem, social workers rated the level of change from pre-rape patterns on a scale from 1 to 4. They were instructed to make their ranking decision assuming a score of 4 is four times as intense as a score of 1. Not all victims were rated on all adjustment problems; many victims in the initial research stages were excluded from these ratings, but the majority of persons with a first and a fourth home visit were scored on each problem.

All adjustment variables were also coded 0 or 1. If the score is 1, an adjustment problem has developed since the rape; if the score is 0, one has not. The following forty-eight independent variables were also selected to be included as part of the analysis for this book:

Victim age

Victim race

Victim marital status

Whether the victim lives alone

Whether the victim lives with her mother

Whether the victim lives with her father

Whether the victim lives with her sister

Whether the victim lives with her brother

Victim's employment status

Whether the victim is a welfare recipient (on public assistance)

Mean income for the census tract in which the victim resides

Number of school years completed by the victim

Victim's history of prior truancy problems (self-reported)

Victim's history of police trouble (self-reported)

Whether or not the victim had had psychiatric, psychological, or mental health assistance prior to the rape

Whether or not the victim had been assaulted physically (nonsexually) before the rape

Whether or not the victim had been sexually assaulted before the rape

The location in which the rape took place

The duration of the assault

Whether the rape was accomplished through the use of tempting[1] by the offender(s)

Whether the rape was accomplished through the use of coercion[2] by the offender(s)

Whether the rape was accomplished through the use of intimidation[3] by the offender(s)

Whether the rape was accomplished through the use of a weapon[4] by the offender(s)

Whether the rape was accomplished through the use of any element of nonphysical force by the offender(s)[5]

Whether the rape was accomplished through the use of roughness[6] by the offender(s)

Whether the rape was accomplished through the use of a nonbrutal beating by the offender(s)[7]

Whether the rape was accomplished through the use of a brutal[8] beating by the offender(s)

Whether the rape was accomplished through the use of choking by the offender(s)

Whether the rape was accomplished through the use of any element of physical force by the offender(s)

Whether the rape event included penile–vaginal intercourse by the offender(s)

Whether the rape event included fellatio by the offender(s)

Whether the rape event included cunnilingus by the offender(s)

Whether the rape event included anal intercourse by the offender(s)

Whether the rape event included sexual contact without penetration by the offender(s)

Whether the rape event included fondling or caressing by the offender(s)

Whether the rape event included any other sex acts[9] by the offender(s)

Whether the rape event included no sex acts by the offender(s)

Whether the rape event included repeated intercourse[10] by the offender(s)

Whether it was a group rape

Whether any strangers were involved in the rape

Whether any relative strangers were involved in the rape [11]

Whether any casual acquaintances were involved in the rape [12]

Whether any friends were involved in the rape

Whether any extended family members were involved in the rape

Whether any nuclear family members were involved in the rape

The victim–offender racial class

The victim–offender age differential

Whether or not the victim had had any previous consenting sexual relations with the offender (self-report)

The principal mode of analysis used in this book is similar to a technique called predictive attribute analysis.[13] The first step in the analysis is to select a dependent variable from the adjustment problems. For example, the problem might be increased fear of being home alone 1 year after the rape. Among 202 victims where this information is available, 50 had increased fear (24.8%) while 152 did not (75.2%).

Each of the forty-eight independent variables is tested against the dependent variable. If any variable is significantly associated with increased fear it is noted.[14] In the example cited, four variables are significantly associated with increased fear of being home alone one year after the rape:

Variable	Value	Percentage with increased fear of being home alone 1 year after the rape
1. Whether any casual acquaintances were involved	Yes	50.0
	No	20.7
2. Victim–offender age differential	Offender is less than 10 yrs. older, or is younger than, the victim	28.5
	Offender is more than 10 yrs. older than the victim	9.3
3. Victim age	18+ yrs. old	31.6
	12–17 yrs. old	19.1
	0–11 yrs. old	9.1
4. Whether the victim had been assaulted nonsexually before	Yes	40.0
	No	21.0

Note that all independent variables not found to be significantly associated are excluded from any further consideration in relation to the dependent variable.

Among the four variables significantly associated with fear of being home alone 1 year after the rape, whether any casual acquaintances were involved in the rape is the strongest association. As a consequence, that variable is used to split the sample into two groups: one group where a casual acquaintance was involved in the rape and a second group where no casual acquaintance was involved in the rape. Each group is called a branch.

The analysis now focuses on each branch. For victims where no casual acquaintances were involved in the rape, three variables are significantly associated with increased fear of being home alone. The victim–offender age differential is the strongest association. Therefore, it is used to make the next split. On the other branch, no variable is significantly associated with increased fear of being home alone. Consequently, that branch is closed and called a terminal group. Figure 2–1 depicts all of the splits, branches, and

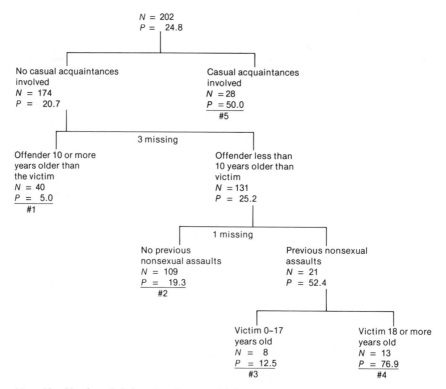

Note: N = Number of victims; P = Percent with increased fear of being home alone

Figure 2–1. Increased Fear of Being Home Alone 1 Year after the Rape.

terminal groups for increased fear of being home alone 1 year after the rape. Note that terminal groups 1, 2, and 3 have small chances of increased fear, whereas groups 5 and especially 4 have good chances of increased fear.

Subsequent chapters will interpret these and other findings. For interested readers, a more comprehensive discussion of the statistical techniques used may be found in the notes following this chapter.

The next four chapters specifically concern victim adjustment. The section on the criminal justice response, which follows the section on adjustment patterns, uses similar methods of analysis.

Notes

1. Following Amir, tempting is defined as: "The victim is offered money or a ride; the offender tries to arouse interest by verbal or nonverbal means." Menachem Amir, *Patterns in Forcible Rape* (Chicago: The University of Chicago Press, 1971), p. 152.

2. "The victim is threatened with bodily harm, or other kinds of verbal violence are employed by the offender." Ibid.

3. "Physical gestures and verbal threats are used." Ibid.

4. "Threats are reinforced with a weapon or other physical object (a stick, stone, etc.)." Ibid.

5. If the rape includes tempting, coercion, intimidation, or a weapon, nonphysical force is included. Ibid.

6. "[H]olding, pushing." Ibid., p. 154.

7. "[S]lapping." Ibid.

8. "[S]lugging, kicking, beating by fists repeatedly, etc." Ibid.

9. For example, insertion of an object into the vagina or anus of the victim, manual penetration of the victim, and so forth.

10. Does not include multiple offenders, only repeated intercourse by the same offender is counted.

11. "[O]ffender is only known visually to the victim without any other contact between them." Amir, *Patterns in Forcible Rape,* p. 233.

12. "[O]ffender becomes known to the victim just before the offense, or she has some prior knowledge about his residence, place of work, name or nickname, but no specific relationships exist between them." Ibid.

13. The technique of data manipulation chosen closely resembles predictive attribute analysis (PAA), where the dependent variables are nominal, and automatic interaction detection (AID), where the dependent variable is interval. In the former case, cross–tabulation was used, and the statistic selected was chi square where PAA generally uses Goodman and Kruskall's tau beta and lambda beta. In the latter case, step–wise analysis of variance was used, and the statistic selected was F. Note that whereas phi is equal to tau beta with dichotomous variables, the stopping rule is based, in

part, on statistical significance typically at the .05 level in this study, rather than a fixed proportional reduction in error or a minimum overall improvement in variance explained. However, each technique, although each may stop at different points, would split exactly the same up to each respective stopping point. For an excellent discussion of PAA in criminological investigation, see Stanley Turner, "The Ecology of Delinquency," in *Delinquency: Selected Studies,* ed. Thorsten Sellin and Marvin E. Wolfgang (New York: John Wiley and Sons, 1969), pp. 27–60. AID is described in John A. Sonquist and James N. Morgan, *The Detection of Interaction Effects* (Ann Arbor, Mich.: Institute for Social Research, University of Michigan, 1964).

14. Using chi square and the .05 level.

**Part II
The Victim's Readjustment to
Living**

3 Adjustment: Overview and Case Studies

In their book *Sexual Assault in America,* Nancy Gager and Cathleen Schurr argue that "it is not helpful to stress 'adjustment' to a society which condones and, in some ways, encourages rape."[1] Indeed, are not the so-called professionals justly criticized for implying that it is the victim's behavior that must be changed, rather than the offender's? Are we really saying that, since societal attitudes and behavioral standards will never change, we have no choice but to make the victim conform to these norms?

In the chapters that follow, the term *adjustment* is used in a very specific sense. No value judgment is implicit in the mention of that term, either in discussion of a general nature or with reference to individual cases. Rather, the authors are simply taking cognizance of the fact that after a sexual assault, one has to and wants to be able to return to school or work, or take care of one's children, or enjoy sexual relations with a lover, friend, or husband.

What has actually been measured as adjustment in the current study is return to the prerape state. Levels of adjustment are based, for the most part, on the victim's own assessment of changes in her patterns of interaction. The appearance of an adjustment problem may be significant only if that particular difficulty represents a departure from prerape behavior. One of the gaps in the research design of this study is the inability to directly measure the victim's prior use of defense mechanisms or to assess what these mechanisms might have meant in terms of mental health or mental illness.

It should be emphasized that whereas rape is a potential crisis for the individual, crisis is not a pathological experience. As viewed by mental health professionals, a crisis can be a turning point in an individual's life for better or worse adjustment on a day-to-day basis. An adjustment problem may simply be an indicator of the individual's driving to reach a more satisfactory level of functioning. One could argue that a rape victim who experiences no changes in her day-to-day living experiences may be having a more difficult time adjusting than one who does experience such changes. In some cases, disruptions in routine behavior indicate a forthcoming level of better adjustment.

Other writers on the subject of adjusting to rape have structured their discussions according to various phases of adjustment. Sandra Fox and Donald Scherl speak of three phases of adjustment: acute reaction, outward adjustment, and integration.[2] Ann Burgess and Lynda Holmstrom refer to "the acute phase: disorganization" and "the long-term process: reorganization."[3] The collection and analysis of data in the current study are organized somewhat according to this latter design. That is, the victim's first interview by a social worker (conducted within 72 hours of when the assault was reported) is regarded as a measure of the immediate acute reaction. The fourth home visit (occurring approximately 1 year thereafter) provides a clue to the prospects for successful long-term adjustment.

One must recognize that adjustment patterns are not easily identifiable in every case. Particularly with child victims, the element of time is of paramount importance in correctly assessing levels of adjustment. The details of a rape may be repressed for many years, only to surface at some later critical point in the victim's life. The child victim who appears to have come away from the incident with no immediate difficulties may be in store for far more serious problems years later. This potential is not reflected in the data, where the victim's adjustment is monitored for only 1 year. For adult victims as well, there is no way to accurately predict from the collected data the long-term effects of rape. Only an extended study, following adult victims for 5 to 10 or more years, and perhaps even longer for younger victims, would be able to yield satisfactory data in this area.

If there is some suitable backdrop against which to consider the many findings that follow, it may be the notion that rape is an extraordinary and disruptive event that must be handled by the victim within the context of the everyday world. The media depiction of rape includes only the extraordinary quality (the violence, the police investigation, the trial), generally ending its inquiry when the jury returns its verdict. One is led to believe that the victim's rape experience comes to an abrupt halt with the final rap of the judge's gavel. In terms of adjustment, however, the victim's difficulties may be just beginning, for it is at this point that the extraordinary event and the ordinary context are mingled. We understand and accept open displays of grief at funerals, but we are likely to view such displays as aberrant if they persist for any significant period of time thereafter. Similarly, a rape victim may find that the emotional support that she has been receiving from others has suddenly been withdrawn, and family and friends are beginning to wonder aloud when she will "snap out of it." When others fail to understand the nature of the adjustment process, the victim's difficulties are likely to be compounded.

The remainder of this chapter focuses on the adjustment patterns that were found in a substantial number of rape cases. The authors' purpose in analyzing these patterns was to define as narrowly as possible the effects on the adjustment process of various sociodemographic and incident-related variables. From a therapeutic standpoint, the advantages of such precision are obvious: the clinician can pursue those areas most likely to be pertinent to each individual case, rather than starting from the beginning and using a general approach for all rape victims. Specific problems can be more readily identified and more effectively worked out.

Adjustment problems were found to occur with some frequency in thirteen areas. The first three areas reflect the level of unfocused anxiety resulting from the rape:

Eating Habits: Case 1

The victim is a 20-year-old, single, black female living with her grandmother, aunt, uncle, and three younger male cousins. One night, while accompanying her aunt's ex-boyfriend to a neighborhood Chinese restaurant, she was told by him that he had to pick up something at his apartment. Once there, he injected heroin into his own arm and then forced the victim, at the point of a gun, to take heroin herself. Feeling dizzy and weak, she was led into another room where, over a 3-hour period, she was forced to engage in cunnilingus, fellatio, and repeated intercourse. When, at one point, the victim attempted to leap from a window, the offender grabbed her and injected more heroin into her arm.

As a result of the assault, the victim's behavior changed dramatically. Her once active social life came to a complete halt, she lost her job because she would not venture far from home, became upset whenever a family member left the house, and, by her own admission, wore out her family and friends by constantly talking about the rape. When she was first interviewed, the assigned social worker noted that the victim's food consumption had decreased markedly. Over the course of 1 year, a substantial weight loss was noticed in the victim.

Nearly one-half (47.3%) of the 598 victims questioned about these changes experienced some noticeable difference in their eating habits after being sexually assaulted. Changes in eating habits shortly after a rape may reflect the level of anxiety brought on by the rape. Increased anxiety may take the form of either nervous overeating or a considerable reduction in food intake. Whether a victim overeats or undereats may be dictated by her prior methods of meeting crisis situations.

Prolonged changes in eating habits may reflect the victim's estimation of her self-worth. After a year's time, overeating may indicate a dislike of self and an effort to make oneself as unattractive as possible. By being unattractive, the victim reinforces her own sense of guilt at having somehow precipitated the rape and simultaneously protects herself (so she believes) from future sexual assaults. Overeating that leads to excessive weight gain would also serve as a means of avoiding social activities and new sexual relationships. On the other hand, where undereating coupled with excessive weight loss is noticed 1 year after the rape, the victim may be portraying herself to the world as pitiful, victimized, and someone to be protected. Rather than saddle herself with guilt over the incident, the victim may see herself as a martyr. Whereas continued undereating may also serve to diminish the victim's attractiveness and sexual desirability, the victim may here be seeking attention, rather than punishing herself.

Sleeping Patterns: Case 2

The victim, a 23-year-old married black woman, had been working the night shift at her job. One night, while waiting for a train on her way to work, a man with a gun approached her and forced her to drive with him to an abandoned building. Once there, he began fondling and caressing the victim and told her that he was punishing her because her husband had had an affair with his (the offender's) wife. Before the offender could rape her, the victim hit him with her pocketbook and sprayed him with a tear gas gun that she was carrying. She then fled.

The victim received no support from her husband. He denied the affair and withdrew from her emotionally. At one point, he accused her of somehow being involved with the offender. In addition, the victim began to receive harassing phone calls from the offender. On one occasion, he attempted to break into her home. As a result of these events, the victim experienced a disruption in her regular sleeping pattern. Her inability to get sufficient sleep continued even after the police tapped her phone and promised to maintain a close surveillance on her house. Her sleeping problems finally ended when she changed to the day shift at work, moved to a safer neighborhood quite a distance from her previous residence, arranged to have an unlisted phone number, and experienced a dramatic improvement in her relations with her husband.

Nearly one-half (49.9%) of all victims interviewed experienced some changes in their sleeping patterns. As was the case with changed eating habits, whether one's difficulties take the form of undersleeping or over-sleeping will depend on the individual and the way in which she views the assault. An inability to sleep often reflects high levels of anxiety and tension, whereas oversleeping may reflect a desire to avoid all situations and interactions with others. One might reasonably predict that 1 year after the rape a victim would be more likely to oversleep than suffer an inability to sleep. Like any other individual, a rape victim could not continue to function while experiencing high levels of anxiety and tension over a 1-year period. If the problem (that is, the assault) has not been satisfactorily resolved, then the victim may be compelled to try to avoid facing the problem altogether. Oversleeping allows the victim greater periods of time during which she need neither deal with the problem nor be faced with her fears or guilt. In fact, the data indicate that 1 year after the rape there is a decrease in the number of victims unable to sleep and an increase in the number of victims sleeping excessively.

Nightmares: Case 3

The victim, an 18-year-old, black, single woman, lived with a roommate and attended a local technical school. As a young girl, she had had difficulties in school and a history of truancy and fighting. Her mother declared her incorrigible and had her referred to a state-managed group home. While there, she obtained a high school diploma and entered technical school. She then established an independent residence.

On her way home one day, she accepted a ride in a passing car. After she entered the car, the driver and a second male passenger drove her to a local park, where they joined up with a third man. The three men spent the next seven hours abusing the victim, beating her severely about the head, chest, back, and face; raping her repeatedly, both vaginally and anally; and forcing her to perform fellatio. After she was taken to the house of a fourth man, she managed to escape and call the police.

When interviewed by a social worker, the victim was outwardly calm. She was able to discuss the rape with little apparent anxiety. However, her grades soon began to slip and shortly thereafter she decided to leave school. She slept less, fitfully when she did sleep, and had strong, persistent nightmares.

Nightmares often occur when an individual is unable to successfully deal with a traumatic event that has recently come to pass. Replaying the event during the sleeping state represents an attempt by the subconscious to integrate the event into the everyday world. The intensity of the fear and the negative feelings surrounding the incident contribute to the disquieting character of the nightmare.

Nightmares often exhibit a repetition compulsion—the victim replays the rape over and over in her mind. One social worker recounts how nightmares initially seem to be reenactments of the rape incident. After several weeks, however, the nightmares may instead become scenarios of how the victim would like the rape incident to have gone. In these revised nightmares, it is the victim who controls the situation, often killing the offender. Through nightmares, the victim achieves mastery of a situation that up until then could not be integrated into everyday experience.

Alone on the Street: Case 4

The victim, a 35-year-old white woman, lived 4 blocks from the factory where she had worked for 4 years. The immediate neighborhood was declining, and there was increased racial tension.

On her way to work one day, a young black male stopped her, put a gun to her head, and motioned her into an alley. He forced her against a wall, the gun against her face, and raped her.

Afterwards, the victim walked to work with her umbrella on her arm, despite the fact that it was raining heavily. She worked through the day, not mentioning the incident to anyone until she told her sister on returning home. At that point, the police were notified.

From then on, she would not go out alone. She arranged for a daily ride to work and, even a year after the rape, would not go to the corner store unless accompanied by her daughter. She keeps her daughter home with her most of the time and fears that her daughter now has no social life because of her demands.

Nearly two-thirds (65.9%) of all interviewed victims experienced an increased fear of being alone on the street after having been raped. This reaction often reflects the geographic circumstances of the incident—if the rape took place in an alley, lot, or back street, the more pronounced will be the victim's subsequent fear of being alone outdoors. However, increased apprehension may also indicate a general alteration in the victim's perception of self following the rape incident. If the victim has up until then viewed herself as an independent, capable individual, the rape incident may serve to shatter her sense of independence and mastery and heighten her feelings of vulnerability. The sense of security that may be destroyed by a different perception of self is illustrated by the following case example.

Case 5

The victim, a white woman in her late thirties, had been married for seventeen years to a black man. They lived in a mostly black neighborhood and had two teenage children. The victim worked at night as a registered nurse.

The woman always saw herself as "being black." Her friends were black, her associates at work were black, and she had always felt comfortable with her neighbors and with black people in general. She had severed most of her ties with her white friends and family members.

On her way home from work one evening, she was raped in an alley by a young, black male. Her sense of "whiteness" was suddenly heightened, in part because her attacker told her that she had been selected as a victim because she was "like all other white bitches." As a result, she felt uncomfortable in her neighborhood and around her black friends. She could not discuss her discomfort with either her husband or her children. She became painfully aware that people would look at her when she was traveling with her family. Subsequently, she withdrew from most of her social activities and took her children with her whenever she needed to go out on errands. Her sense of security within her home and her community had been completely shattered.

Alone at Home: Case 6

The victim, a 38–year–old black woman, had been separated for many years and was living with her father, sister, and two nieces. She had been employed for approximately 4 years and had had no current or recent sexual involvements with men.

One day, while her family was away, an intruder entered through the unlocked front door. The victim awoke when she felt someone on top of her, but she was able to see only a knife. When she began to scream, her attacker covered her face with a pillow. She was ordered to wrap her legs around the offender and "act like you're enjoying it." When she tried to push the pillow away from her face because of difficulty in breathing, the rapist shouted "I'll kill you."

The victim was raped twice, and her purse was taken. She is convinced that she recognized the rapist's voice and believes that she knows him. She is terrified of being home alone, and under no circumstances does she allow men to enter her home when she is alone: "I don't want any male friends visiting. How will I know it wasn't him?"

Soon she began to believe that the rapist was a soldier whom she had previously known and who was home on leave at the time of the rape. Still, her fear of being home alone did not diminish.

As one might expect, a victim who has been raped in her own home is more than twice as likely to experience a subsequent increased fear of being home alone than a victim who was raped elsewhere (72.2% versus 34.4%). As was the case in the previous category, however, the problem may exist independently of any geographic origins. Once again, resultant difficulties may reflect the victim's feeling that she can no longer master her environment, regardless of where the rape occurred. Physical changes in her environment—moving after the rape, changing locks on doors, securing windows—may enable the victim to eventually feel safe again in her own home. However, when the fear of being home alone is related to doubts concerning her ability to cope with life in general, the victim's fear is likely to persist. If she believes that the rape occurred at least partly because of an error in judgment on her part (letting the "wrong man" into her house, leaving the door unlocked or the window open, and so forth), then physical measures alone will probably not restore a sense of security to her.

Social Activities: Case 7

The victim, a 16-year-old white female, lived with her parents. She had had some difficulties in her family relationships. She had been cited at least ten times for truancy and had been arrested once as a runaway when she had gone away for a weekend without telling her parents.

One night, while her parents were away, the victim went outside when she heard an ice cream truck. On her way back to the house, a man held a knife to her throat and forced her into a car where another man was waiting. While the men drove to an abandoned house, the victim was forced to remain on the floor of the car. She was punched in the mouth when she tried to scream and was choked to prevent her from making a sound while passing a police car. She was raped by both offenders and then released. She found herself in an unfamiliar neighborhood and telephoned a neighbor for assistance on returning home.

The victim told her parents only that she had been jumped. They discovered that she had been raped when they found in her possession a booklet provided by Women Organized Against Rape. Her parents provided no support and seemed to blame her for the incident.

She desperately wanted no one else to know that she had been raped. However, the police questioned all her friends and neighbors and, when asked, admitted that they were investigating a rape. Because the victim's face was badly swollen, everyone deduced that it was she who was the victim.

The victim was fearful that her friends and neighbors would "come down on her," since she had only told them that she had been jumped. As a result, she attempted to avoid all interactions. She stopped her once active social life. She effectively left school and rarely ventured from home.

A year after the rape, her spirits had improved somewhat as she contemplated moving to a new location where she could begin again.

One measure of the difficulties faced by rape victims in adjusting to the incident is the extent to which normal social activities are modified. One-half (50.3%) of all victims studied reported some change in their social activities immediately after the rape. Invariably, this involved a curtailing or complete elimination of such activities. "Social activities" denotes those activities that are not necessary for an individual's day-to-day functioning. As such, they require the greatest trust in oneself and the greatest sense of security in interpersonal relations. It is therefore to be expected that obstacles to adjustment will arise in this area.

A decrease in social activities may also reflect the victim's difficulty in dealing with the sexual component of rape. It is the sexual aspect, rather than the aggressive aspect, that is likely to be the source of the victim's reluctance to resume normal social interactions. Particularly in heterosexual social relationships, the victim's sense of vulnerability is heightened, and her ability to trust herself is put to a severe test. Because the victim may begin to see herself as being "bad" or "that type of woman" (particularly if the issue of victim precipitation has been raised), a decrease in social activity may represent a subconscious desire to avoid these labels.

The following two cases illustrate how societal attitudes regarding the so-called appropriate socialization of females can affect postrape adjustment.

Case 8

The victim, a woman in her late twenties, lived with her two young children in a high-rise housing project, where she had resided for approximately 9 years. She was raped in the elevator of her apartment building when returning home late one night from a social activity. When discussing the rape, the victim spoke in a matter-of-fact fashion and displayed virtually no emotion. She stated that since she lived in the housing project, she had expected to be raped at some point. Now that the rape had occurred, she realized that she could no longer take the risks that she once did. Since she had finally been "caught," she would have to accept the natural consequences of the rape, namely a curtailing of her social activities.

Case 9

The victim, a black woman in her early twenties, lived with her mother and sisters. She often visited a neighborhood bar for several drinks after returning home from work. One evening she was approached in the bar by a man who bought her several drinks and asked her to accompany him to another bar. She agreed to go with him. After leaving the second bar, the offender offered to drive her home, but instead drove her to a street with many abandoned buildings and raped her in his car.

Returning home, the victim was confronted with the angry reactions of her mother and older sisters. They told her that they hoped she had finally learned her lesson, and they implied that if she continued to frequent bars after work, she would again be punished by being raped.

The following six adjustment categories involve the degree to which the victim's attitudes and interactions concerning the opposite sex are changed as a result of being raped.

Feelings toward Known Men: Case 10

The victim, a 44-year-old black woman receiving public assistance, had been working in a factory for 12 years before being laid off 2 months prior to the rape. During those 2 months she had been drinking fairly heavily.

Her marriage had ended in divorce 15 years earlier. She had spent 1 year in jail and 2 years on probation for attempting to kill a man with whom she was involved, and who had been beating her. She had been involved with only two men in the last 12 years, each relationship terminating when her lover began to beat her brutally.

One weekday afternoon, the victim's godson came to her house and, during an argument, hit her in the eye. The victim was knocked to the ground, her eye badly injured. Her godson then kicked her with his boots, pulled out a knife, and, with the knife held to her stomach, raped her anally. As soon as he had climaxed, he cried "Oh my God, Aunt _____, look at your eye! Look what I've done!" and ran out of the house.

The victim already harbored some negative feelings toward men that she knew, but after the rape these feelings became extremely intense. Because the victim knew the rapist so well, she felt that "if he'd do it, why not everyone?"

Whereas an increased fear of known men can be expected to result from a rape in which the victim is previously acquainted with the offender, several other factors may also precipitate this reaction. As with several of the categories already discussed, a fear of known men following a rape may be indicative of the victim's general loss of trust in herself and in others. If she has been raped in the offender's home or car, she may no longer trust her judgment. In addition, the motives of others, even those who have been close to her, may become suspect in the face of what she perceives as misplaced trust. If the victim has previously suffered from emotional distress of one form or another, the rape is likely to reinforce her pessimistic world view. Under such circumstances, specific fears may be replaced by a general mistrust of all men, based on the assumption that to be overly cautious is safer than to not be cautious enough.

Feelings toward Unknown Men: Case 11

The psychiatrist who counseled this victim wrote: "This unhappy twenty-one year old, unmarried, unemployed black female has always felt rather lonely, frightened, and depressed. For the past two years she has had episodes of depression manifested by a subjective feeling of sadness, loneliness, anorexia, insomnia and frequent crying spells. Her depression is usually accompanied by anxiety and a tendency to avoid people. She has always feared males and found it difficult to trust them. She has always had some confusion and conflicts regarding sex which she has attempted to handle by avoiding men. ('When I was young, my mother and father caught me listening at their bedroom door . . . they scolded me and told me sex was bad and I was bad for having such thoughts . . . mother would never leave me alone with a boy . . . my girlfriend told me sex was painful.')"

The victim lives in a high–crime area with a gang problem. One day she entered a house in which she expected to find a male friend. Instead, three young men whom she knew casually were inside. They grabbed her, pulled her upstairs, and all three men raped her. They then stood around and watched her try to dress. The victim was unable to put on all her clothes and finally picked most of them up and ran home.

The rape incident intensified all her symptoms, and she became unable to cope with her feelings and conflicts. She vowed never to engage in sexual relations again and began to view all men as evil. These negative feelings were directed in particular at men whom she did not know, such as those whom she had to confront when walking on the street.

Over one–half (57.5%) of all victims in the current study experienced increased negative feelings toward unknown men immediately after being raped. As one would expect, this reaction was most common among victims who were not previously acquainted with their attacker. Where at least one total stranger was involved in the assault, 67.5% of those victims subsequently experienced increased negative feelings toward unknown men. Where at least one "friend" took part in the assault, this reaction was found only 38.5% of the time, as opposed to 61.8% in those cases where no "friend" was involved.

Once more, however, the problem may stem from more than the prior relationship (or lack of same) between victim and offender. The victim may question her previous feelings of self-mastery and trust and may now feel uncomfortable when confronted with any unfamiliar situation. And, if she feels incapable of handling new situations, she may also doubt her ability to deal with people whom she does not know. As a result, she is likely to generalize about men, particularly those about whom she has no prior knowledge. Rather than attributing to all unknown men the motives of the rapist whom she did not know, the victim may simply be reacting to feelings of uncertainty resulting from her lack of background information about such men.

Heterosexual Relationships: Case 12

The victim, an 18-year-old, single, black female, had had a history of poor relations with her family. Although she lived with her mother and three brothers, she had always felt closer to her father. Her mother admitted that she held little affection for the victim, and described her as a "bad girl." The victim had been arrested twice as a runaway and suspended from school for truancy. When a mental health worker referred both mother and daughter for counseling, the mother instead turned the victim over to the authorities as incorrigible.

The victim had had regular sexual relations with her boyfriend. One night, a man whom she had met for the first time earlier that night knocked on the door. When he learned that her boyfriend was asleep, he pushed the victim into a front room and raped her. Whenever she cried or begged him to stop, he struck her with a stick that he held in his hand. The attack continued for over 2 hours.

When the victim ran to her boyfriend and told him what had just happened, he called her a liar. She soon began to suspect that she had been "set up." When the case came to trial, her boyfriend testified that she had consented to sexual relations with the intruder.

The victim's mother made repeated nasty remarks about the incident. Her father was supportive at first but then told the victim that he was disappointed in her. Over the next year, both parents continued to make it clear that they blamed the victim for the rape.

Soon after the rape, the victim found that she no longer liked being in the company of men. In their presence, she was nervous. She began to harbor angry feelings toward men, unlike any she had ever had before. One year later, she had become convinced that no man could be trusted and that all men blame women for being raped. She found a new boyfriend but did not have sexual relations with him. She suspected that her intimacy with her prior boyfriend had led to her rape and she did not want to make that same mistake again. She avoided other men when possible.

Increased negative feelings toward men need not always be translated into substantive behavioral changes. Two-fifths (40.2%) of the rape victims in the current study did experience worsening interactions with men immediately after the rape. This characterization was applied to anything from palpable fear or anxiety when in the presence of men in social situations to a vague uneasiness when dealing with the mailman, the newspaper boy, a male neighbor or coworker, or an unknown man on the street. As with negative feelings toward known and unknown men, the victim may feel that she cannot afford the luxury of carefully assessing the motives of each male that she encounters. Her rule of thumb is to assume the worst, and her negative feelings are here of sufficient magnitude to materially affect the quality of any interactions that she has with men.

Relations with Husband/Boyfriend (for victims 12 or more years old): Case 13

The victim, a 44-year-old, married, black female, lived with her husband. Her parents had provided her with a stable home life emphasizing traditional values. The victim was deeply religious and very close to her "prayer partner," another married woman living in the same neighborhood. Although childless, the victim and her husband had raised a nephew, who was then in college.

While on her way to the corner store early one Sunday morning, the victim was approached by a young black man who then put a knife against her stomach and threatened to kill her if she failed to cooperate. The victim did not scream or offer any resistance, but instead accompanied the offender to a vacant lot where she was forced to engage in fellatio and penile-vaginal intercourse. The offender then robbed her and fled.

After the rape, the victim's previously excellent sex life deteriorated, as did the rest of her marriage. Her husband accused her of being too emotional about the rape and insisted that she not think or talk about it. He was also annoyed that she had told so many friends and neighbors about the incident, feeling embarrassed that others knew about it. Finally, he was angry that she was now spending so much of her time with her "prayer partner." Their marital relations, which had been strong and healthy before the rape, continued to decline.

Approximately one in four rape victims (26.9%) experienced worsened relations with her husband or boyfriend as a result of the rape. Much of the problem may stem from a breakdown in communication. The victim's husband or boyfriend may feel either that the victim does not wish to interact with him at this time or that she is upset with him because of his failure to prevent the rape. His own feelings of guilt or inadequacy may prevent him from expressing his concern over her well-being. If this results in the victim's emotional needs not being met, she may become less able to cope with what has happened to her. If her husband then becomes less patient with her, a serious adjustment problem is likely to develop.

Many sympathetic men who have their own difficulties in dealing with the victimization of their wives or girlfriends feel that this is not the time to deal with their own feelings. The repression of these feelings is likely to inhibit the normal flow of communications and result in increased tension between the victim and her partner. In addition, the victim's husband or boyfriend may experience feelings of guilt if his reaction to the rape is different from what he had thought it would be. For example, he may come to realize that his liberal posture regarding the possibility of his wife's engaging in extramarital sexual activity may not reflect his true feelings. He may try to relieve his feelings of guilt or inadequacy by blaming the victim for the rape, accusing her of either complicity or inadequate resistance. This is most likely to occur if there is no overt evidence of brutality in the rape incident.

Sexual Relations with Partner (for victims 12 or more years old): Case 14

The victim, a 22-year-old black female, had been seeing her boyfriend for five years. They had a son, age four. Although her boyfriend steadfastly refused to marry her, he still maintained a stable and consistent relationship with her. The victim lived with her mother and five brothers and sisters, supported by public assistance while obtaining job training.

The victim's boyfriend maintained that he was entitled to two or three "nights out with the boys" each week, during which the victim was expected to stay at home. Instead, she often visited her friends and would sometimes stop at a male neighbor's home, where wine and marijuana were made available to the females in the neighborhood. While at his house one evening, she became sick after smoking marijuana and drinking wine and went upstairs to the bathroom.

As she was about to rejoin her host, she found him waiting for her outside the bathroom, a knife in his hand and not wearing any pants. The victim was dragged back into the living room and raped.

The victim's boyfriend was outraged at the offender for assaulting her, but he was also angry with her for being alone with the offender in his house. The other women in the neighborhood doubted the victim's account of the incident because the offender had been so nice to them and had even lent money to some of them from time to time.

The victim had a great deal of difficulty adjusting after the rape. She revealed to her social worker that she had been raped before at the age of fifteen. An added crisis occurred when a not-guilty verdict was handed down by the court. Her boyfriend was distressed by the verdict, and refused to see or to talk to her for several weeks thereafter. Although they maintained a relationship, there was a lessening of communication between them, as well as a substantial reduction in sexual activity.

Nearly one-half (46.6%) of the adult victims in the current study experienced a worsening in sexual relations with their partners following the rape. The problem may be as much the result of a cultural bias concerning the communication of sexual matters as of the nature of any specific communications between the victim and her partner. That is to say, most children learn about sex from the parent of the same sex, and they discuss sexual matters exclusively with members of the same sex. When adulthood is reached, there is the sudden expectation to communicate sexual needs and feelings to members of the opposite sex, in spite of a lack of prior experience in doing so in childhood or adolescence. And, at a time when open discussion of sexual needs and feelings may be called for, this inability to communicate openly and honestly can lead to a deterioration of sexual relations between the rape victim and her partner. This possibility is illustrated by the following case.

Case 15

The victim, an attractive professional woman in her mid-twenties, had been involved with a married man for approximately 3 years in a relationship characterized by the victim as warm, open, and caring. One night, the victim awoke to find a man standing over her bed, a knife in his hand. When he was unable to affect penetration because of impotence, he forced the victim to fellate him.

When the offender left, the victim quickly telephoned her boyfriend, who rushed to her apartment. He expressed a desire to have sex with her immediately, stating that if you fall off a horse you should get back on as quickly as possible. The victim was bothered by his failure to appreciate what she felt at that point and was unable to understand that his seemingly insensitive actions may have been emanating from his concern over her well-being. Their relationship steadily worsened and was eventually broken off altogether.

For many victims, being raped is equated with committing adultery. Although the victim recognizes that she did not consent to sexual relations with her attacker, she is unable to escape the fact that she has had sexual relations with another man. If the victim found herself sexually aroused in any way, even if only within the context of physiological response to sexual stimuli, her feelings of guilt may be heightened. The tendency of victims to blame themselves for infidelity is often encouraged by husbands and boyfriends, who make it clear to the victim that she is regarded as property. As such, she is expected to be faithful and to refrain from any seductive or otherwise inappropriate behavior. When a deviation from this code of conduct results in a rape, it is the victim who finds herself accused of having violated her partner's trust. Their sexual relationship may no longer be viewed as monogamous, and the character of their future sexual involvement may be radically altered.

Feelings Concerning Sexual Attractiveness (for victims 12 or more years old): Case 16

The victim, a 19-year-old black female, lived with her common-law husband. While she was visiting at the home of a girlfriend, several male acquaintances of her friend joined them. After all had been drinking for a while, the victim heard her friend screaming. She ran to her friend's bedroom to find several of the men holding her down and raping her. When the victim attempted to intercede, she was dragged into another room and beaten and raped repeatedly. She kept screaming until a blow to the eye knocked her out.

The girlfriend's husband arrived and called the police. One offender was apprehended, but was acquitted at a jury trial through a defense of consent.

Everyone in her neighborhood knew or suspected that the victim had been gang-raped. As a result, the victim was ashamed whenever she went out and was convinced that no decent man could ever find her sexually attractive.

Fewer than one in five (18.7%) adolescent and adult rape victims reported insecurities concerning sexual attractiveness as a result of being raped. Whether a victim views herself as being any less sexually desirable because of the rape incident may depend largely on the emotional support system available to her. If the family and friends of the victim fail to provide her with this needed support, she may feel that the rape has effected certain basic, detrimental changes in her. And, if her own family can no longer accept her, how can she expect others to view her as an attractive and sexually desirable woman? Conversely, an outpouring of warmth and reassurance from family and friends is likely to have a positive impact on the victim's self-image and convince her that she is essentially the same person that she was before the rape.

This phase of adjustment may also be significantly affected by the victim's prerape feelings concerning her sexual attractiveness. If she has had problems with self-image in the past, the rape may be interpreted by her as confirmation that no man could ever relate to her as a normal human being.

The final category to be considered involves the effects (both positive and negative) of interactions with family members (other than her husband) on the victim's adjustment to rape.

Relations with Family Members: Case 17

The victim, a 23-year-old, single, black woman, had a long history of truancy, fighting, and running away from home. She had spent 3 years in a juvenile institution, where she became a heroin addict. When neither her mother nor her father would house her, the victim and her two young children moved in with her grandmother and uncle.

One night, the victim awoke to the screams of her 4-year-old daughter. When she entered her daughter's room, she found her uncle raping and choking the child. During the fight that ensued, the victim was also raped and choked. The victim's grandmother called the police and another uncle of the victim.

The other uncle threw the offender out of the house. However, the victim's grandmother began placing pressure on the victim to drop all charges, arguing that the victim had only been trouble while the uncle had not. The victim, who would have had no place to go, dropped the charges. Tensions increased until finally the victim and her children were forced to leave the house, and the offender returned home.

The victim was unable to secure assistance from any member of her family. As an outcast, she tried unsuccessfully to reopen the case against her uncle.

Case 17 illustrates only the negative impact of family relations following a rape. In fact, of the thirteen adjustment responses being considered, worsened relations between the victim and family members is the least likely to occur. In most instances, a family support system improves the victim's postrape perception of herself, as well as restoring to her a sense of normalcy in her relationships that is more difficult to reestablish with casual acquaintances, friends, or boyfriends after a rape incident. Because of the reassuring effect of such a normalization, the victim may sometimes prefer that her family act as though nothing had happened, even at the expense of some of the care and emotional support that she has been receiving, as is illustrated in case 18.

Case 18

The victim, a 15-year-old girl, had been raped by several boys at a party. She felt some guilt over the incident because she had gone to the party against her father's wishes. Her family, however, was very supportive. Her father, in particular, was quite upset that her first sexual experience should occur through a rape. Not a week went by without his bringing her some new clothes. Day after day, her mother prepared the victim's favorite meals, and her older brothers and sisters began to take her out with them, whereas previously they had refused to do so.

Although the victim was grateful for this outpouring of warmth and support, her initial guilt feelings returned to plague her. She felt that perhaps she did not deserve all the care and attention that she had been receiving. She then set out to see how much she could get away with. She stopped cleaning her room and refused to help her mother with household chores. Finally, in frustration, her father yelled at her and confined her to the house for a week. She joyously told her social worker of the incident, exclaiming, "He yelled at me! He finally yelled at me! Now I know that things are back to normal."

The data seem to support the theory that individual family members serve different functions during the adjustment process. Both father and mother may be cast in the role of protector, but father may also play an important role in restoring the victim's willingness to recognize individual differences among the men that she encounters. Both brother and sister may offer the victim peer support, and brother may also help to allay the victim's concerns over her physical safety. Mother may provide the victim with a strong base of emotional support that has a positive impact over a wide range of possible adjustment patterns. There exists the strong possibility that victim-family interactions operate on two distinct levels. For example, a victim may resent her parent's attempts to alter her social activities or her circle of friends, yet may, at the same time, feel more physically and emotionally secure because of her parent's presence in the home. In some cases, however, this tacit support may be outweighed by interactions that essentially redefine the victim-family relationship (for example, where they blame rather than support her), or aggravate an already difficult relationship (for example, where the victim has been a truant or a police problem).

In chapters 4 and 5, the authors explore various interpretations for some of the more striking correlations found to exist between the adjustment patterns and various victim- and incident-related variables. It cannot be overemphasized that the correlations uncovered in the current study merely represent probabilities. There is no such thing as a so-called typical rape victim for any aspect of adjustment being considered. To say that a particular correlation will occur 95 times out of 100 is also to recognize that 5 times out of 100 it will not occur. It is the authors' contention, however, that awareness of these probabilities may provide the clinician with valuable clues as to the likely course of postrape adjustment in particular cases, and it may eventually lead to the treatment of rape victims as individuals, rather than as stereotypes.

Notes

1. Nancy Gager and Cathleen Schurr, *Sexual Assault: Confronting Rape in America* (New York: Grosset and Dunlap, 1976), p. 126.

2. Sandra Sutherland Fox and Donald J. Scherl, M.D., "Crisis Intervention with Victims of Rape," *Social Work* 17 (January 1972): 37–42.

3. Ann Wolbert Burgess and Lynda Lytle Holmstrom, *Rape: Victims of Crisis* (Bowie, Md.: Robert J. Brady Company, Prentice-Hall, 1974), pp. 37–50.

The Victim

Media depictions of rape have promoted a system of classification based almost solely on the character of the incident. If the victim has been subjected to excessive brutality, threatened with a weapon, assaulted by more than one offender, perhaps over a considerable period of time, or forced to engage in acts of sexual deviance, then one is justified in describing the incident as a "bad" rape. On the other hand, a rape incident in which the victim has suffered no visible physical injuries or has been assaulted by an acquaintance is to be viewed as somehow being of a less serious nature. Indeed, in either of the latter two scenarios the victim is often placed in the position of having to demonstrate her own integrity to the satisfaction of police, detectives, judge, jury, husband, boyfriend, family, or friends.

From the standpoint of the victim's postrape adjustment, however, the amount of violence to which the victim was subjected is often of secondary importance. Rather, factors such as the victim's age, marital status, and employment status are significantly more likely to affect certain aspects of her adjustment than is the extent to which she was brutalized. In this chapter the authors focus on some of the victim factors and the ways in which they affect the adjustment process.

Age

In the research design used in this study, rape victims were categorized as either adult victims (18 or older), adolescent victims (12 through 17), or child victims (under 12). The data indicate that, at least in the short run, adults are most likely to face adjustment problems, with adolescents less likely and child victims least likely. The difficulties that confront adult victims probably come from a combination of factors. In the first place, adults are less likely to have the home support that younger victims usually receive and are generally unable to retreat into the confines of the home. Adult victims are more likely to be married, and, as discussed later, the marital relationship is often a source of increased tension and anxiety for the victim. Adult victims are more likely than younger victims to be employed, compelling them to interact casually with large numbers of people every day, both during working hours and traveling to and from work. These factors are discussed in detail in subsequent sections of this chapter. In this section, only those factors that involve intrapsychic and developmental differences among age groups are addressed. Table 4–1 summarizes the significant correlations between victim age and likelihood of adjustment problems immediately following the rape.

Adulthood encompasses a wide range of psychosocial and economic stages. The young adult is often preoccupied with her sexuality and its role in the formation of intimate personal relationships. She is just beginning to feel confident about her maturity and her newly established adult status. If a rape incident drives her back to her family or to total dependence on her husband, her sense of maturity may be shattered, often for a long period of time.

Many adult victims are in the process of raising families. The demands placed on a woman at this stage in her life are considerable. Adult women with families are particularly concerned about how the incident will affect other family members. Postrape adjustment difficulties often prevent these women from effectively carrying out the responsibilities of mother, homemaker, and wife.

To older women, the sexual aspects of the rape incident are probably of less concern than the aggressive elements. Older women are, after all, more likely than younger victims to be physically incapacitated by any injuries resulting from a sexual assault. While seeing herself as more physically vul-

Table 4–1
Summary of Adjustment Variables Associated with Victim Age

	Age of Victim	Percent with Change
Change in eating habits	18+	67.0
	12–17	41.9
	0–11	13.6
Change in sleeping patterns	18+	67.9
	12–17	41.4
	0–11	24.8
Increased fear of streets	18+	76.6
	12–17	57.9
	0–11	28.2
Increased fear of being home alone	18+	55.3
	12–17	29.0
	0–11	18.8
Change in social activities	12+	53.1
	0–11	17.9
Increased negative feelings toward unknown men	18+	66.1
	0–17	46.5
Worsened heterosexual relationships	12+	42.1
	0–11	16.7

nerable, an older woman is less likely to identify herself as seductive or "rapeable." She may experience a great deal of cognitive dissonance as the result of being sexually assaulted. In addition, she may live alone, lacking a supportive family network to help her through the postrape period.

In our society, adults are held fully responsible for their actions. They expect to be in control of themselves and of their environments. When a rape incident shatters this sense of mastery, a victim tends to develop feelings of guilt and may believe that she has only herself to blame for her misfortune. Adult victims are especially likely to judge themselves harshly concerning any ambiguous elements of the rape. The word ambiguous is used here to describe those aspects of the rape that are not usually associated with or found in the context of aggression. This would include not only incidents where "fondling and caressing" of the victim occurred but would also encompass those situations in which the victim was assaulted by a friend or casual acquaintance. In such instances, the victim–blaming attitudes of others (police, husband, friends) contributes to the tendency of the adult victim to blame herself.

Finally, an adult victim is often in the position of having to admit that she has achieved a certain permanence in her lifestyle. Particularly with regard to older women, this is the neighborhood in which she will probably continue to live and the type of work or other activity that she will probably continue to perform, perhaps for the rest of her life. And, within this life, she was raped. If the victim were able to imagine an escape from her surroundings—even only the possibility of an escape at some point in the distant future—her adjustment problems would probably decrease. If she could only change her environment radically, she might feel more secure about ruling out the prospect of a reoccurrence. However, since this is rarely possible, she will stay at home more (feeling less secure while there), walk alone outdoors less, restrict her social activities, and interact with men only with a great deal of suspicion and some degree of hatred.

Adolescents are less likely than adults to experience adjustment problems over the first year following the rape. This is because adolescents can solve the problem of rape in the same way that they are able to solve so many of the problems of adolescence—by returning to the home and temporarily abandoning moves toward independence. However, the authors hypothesize that adolescents are likely to experience more adjustment difficulties as they become adults so that they catch up with adult victims over the long run. The need to solve all of the problems inherent in developing an intimate heterosexual relationship can be postponed by the adolescent, but they must eventually be confronted during adulthood.

The adolescent who is raped experiences this attack at a time when she is involved developmentally in trying to maintain a steady self-concept and to establish an independent social identity while undergoing substantial physiological changes and intrapsychic reorganization. Psychosexual drives become the focus of the adolescent's attention. As she strikes out on her own, the relationship between parent and child becomes conflict-ridden. She mistrusts most adults.

The aggressive component of rape disrupts the adolescent victim's view of her increasing autonomy and capacity to deal with her social environment at a period in her life when affirmation of her individuality and ability to cope with external reality and with her own drives is critically important. The rape may result in her viewing the possibility of independence with a great deal of pessimism. She may retain strong reservations about interactions with others and the transfer of emotional investment from her family to other persons. However, the victim's family may often feel out of control and unable to manage its adolescent child, particularly if the rape resulted from her being in the type of social situation that would tend to underscore her emerging independence. Her family may, therefore, withhold its support and instead try to make her feel guilty about her participation in the rape.

The sexual component of rape may lend credence to the victim's frightening fantasies about the nature of human intimacy. If the rape incident becomes the basis for her attitude toward sexuality, she is likely to devalue her own future sexual role. Furthermore, the level of anxiety and the affective and physiological arousal in her reaction to either the aggressive or sexual component of rape may leave her with a mental impression of her own vulnerability, passivity, and loss of control. Perceiving herself in this way is likely to serve as a deterrent to receptivity, tenderness, and spontaneity in her pursuit of sexual gratification in the future. Adolescent girls who are already sexually active are often engaging in sexual activity primarily to please or hold onto a boyfriend. They may find sexual relations pleasant, but they may at times feel that the pleasure derived from sexual activity falls short of their previous expectations. The rape may reinforce the negative aspects of their feelings about sexuality.

Some of the consequences of rape in adolescence are related to the state of personality development and physical maturation in which the victim presently finds herself. The young adolescent girl, unsettled by the psychobiologic changes of puberty, is beginning to give up her passive, dependent claims on her mother while seeking to establish new, often idealized, friendships with both males and females. Rape may interfere with this project more or less decisively. The young adolescent victim may turn away from her peers and back to her mother's protection. This anxiety is often met by the complementary concern of her mother. The adolescent is highly alert to her mother's level of distress as a barometer of the seriousness of her (the victim's) own injury and may find some security in her mother's closeness and involvement. On the other hand, the victim's mother or other family members may become so distressed over the rape that the ability to emotionally support the victim is seriously hampered. This is likely to occur when, as a result of the rape, an adolescent's prior sexual activity is discovered, or where the victim's family is unable to cope with the idea that the victim has now been identified as being sexually desirable. When the rape has resulted from association with a more sexually experienced, and often older, female peer, the young adolescent girl may express more despair and disappointment regarding her girlfriend than the offender. This often painful rejection may cause difficulties in the development of subsequent relationships with other females.

Prone to fantasy and limited by scant social experience and sexual knowledge, the young adolescent victim frequently deals with the consequences of rape in vague, global terms (for example, "a cloud over my future"), while regarding the actual experience of rape as having literally and catastrophically forced her to cope with sexual problems as an unequipped and frightened child. Adolescent peer groups often still divide girls into good-girl and bad-girl categories. Adolescent rape victims are often afraid that they will, by virtue of the rape, be placed in the bad-girl category.

Fear of venereal disease and pregnancy may persist for years after the rape of the early adolescent who has just been introduced to such matters. This may be due to the panic level anxiety aroused by the actual experience of being raped, and the fear may be heightened if the incident involved multiple offenders. The victim may continue to feel dirty, contaminated, and ruined, even after medical examination, treatment, cleansing showers, supportive counseling, and psychotherapy.

During middle adolescence, there is already a foundation of precedents and accommodations to physical change. Heterosexual relationships are more structured, emotionally meaningful, and capable of meeting the adolescent's needs. During this phase, the adolescent girl achieves further psychological separation from her parents. She becomes less bound by internalized admonitions and also potentially less protected by parental support. She is able to appraise more realistically her social interactions and to develop distinctive interests and skills that can help to sustain her motivation and sense of competence in difficult times. Her reaction to rape is more likely to be based on realistic considerations than is the case with younger victims.

The teenager in middle adolescence is more amenable to pursuing her trial-and-error dealings with the adolescent community, as well as her active negotiations with her parents over the issue of controls. The support of her peer group, a good relationship with her boyfriend, family understanding and support, ongoing academic interests, and tentative life goals can all greatly assist the adolescent rape victim in renewing her confidence and motivation. The adolescent who is narcissistically entrenched or limited by a rigid superego may have considerably more difficulty in trying to overcome self-doubts and a depressive outlook.

The experience of rape in late adolescence, when the individual has already begun to stabilize her ego organization and take on a definitive sexual identity, can be met with even more resources. However, the reactions of family, peers, and/or boyfriend are often decisive, either generating substantial emotional support or seriously aggravating postrape difficulties. The victim's long-term ability to seek and find a loving relationship and sexual gratification will almost certainly be affected by the rape and her immediate response patterns.

All adolescent rape victims share the problems associated with the management of a spoiled identity—they are always "discreditable."[1] If the victim manages to escape her immediate environment when she enters adulthood, does she tell her new friends that she has been raped? And what about a boyfriend? At what stage in their relationship does she tell him? All the tensions surrounding this decision-making process may persist for years.

The marked difference in adjustment patterns between adult victims and late adolescent victims should be noted. One may question the notion that adjustment patterns are susceptible to such fine distinctions based on age. Obviously, the adjustment problems of a 19-year-old rape victim may more closely approximate those of a 17-year-old adolescent victim than those of a 50-year-old victim. However, even a 19-year-old victim may feel that her lifestyle has already taken on a quality of permanence. If she is out of school, married, and working, she may not be able to foresee ever moving to a new environment. In many ways, her reaction to rape will be based on the same psychological premises as those of the considerably older victim. The 17-year-old victim is more likely to still be in school and less likely to be married or working at a job that she will be tied to for years. In spite of the seemingly insignificant age difference, the adolescent victim is often in a far better position than the young adult to imagine an escape from the environment within which she was raped.

Finally, child victims of rape exhibit the fewest short-term adjustment problems. In many cases, the nature of the event (or events) is merely confusing. Whereas the event is disturbing to the victim, it is perhaps no more disturbing than so many other aspects of a child's life. In the first year following the rape, the victim's family may deliberately maintain an "everything-is-normal" posture. These efforts, combined with the child's natural tendencies to forget and to replace bad feelings with good feelings, usually result in the appearance of few adjustment problems. For example, one child victim told the psychiatrist, "when I remember about it (the rape) I keep trying to think about good things like Christmas and it goes away."

Several other factors relating directly to differences in age may contribute to the relative absence of short-term adjustment problems in child rape victims. First, the needs of children are usually met by a relatively small, closed circle of family and friends. On the other hand, adults and, to a lesser extent, adolescents engage in much broader interactional patterns. Their needs tend to be met through a variety of relationships that are of a less fundamental nature than those of children. For example, adult females will often have close friends in whom to confide, casual acquaintances with whom to share specific interests or hobbies, and sex partners to meet their sexual needs. Because the adult rape victim must interact with this wider circle of individuals to have her needs met, she must place herself in a position of greater vulnerability. She will thus be more prone to short-term adjustment difficulties. In addition, the manner in which children satisfy certain basic physiological needs may be more reflective of actual needs than is the case with older individuals. From the standpoint of adjustment, this means that child rape victims may not suffer drastic changes in eating habits simply because their habits are probably more in line with the body's nutritional needs than are the eating habits of older victims. An adult rape victim could probably drastically reduce her food intake without presenting a serious threat to her survival; a child victim probably could not. Similarly, the need for sleep in younger victims cannot be denied to the extent that it can be in older victims, where external drugs (for instance, coffee) can be relied on to compensate for inadequate amounts of sleep. And, in matters of both eating and sleeping, the child victim is likely to be closely monitored by other family members.

Some of the research findings on child victims are disappointing in regard to the paucity of conclusions that can be drawn about the effects of childhood rape. In many ways, the research instruments were not sensitive enough. Gross changes were recorded, but periodic interviews at 3, 7, and 11 months did not provide adequate information concerning the more subtle psychological changes that may have been taking place within the child. The theoretically critical response of the victim's parents was not sufficiently documented. Indeed, 1 year is not a suitable follow-up period over which to examine the possible long-range effects of rape—a 5- or 10-year study would probably be needed for this purpose. What the present study measured was primarily the absence of response in child victims, presumably because of the need of the victim's mother to minimize the severity of the sexual assault to the interviewer.

Most of the negative changes in child victims were found to have taken place immediately following the rape incident. In many cases, subsequent home visits failed to uncover substantial negative change unless the offender (if a family member) remained in the home or the victim was anxiously anticipating a court appearance. The changes that did appear were often difficult to attribute to the rape, as they may have reflected normal developmental growth and change.

However, these well-adjusted children could just as easily have been pseudo-adjusted. The authors hypothesize that these children, to the extent that they have repressed the rape incident, will experience considerable adjustment problems once they reach puberty, begin dating or having sexual relations, or give birth to children of their own.

Joseph J. Peters, M.D., founded the Center for Rape Concern, in part, because of the alarming number of patients in his private practice whose problems could be traced primarily to incidents of childhood rape. He published six case histories to illustrate this pattern.

The first two cases involve forcible rape by a friend acting as a baby-sitter, with future problems being attributed, in large part, to the silence imposed on the victim by her mother. The next two cases involve adolescent girls who were seductively flattered by their fathers, and who ran away from home when intercourse was attempted. In each of these cases, Dr. Peters felt that the lack of a parental heterosexual relationship after which to pattern her own relationships may help to explain the first victim's inability to select a suitable male companion, and the second victim's inability to become seriously involved with any man. The last two cases involve two sisters who were subjected to repeated preoedipal rape and sexual assault. The poorer prognosis in the case of the older sister was attributed to her never having had the opportunity to confront and work through her rape experience and parental relationships. Her younger sister did have this opportunity, following an hysterical episode at the birth of her first child, whom she believed was the result of her earlier sexual relations with her father.[2]

Dr. Peters suggested that childhood rape victims who show little emotion immediately after the incident are actually storing up "psychological dynamite" that may explode at some later critical point in their psychosexual development (courtship, marriage, childbirth). He contrasted the typically withdrawn child victim to the typically tearful adult victim and described working with child victims as a process of "defusing a psychological time bomb."[3]

Marriage and Family Relationships

A rape victim who lives with her mother, father, sister, or brother will be significantly less likely to experience adjustment problems than will a victim who lives with her husband. Relations between a victim and her family (other than husband) decline in only one case in seven. Often, they improve. The marriage relationship does not provide the same level of support, and it nearly always has a negative impact on the adjustment process.

The problems confronting a married rape victim may be attributed to any of several factors. First, a married woman is less likely than a single woman to view herself as a potential rape victim and might therefore feel more guilt over being raped. Many older married women do not define themselves as being seductive or particularly sexual. When a rapist labels them as being sexual, they may have a great deal of difficulty in incorporating this idea with their prior self-images. Uncertain now of how others perceive her, the rape victim may find interacting with others a painful, anxiety-producing process.

Whereas the married rape victim may blame herself for her victimization, in most cases her adjustment problems are due, at least in part, to the reaction of her husband to the rape and/or how she perceives his reaction. In many cases, communication between husband and wife following a rape becomes a matter of extreme confusion and uncertainty. Does he try to show her that he still loves and cares for her by having sexual intercourse with her soon after the incident? For some women, this would be an appropriate reaction; others may construe it as inconsiderate and insensitive. If her husband tries to avoid selecting an improper approach by withdrawing from her as much as possible, the victim may sense that he now views her as defiled or contaminated and would rather not be married to her anymore. Husbands who need to work through their own reactions to rape are not often given the opportunity to do so. They may, therefore, harbor some resentment against their wives for causing them this emotional anguish.

In each of these instances the victim is blamed, either by herself or by her spouse, not for the rape itself but rather for her failure to communicate her feelings to her husband following the rape. In many cases, however, the victim may find that her husband blames her for being raped. She may be subjected to fierce interrogation from him regarding the extent of her resistance and/or revulsion, and she is likely to be extremely dismayed upon discovering that her anticipated primary source of emotional support has become her most determined accuser.

The husband of a rape victim is likely to rely on one of two theories to justify his victim-blaming posture. First, he may accuse her of complicity, insinuating that the rape allegation is merely being used to explain away an extramarital liaison that has, or was about to, come to his attention. In cases where the victim was raped by a casual acquaintance or friend, or in the offender's apartment, the likelihood of such an accusation is increased. And secondly, the victim's husband may blame her for failing to offer adequate resistance in the face of the assault. He may argue, either expressly or by implication, that her failure to resist must indicate that she enjoyed having sexual contact with the offender. Victims who bear no overt physical injuries are most likely to be confronted with this sort of accusation.

The reasons behind these victim-blaming postures are best understood through an examination of the husband's role in the marriage. He is a protector and provider and a rape incident may indicate to him that he has failed in this role, and he may feel unsure about his ability to adequately protect his wife in the future. By blaming the victim, however, the failure is no longer his. It was she who failed to offer adequate resistance and, therefore, she who must be held accountable for any subsequent difficulties. Furthermore, the blamed victim may be viewed by her husband as a legitimate outlet for his own anger and frustration over the incident.

Even if a victim is not blamed for a rape that left her with no visible physical injuries, her experience may intrude on her normal sexual relations with her husband. This is particularly true if the rapist has incorporated some element of tenderness (for example, fondling and caressing—see chapter 5) in the assault. As a general principle, one can speculate that the more a rape incident mimics elements of the victim's normal love-making experiences, the greater will be her difficulty in segregating the rape from the love-making process. If the rape victim is accustomed to being treated insensitively during sexual relations, the similarities may be even more disturbing to her. Sexual relations may come to be viewed as rapelike, and sexual relationships are likely to suffer. If the victim is married, the whole marital relationship may deteriorate if the problem is not quickly addressed and effectively worked out.

In some cases, married rape victims have fantasized, at some point prior to the assault, about having sexual relations with someone other than their husbands. Even in good relationships, this is not at all uncommon. When such a woman is raped, she may feel that she is being punished for the adulterous behavior in her fantasies.

A married woman is nearly twice as likely to experience worsened relations with her husband than is an unmarried woman with her boyfriend (45.5% versus 23.5%). The victim's husband is, after all, identified with her. Her difficulties are also his own and will continue to be so until they are resolved. He is unable to sidestep the problem, and he may become impatient if it persists. A boyfriend, on the other hand, can afford to be a bit more patient. His day-to-day contact with the victim is likely to be more limited than that of husband and wife. He is not likely to be identified with the victim to the same extent, and he may not feel the same sense of failure in his role as protector that a victim's husband may feel. If her problems ultimately become too much for him, he can gracefully exit from the relationship.

A married rape victim is more than twice as likely to experience worsened relations with other family members (that is, not including her husband) than is an unmarried victim (34.1% versus 15.3%). It appears that the divisive impact of rape on a marital relationship may spill over to other family members, who may feel compelled to lend their support to one side or the other. Some may agree with the victim's husband that the victim placed herself in danger, failed to offer adequate resistance, or should have expected that something like this would eventually happen, and so forth. Others may feel that the victim's husband has failed to offer his wife any emotional support, has no right to hold her accountable for the incident, or has been far too impatient with her, and so forth. The conflict between the victim and her husband is likely to be viewed by family members as a clash of personalities, not terribly different from many other marital problems. Even where no conflict between the victim and her husband has yet been observed, family members may feel the need to "get in the first blow," in anticipation of the issue of blame eventually being raised. With an unmarried victim, however, the problem is better defined. Since there is no other personality represented (except in cases where the offender is a family member), not to side with the victim is to side with the rapist. And, although this may occur in cases where the victim has previously been labeled a bad girl (a history of truancy or police trouble—discussed later), in most instances it does not.

Family support plays a vital role in mitigating the severity of postrape adjustment difficulties in almost every area that was tested. The presence in the home of one or more family members (mother, father, sister, or brother) significantly reduces the likelihood and/or the intensity of the following adjustment problems frequently occurring immediately after a rape incident:

Change in eating habits

Change in sleeping patterns

Increased nightmares

Increased fear of being home alone

Worsened heterosexual relationships

Insecurities concerning sexual attractiveness

Whereas the presence in the home of any family member is assumed to aid in restoring to the victim some sense of physical security, other more specific functions appear to be served by individual family members (see chapter 3). Often the support of family members is in sharp contrast to the reaction of the victim's husband, as already detailed. For example, whereas a married woman will suffer a more severe increase in her insecurities concerning sexual attractiveness—probably because her own fears in this area are aggravated by her husband's failure to emotionally support her—a victim living with her mother is likely to receive continued reassurance that she is still attractive and sexually desirable. It was also found that a victim who lives with her father is significantly less likely to be experiencing increased negative feelings toward known men 1 year after the rape than is one who does not live with father (19.4% versus 39.3%). The presence of father in the household is likely to undermine any stereotyping that may have been brought on by the rape. Here is, after all, a man whom she knows and who is not out to take advantage of her. And, if there is at least one obvious exception to her recently adopted rule that all men are alike (that is, like the rapist), are there not likely to be others? As discussed, the relationship between the victim and her husband, particularly the sexual component of that relationship, may reinforce any negative feelings that the victim has previously harbored against men.

Table 4-2 presents partial sets of data illustrating the likelihood of occurrence of various adjustment problems immediately after the rape (variables presented in order of strength of association).

Marked differences in adjustment patterns between the married and unmarried rape victim may be due to a fundamental difference between the type of support expected from her husband and that which is expected from other family members. A rape victim will respond primarily to the form and substance of her husband's communications with her. If he appears to be blaming her for the rape, she may begin to experience increased feelings of guilt, with a consequent worsening of the marital relationship. However, even if her husband feels only compassion for her, his inability to effectively communicate his feelings to her may lead to equally serious adjustment problems because of her feelings of rejection. A rape incident can have a profound impact on many facets of the marital relationship, and in many cases nothing less than the actively expressed support of the victim's husband is needed to facilitate the adjustment process. The support offered by other family members, however, can be of a more passive nature yet still be effective. The data suggest that it is the mere presence of other family members that has a positive effect on adjustment—not necessarily the communicational aspects of these relationships. For example, the victim who sleeps in proximity (in the same or a nearby room) to a sibling is presumed to have a greater sense of security at bedtime, which translates into fewer disruptions of her normal sleeping pattern. This type of peer relationship, combined with the protective role of male family members, probably explains the correlation between "victim lives with brother" and the relative infrequency of increased nightmares. The presence of any family member makes the home a less threatening place to the victim.

The correlation between "victim lives with mother" and decreased likelihood of eating or sleeping changes may represent a more active role. Particularly with a younger victim, eating and sleeping are likely to be more closely monitored by the victim's mother. In some instances (for example, "increased insecurities concerning sexual attractiveness"), the role of the

Table 4–2
Variables Associated with Adjustment Difficulties

Variable	Value	Percent with Change
Change in Eating Habits		
Victim lives with mother	no	60.9
	yes	38.9
Victim lives with brother	no	55.9
	yes	37.8
Victim's marital status	married	81.4
	not married	51.2
Victim lives with sister	no	54.3
	yes	38.1
Change in Sleeping Patterns		
Victim lives with mother	no	63.2
	yes	41.4
Victim lives with brother	no	58.9
	yes	39.9
Victim lives with sister	no	56.4
	yes	41.2
Victim's marital status	ever married	67.5
	never married	50.8
Increased Nightmares		
Victim lives with mother	no	40.0
	yes	24.8
Victim lives with brother	no	36.7
	yes	24.1
Increased Fear of Being Home Alone		
Victim lives with mother	no	58.9
	yes	30.2
Victim's marital status	ever married	64.1
	never married	36.4
Victim lives with father	no	49.2
	yes	25.2
Victim lives with brother	no	52.1
	yes	30.8
Victim lives with sister	no	50.0
	yes	32.6

victim's mother in actively providing reassurance to the victim approximates the degree of support that must be, but often is not, offered by the married victim's husband. In some instances, however, the overactive support of family members may be counterproductive (see case 18 in chapter 3). Even where family relations deteriorate to some degree, the continued presence of family members in the home may nonetheless enable the victim to regain a sense of physical and emotional security. Disagreements with her parents over, for example, the victim's continued participation in certain social activities may often be of relatively minor importance within the context of postrape adjustment.

A victim who was married but is no longer, is more likely to be living alone than a victim who has never been married. The rape incident may make her suddenly aware of her increased vulnerability in her present living situation. She is significantly more likely than an unmarried victim to experience a change in sleeping pattern and an increased fear of being home alone.

Finally, the only instance in which being married decreases the likelihood of change is with respect to social activities 1 year after the rape. This is readily explained by the fact that the married victim's social activities are rarely directed toward the pursuit of new heterosexual relationships and thus do not typically involve a very high degree of risk. In addition, these activities are often performed in the company of a protecting male, her husband. She therefore need not feel the same sense of urgency regarding a curtailment of her social activities as would an unmarried victim.

Prior Problems

A rape victim who has experienced certain types of problems in the past appears to be predisposed to adjustment patterns that reflect these prior problems. For purposes of discussion, a distinction has been drawn between problems that are primarily interpersonal and those that stem mostly from intrapsychic factors. In the first instance, the adjustment process may be significantly affected by the manner in which others react to the victim. If past activities have already earned her the label of bad girl, then she is more likely to be blamed for the incident and less likely to receive the support of others. In the latter instance, the victim's own view of herself and her environment may have a substantial impact on the way in which she adjusts to the incident. If she already views her world as dangerous (because of a previous assault) or otherwise troublesome (evidenced, perhaps, by a need to seek psychiatric assistance), then she is likely to have a higher level of chronic anxiety at the time of the rape and therefore less reserve strength and more vulnerability.

Whereas the distinction between interpersonal and intrapsychic problems may be of some theoretical value, there is bound to be some overlap between the two categories in practice. A victim who has been labeled by others as bad may, at some point, begin to view herself in this manner. In many cases, a history of police trouble or truancy may lead to adjustment difficulties primarily because of a poor self-image (for instance, "maybe I did bring this upon myself") rather than because of the accusations of others. Similarly, a victim who has previously exhibited a depressive personality may have already isolated herself from potential sources of emotional support. Her adjustment problems may stem, in large part, from the absence of any supportive interpersonal communication. With these possibilities in mind, each category of adjustment problem is discussed.

Interpersonal Problems

Rape victims with a history of trouble (police trouble or truancy) are more likely to be blamed by others, or to blame themselves, when raped. Of particular interest are such a victim's deteriorating relations with members of her family. If a victim has a history of truancy or has been in trouble with the police, her victimization is likely to be viewed as just one more item on a long list of misdeeds. Her past behavior raises a near conclusive presumption that she is once again at fault. Even 1 year after the rape, 30% of all victims who have had prior police trouble are still experiencing worsened family relations, as are 26.3% of those victims with a history of truancy. Additionally, a history of police trouble results in a threefold increase in the intensity of worsened relations with husband or boyfriend over what it is where there is no such history. This, too, occurs 1 year after the rape, indicating that a bad-girl or bad-woman label is not easily discarded following a rape incident. In some instances, it is possible that the incident is viewed as another victim-precipitated misdeed only after the immediate emotional responses of the victim and others have subsided somewhat. The negative criminal justice response likely to confront this type of victim (see part III) may serve to further reinforce the nonsupportive responses of those close to her.

The individual who is involved in activities that are labeled delinquent may feel that the rules of society do not apply to her own behavior. She may feel that she is above these rules and, in certain ways, invincible. When she believes that she is punished for not abiding by these rules (that is, by being raped), her sense of power is greatly diminished. All heterosexual relationships now present the possibility of further victimization without redress. Under these circumstances, she is likely to become extremely defensive in all interactions with members of the opposite sex. Because of the nature of her victimization, she may even feel justified in blaming males, in general, for the unflattering characterizations that have been applied to her because of her involvement in other incidents and activities.

Over three-fourths (77.4%) of those victims who had had previous trouble with the police had modified their social activities within the year immediately following the rape, as opposed to only one-half (50%) of those who had not had such trouble. A history of truancy is found to be similarly associated with a change in social activities at this point (69.2% of truants versus 49.7% of nontruants reduced their social activities). The association of these two variables with the intensity of change is even stronger. When one considers the other factors that attach to these variables, the reasons for this correlation become clearer. A victim who has been an habitual truant or police problem is likely to have been associating with others who are similarly disposed. It is not improbable that, in many cases, the assault arose directly from this association. A common scenario may proceed along the following lines: The victim and several other students (some of them male) cut school. They retire to some undisclosed location in order to "get high." Things eventually get out of hand. The victim loses control over the situation and is raped by one or more male companions.

For the victim with a history of police trouble, the incident may be a slightly more serious variation on this theme. In either case, the victim may decide that she would be a lot better off without these "friends" and may change her activities, and her companions, accordingly. Whether or not the rape has stemmed directly from some aspect of her lifestyle, any subsequent change in her social activities may reflect just how much room for change there was. Stated otherwise, the adoption of a life-style that allows for social interaction only in limited, riskfree situations may represent only a moderate alteration for some victims and just a slight change for others. In the case of a victim with a history of truancy or police trouble, the change to such a restricted lifestyle is more likely to be a substantial one. In this instance, the change must be characterized as a positive adjustment pattern.

Intrapsychic Problems

A rape victim who has been assaulted on one or more occasions prior to the rape, or who has previously suffered from emotional problems of sufficient severity to merit referral to a psychiatrist, is more likely than other victims to harbor a somewhat pessimistic outlook on life. The authors hypothesize that a successful postrape adjustment depends on the victim's fully believing that the event is past, that it was a horrible tragedy but one that is not likely to reoccur. If a negative worldview leads the victim to instead view rape as a normal consequence of living, or if prior problems otherwise compound the crisis, adjustment difficulties emerge.

One-half (50.5%) of all interviewed rape victims who had been sexually assaulted in the past experienced increased negative feelings toward known men immediately after the rape, whether or not their attackers were previously known to them. Slightly under one-half (49.3%) of those victims who had suffered a previous nonsexual assault also faced this problem. The effect of multiple assaults is apparently cumulative. On one level, the victim may no longer be willing or able to distinguish one attacker from another in terms of motivation. On another level, she may attribute these same motives to all men, feeling that her future safety requires nothing less than this kind of universal mistrust. As one would expect, there is a greater tendency toward such a sweeping indictment where the previous assault is sexual in nature, and the role of male as predator has already been underscored. One year after the rape, however, the victim may once again be able to accept the idea that her assaults are "past," provided that she has not been victimized again in the interim. At this time, her adjustment patterns are not significantly different from victims who have been raped once, with the only exceptions being a greater fear of being home alone and more intense nightmares.

A similar phenomenon is seen for victims who had received psychiatric assistance at some point prior to the assault. These victims experienced a significantly higher mean increase in negative feelings toward known men immediately after the rape than did those victims who had not received prior psychiatric assistance. However, there is no significant difference between these groups 1 year later. A victim who has suffered previous emotional problems is likely to view the rape as further evidence of her inability to come to terms with her environment. Her tendency to trust no one becomes readily understandable. But, as in the previous instance, her freedom from further assaults over a year's time may help to erase the victim's fear of impending doom and may result in an increased willingness to recognize motivational differences among males, particularly among those with whom she is acquainted. The quality of her heterosexual interactions is likely to improve.

A victim who has been nonsexually assaulted on at least one previous occasion may, in time, likewise come to view the rape as part of a pattern of possibilities inherent in her everyday activities. If she has attempted to be more cautious following the nonsexual assault, then she is liable to interpret the rape incident as an indication that limited measures do not help. Even the victim's own home may become the focal point of fears regarding further victimization. And, although not available in the data, one can reasonably conjecture that a victim who has been assaulted in the past is more likely to be blamed by others for the rape incident. She may be confronted by family members who demand to know "why you keep putting yourself in these situations." The correlation between previous nonsexual assaults and the intensity of worsened family relations immediately following the rape may be due, in part, to this type of interaction. Equally likely under these circumstances is an overprotective reaction from other family members. The level of tension existing in the victim's home can be expected to increase considerably if her family attempts to oversee all aspects of her life, with a consequent increase in adjustment difficulties.

Employment Status

In practically every area of adjustment considered in this study, the working victim will have a more difficult time than the nonworking victim. The working woman is forced to interact with men, both in the office and on the street, at a time when she would prefer not to. She is likely to become extremely defensive, and perhaps even openly resentful. She is faced with the enormous task of coping with these problems on a daily basis. A strong correlation between employment status and negative postrape psychiatric prognosis suggests that difficulties of this nature have an immediate, quite noticeable effect on many victims.

Employment status has a particular bearing on the rape victim's increased negative feelings toward unknown men. Because a working woman is compelled to interact with a substantial number of unknown men every day, she may begin to feel extremely vulnerable. She may blame all unknown men for her continued uneasiness. Her problems may even be aggravated by subtle reminders that the business world is still essentially a male domain. More than three of every four (77.8%) employed rape victims experienced increased negative feelings toward unknown men immediately following the rape, whereas only half (52.3%) of those who were not employed experienced this reaction. In general, those males with whom she is acquainted pose no such extraordinary threat to the working woman—she continues to trust those who have, up until that time, been trustworthy. It is worth noting that 1 year after the rape, employment status is no longer significantly correlated with increased negative feelings toward unknown men. Whereas having to face the world may cause severe problems initially, it may also help to set some things back into the proper perspective in a shorter period of time than would normally be required.

One year after the rape, the victim's employment status has become the variable most strongly associated with the likelihood of increased nightmares. There seems to be implicit in this and other findings the requirement that a distinction be drawn in the victim's mind between the rape, on one hand, and her everyday life, on the other. This is especially true when the rapist is a casual acquaintance of the victim (see chapter 5—victim–offender relationship), perhaps someone whom she sees at work, or on the way to work, every day. The victim cannot find solace or security in returning to her everyday routine, for in her mind she is merely placing herself in continuing peril. Rape is no longer the isolated incident that can be avoided by locking the door at night but rather a real danger built into every facet of her life—an unavoidable horror. Unless the employed rape victim is able to segregate the rape from the particulars of her everyday life, the rape will continue to contaminate her life. The persistence of nightmares 1 year after the incident suggests that she may only be pseudo-adjusted in her attitude toward unknown men. In other words, she might not have overcome her negative feelings but merely forced them from the level of consciousness so that she might again perform her day-to-day activities. These repressed feelings will emerge during the sleep state in the form of nightmares.

Only with regard to the intensity of worsened sexual relations with one's partner immediately after the rape does one find that the unemployed victim has a significantly worse reaction than the employed victim. One may conjecture that, rather than describing one or more direct causal links between variable and adjustment pattern, the appearance of this particular correlation defines, in part, the socioeconomic status of the victim and her partner. And, it is from this status itself that certain adjustment difficulties may arise. That is to say, a victim who is 18 or more years old, does not work, and does not have a high school education (another significantly associated variable), may belong to a socioeconomic class that typically harbors strong feelings concerning the territorial aspects of sexuality. The victim's partner may feel that, from the standpoint of their sexual relations, the victim is no longer exclusively his. He may see his own reputation as being in more danger than hers. If there is no evidence of brutality accompanying the incident (another significantly associated variable in this category), the tendency to blame the victim, whether to save face or to vent his anger, is likely to increase substantially.

Education

The overlap between victim age and other sociodemographic variables is most clearly illustrated in the case of the variable "number of school years completed"—the rape victim who has completed 12 or more years of school is nearly always an adult (18 or more years old). With only four adjustment categories does one find education to be either more strongly associated than victim age or correlated independently of victim age. Just as a victim's tendency to view the rape in global terms (for example, "I can no longer trust any man," or "I can no longer feel safe any time that I am alone") appears to increase with the victim's age and the greater permanence of her lifestyle, the educated victim may be even more prone to this type of thinking. She is more likely to intellectualize about certain aspects of her experience and may view the implications of being raped as extending far beyond the immediate physical and emotional trauma. Her adjustment may be hindered, to some degree, by this tendency to envision the worst possible consequences of rape and to assume that they will eventually apply in her own case. This may explain, in part, the significantly worse reactions, in the form of increased nightmares and an increased fear of being home alone, found among high school-educated rape victims. It may also play a role in those areas in which the effects of education are probably included within the more strongly associated variable of victim age.

The only two areas in which "school years completed" is inversely related to adjustment difficulties (that is, the better educated victim will have fewer difficulties) are sexual relations with partner and relations with family members. As was the case with employment status, the role of the victim's educational background in worsening sexual relations after a rape may be primarily one of defining that victim's (and often, presumably, her partner's) socioeconomic status. The relationship among socioeconomic status, rape violence, and adjustment to rape has already been considered (as discussed under the variable of employment status). As for worsened relations with family, the greater intensity of change for victims without a high school education may be due to a number of factors. The adult victim who has previously dropped out of school may have already been having family trouble. The rape may provide family members with what they see as new justification for maintaining their victim-blaming postures. The child or adolescent victim, who is unlikely to have yet completed 12 years of school, may experience an even greater worsening of family relations because of the likelihood that she still lives at home. The combination of these factors may explain the absence of victim age as a significantly associated variable in this area.

Summary

The course of a victim's postrape adjustment often depends primarily on factors not related to the actual rape incident, such as the victim's age, marital status, and employment status. Prior problems may predispose a rape victim to a difficult period of adjustment, even though the nature of her assault may be characterized by both the media and the courts as relatively mild.

The authors found that adult victims (aged 18 or over) have significantly more short-term adjustment problems than either adolescents (aged 12-17) or children (aged 0-11). However, it is hypothesized that both adolescent and child victims will eventually catch up with adult victims in the long run, experiencing more serious adjustment problems as they become adults. This is because the postponement of adjustment problems is often mistaken for the absence of adjustment problems. Such problems may lie dormant for years, only to appear at some critical point in the victim's psychosexual development (courtship, marriage, childbirth). A 5- or 10-year follow-up study would be needed to accurately document the unfolding of latent rape-related difficulties.

The adult rape victim is more likely than a younger victim to be married, employed, or high school educated. However, each of these variables impacts on the adjustment process in a unique way. While a victim living with her parents and siblings is likely to receive their emotional support in most instances, a married victim is often blamed for the rape—by her husband on the grounds of complicity or lack of adequate resistance and/or by family members who feel compelled to take sides during any marital difficulties that result from the rape. The employed victim must go out into the world every day, confronted by unknown men at her job and on her way to and from work. A high level of anxiety is likely to plague her for some time, particularly if she was raped within this everyday environment. The better-educated rape victim is more likely to be concerned about the more remote implications of having been sexually assaulted, thus hindering her adjustment in certain areas.

Finally, the rape victim who has traditionally been blamed by others because of participation in delinquent activities (truancy or police trouble) is also likely to be blamed for her involvement in the rape incident. If she already has a poor self-image, either because of such interactions with others or because of intrapsychic difficulties (brought on by previous assaults or by problems requiring psychiatric assistance), adjustment problems are likely to emerge.

Notes

1. Erving Goffman, *Stigma: Notes on the Management of Spoiled Identity* (Englewood Cliffs, N.J.: Prentice-Hall, 1963), p. 41.

2. Joseph J. Peters, "Children Who Are Victims of Sexual Assault and the Psychology of Offenders," *American Journal of Psychotherapy* 30 (July 1976): 407.

3. Joseph S. Peters, "Child Rape: Defusing the Psychological Time Bomb," *Hospital Physician* 9 (February 1973): 46.

The Incident

The terms *rape* and *sexual assault* encompass a wide range of possible situations. Factors such as the amount of violence involved, the performance of any sexually deviant acts, the number of attackers, the presence of a weapon, the location of the incident, and any prior relationship between victim and offender are all important in predicting the specific adjustment problems likely to confront any given rape victim. Even a rapist's pretended displays of tenderness during the incident may have a profound impact on certain aspects of the adjustment process. Unfortunately, media depictions of rape gloss over most of these finer details, generally focusing only on those one or two bits of information that are relevant at the trial stage (for example, the victim was previously acquainted with the offender). The adjustment process itself is largely ignored.

The criminal justice system does not ignore these finer details, but it often misinterprets their significance. What is likely to be viewed by both the courts and the media as a somewhat less serious assault (for example, victim and offender previously acquainted, the incident arising out of normal social activity, no visible physical injuries) often leads to far more severe adjustment problems then a brutal, back–alley gang rape, irrespective of any sociodemographic differences among victims (see chapter 4). The conventional wisdom seems to be that a case of rape involving difficult elements of proof (what the authors term an ambiguous rape, discussed later) will have a less traumatic effect on the victim. In most cases, exactly the opposite is true. In this chapter, the authors examine the relationships between these incident factors and the adjustment process.

Rape Violence

Among the variables that describe the violence component of a rape are the following:

Brutal beating

Nonbrutal beating

Physical force

Nonphysical force (threats)

Coercion

Intimidation with a weapon or object

Choking

Number of attackers

Roughness

Since all rape incidents include one or more elements of violence, characterizations on the basis of rape violence must focus on subtle differences in degree. From the standpoint of adjustment, however, even such subtle distinctions may be of little value to the clinician. Although adjustment difficulties are likely to increase proportionately to the level of brutality, the types of adjustment problems likely to confront a rape victim may depend more on the specific nature of that violence (for example, choking, as opposed to intimidation with a weapon). Furthermore, in many instances a relatively low level of rape violence serves as the direct cause of equally serious adjustment problems. Rather than the anticipated correlation between rape violence and adjustment difficulties (figure 5-1), the authors obtained a model quite different (see figure 5-2).

The problems characteristic of a relatively nonbrutal rape (point A) are generally of a different nature, but no less serious, than those likely to face the victim of an extremely brutal rape (point B). The specific problems arising at each end of the continuum are now detailed.

If rape constitutes an invasion of the victim's territorial rights over her own body, a brutal rape must be a double invasion. The victim must now deal not only with the sexual and aggressive aspects of rape but also with a reinforced sense of her own mortality and vulnerability. A brutal rape is likely to shatter the victim's basic sense of trust and security in herself and her environment. Unlike many of the victim factors (see chapter 4), which tend to become less strongly associated with adjustment difficulties 1 year after the rape, the brutal aspects of rape continue to affect adversely adjustment 1 year later. Indeed, certain violence-related variables often become more strongly associated with adjustment problems 1 year after the rape. In particular, life-endangering variables like "choking" and "intimidation with a weapon" are just beginning to appear as significantly associated with various adjustment difficulties. The authors hypothesize that these delayed or increased correlations are because of a change in the way in which the victim views her experience over time. The victim must first deal with the immediate trauma of having been raped. Whether she is primarily concerned with the aggressive or the sexual aspect of her victimization, she may not fully appreciate any actual threat to her life, except in a vague, general sense. With the passage of time, however, the details of the incident are

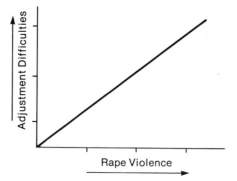

Figure 5-1. Anticipated Correlation between Rape Violence and Adjustment Difficulties.

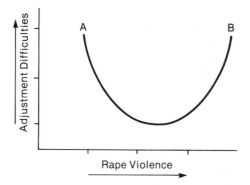

Figure 5-2. Actual Correlation between Rape Violence and Adjustment Difficulties.

likely to be sorted out by the victim in a more rational manner. She may only then realize the extent to which her life had been endangered. With regard to choking, it is unlikely that any adverse effects will decrease over time, because a rape victim is not likely to have subsequent experience with this type of situation. She may be in contact with men who do not rape, and with guns or knives that are not pressed against her head or throat. Her sensitivity to men, and even to weapons, may thus be lessened in some cases. However, it is impossible to imagine a subsequent experience with choking that would serve to reduce her anxiety.

Bearing the adverse effects of these life-endangering variables in mind, one can more readily explain the appearance of various adjustment problems. For example, the victim's family may often harbor some expectations regarding an appropriate time frame for adjustment, and they may become impatient with the victim when these expectations are not met. A victim who is still afraid to be alone on the street 1 year after being raped—and 76.7% of all victims who were choked fall into this category—may be accused by family members of not making a concerted effort to readjust to living, of wallowing in self-pity. Family relations can be expected to worsen at this point. This situation provides a clear illustration of the difficulties confronting the rape victim in having to deal with an extraordinary and disruptive event within the context of the everyday world (see chapter 3).

When an individual comes face to face with a life-endangering situation (for example, an automobile accident or a heart attack), one often witnesses a marked change in that individual's subsequent life-style. He may try to seek more satisfaction for himself by becoming more job oriented, more family oriented, and so forth, but this change will usually incorporate a decrease in risk-taking behavior. The rape victim, however, is more likely to exhibit a withdrawal from existing activities, rather than some positive changes in them. A decrease in risk-taking behavior becomes the focus of her altered life-style—not an incidental aspect of it. Unfortunately, such measures are unlikely to restore a sense of security to the rape victim, since her feelings of vulnerability stem from her being a female. Unlike the victims of accidents and illnesses, the rape victim can do nothing to lessen or erase the perceived source of her vulnerability. If she has been the victim of a brutal rape, her efforts to avoid potentially dangerous situations are likely to be exhaustive even 1 year after the rape. The violent aspects of the incidents will continue to effect a decrease in her social activities, have an adverse impact on her heterosexual relationships, and even keep her in fear of venturing outdoors alone.

Rape violence has an immediate impact on adjustment in regard to increased nightmares. The more brutal that a rape incident is, the less likely that a victim will be able to consciously deal with it. She may repress most details of it and attempt to deny the violent aspects altogether. Not surprisingly, four of the five variables significantly associated with increased nightmares 1 year after the rape describe elements of rape violence.

As stated earlier, serious adjustment problems can also result from the absence of excessive rape violence. If the element of roughness is missing from a rape, the victim is more likely to experience worsened sexual relations with her partner immediately after the rape, as well as a more severe worsening of sexual relations with her partner 1 year after the rape. A victim's husband, boyfriend, or lover may consider bruises or torn clothing the only evidence that a rape has actually occurred. In the absence of such tangible evidence, a victim is likely to find herself accused of failing to offer adequate resistance ("you enjoyed it") or even of trying to cover up other sexual activity by alleging rape. As detailed in chapter 4, to blame the victim for her involvement in the rape incident is to relieve one's own feelings of guilt or inadequacy, as well as to identify a suitable outlet for one's anger or frustration over the incident. The victim may, herself, begin to wonder whether she could have avoided her victimization, either by participating in safer activities or by offering greater resistance when attacked. It is apparent that, insofar as rape violence is concerned, a victim finds herself in what is essentially a no-win situation—either she suffers the trauma of a brutal rape or she is accused of complicity if she does not.

Sexual Acts

The study contains data concerning the following variables relating to sexual acts:

Penile-vaginal intercourse

Contact without penetration

Fellatio

Cunnilingus

Rectal intercourse

Fondling and caressing

Length of assault

Repeated intercourse

(These last two variables overlap considerably with the assault elements of the rape.)

In examining the effects of sexual acts on the adjustment process, one finds a pattern similar to that found in the area of rape violence. That is, adjustment difficulties will be most severe at either end of the continuum of sexual acts. (see figure 5-3). At point *A* would be found variables like "fondling and caressing" and "contact without penetration." Point *B* would include variables describing deviant sexuality (for example, "rectal intercourse"). It should be noted that a single rape incident may include elements from both ends of the continuum. Adjustment problems associated with both extremes of sexual activity (for example, rectal intercourse and fondling and caressing) could then be expected to emerge. In contrast, the inclusion of elements at one end of the rape violence continuum would, in most instances, exclude by definition elements at the other end.

The effects on the victim of specific sexual acts perpetrated during a rape incident may depend primarily on the victim's prior set of beliefs regarding sexuality and moral standards. For example, a young adult who

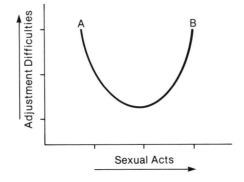

Figure 5-3. Correlation between Sexual Acts and Adjustment Difficulties.

was forced to perform fellatio on her attacker stated that she was relieved that he could not maintain an erection and penetrate her. An older victim, under virtually identical circumstances, was horrified at having to perform fellatio and would have preferred that penetration had occurred instead. Inability to feel comfortable with one's own sexuality may also contribute to adjustment difficulties arising from the sexual aspects of rape. A victim may experience feelings of guilt if her body responded, in some way, to sexual stimulation during the rape. Even involuntary responses to sexual stimuli, such as a hardening of the nipples or lubrication in the vagina, may lead the victim to believe that she somehow desired or enjoyed the incident. If the victim has, at one time or another, fantasized about having sexual relations with someone other than her husband or boyfriend, her guilt feelings over responding to sexual stimuli during the rape are likely to be severe.

It appears that the sexual aspects of rape are always on the periphery of consciousness, having greatest impact on diffuse activities like eating and sleeping, surfacing in the middle of the night as part of a bad dream or as feelings of fear or anxiety when alone on the street or when interacting with men. As is the case with extremely violent rapes, certain sexual aspects of rape may be impossible to deal with on a conscious level. Over half (56.7%) of the victims who were subjected to rectal intercourse experienced an increase in nightmares immediately after the rape, as compared to only 29.6% of those victims who were not subjected to rectal intercourse. One year after the rape, rectal intercourse still ranks second in strength of association with the extent to which nightmares have increased.

In their prognoses for rape victims, psychiatrists predicted that most rape incidents not involving penile–vaginal intercourse would not result in adjustment problems. It appears that a completed sex act serves to set the incident apart from other types of assaults, in the minds of both the victim and those with whom she regularly interacts. The rape victim may sense that others now view her as contaminated, and, in some instances, one who has maintained a monogamous relationship with the victim may indeed view her in this light. The child or early adolescent, whose peers are not yet sexually experienced, is often labeled a bad girl when the fact of her sexual victimization becomes known. Penile-vaginal intercourse, or "completed" sex, appears as a variable significantly associated with adjustment problems more frequently than does any of the other variables relating to sexual acts.

Special attention should be paid to those variables that are not usually associated with sexual aggression—those that the authors view as ambiguous within the context of rape. "Fondling and caressing" is the prime example of such a variable in the category of sexual acts, and it is typical, in its effect on adjustment, of ambiguous variables in other categories (for example, the absence of roughness, victim and offender previously acquainted). When a rape incident contains several ambiguous elements, it becomes more difficult for the victim to mentally segregate the rape from her everyday life. Displays of tenderness during normal love making may become a source of anxiety to the rape victim who has experienced a similar display during the course of a rape. If a rapist can exhibit tenderness, then perhaps her lover can exhibit the aggressive and hostile qualities that went along with this tenderness. In cases where there is contact without penetration, the effects of this ambiguity are likely to be especially dramatic. The wolf dressed in sheep's clothing may lead to a distrust of all sheep, and rape may come to be perceived as a possibility inherent in all normal activities and interactions. It is not surprising to find that "fondling and caressing" and "contact without penetration" are significantly associated with changes in sleeping patterns, increased nightmares, fear of being home alone, worsened heterosexual relationships, and increased insecurities concerning sexual attractiveness. The effects of ambiguous variables relating to other aspects of the rape incident are discussed further.

Victim-Offender Relationship

Several types of victim-offender relationships lead to adjustment problems in a fairly predictable manner. A rape victim who is previously acquainted with her attacker, even if he is no more than a relative stranger to her, is significantly more likely to experience increased negative feelings toward known men than is a victim who is raped by a total stranger. Approximately two-thirds (67.5%) of all victims raped by at least one total stranger experienced increased negative feelings toward unknown men immediately after the rape. If no total strangers are involved in the incident, or if one or more relative strangers are involved, the likelihood that the victim will experience worsened heterosexual relationships is significantly increased. These findings suggest that a rape victim will tend to project her negative feelings toward her attacker onto all males with whom she shares the same type of prior relationship (for example, friends, acquaintances, strangers).

The most severe adjustment problems are found to result in cases where the offender is a casual acquaintance or relative stranger. In these cases, the following logic seems to be operating: If a woman is raped by a stranger, she is likely to harbor negative feelings toward all unknown men and therefore attempt to avoid them. To some degree, this can be accomplished (by eliminating most social activities, never venturing far from home). If a victim is raped by a close friend or family member, she is likely to avoid that individual where possible or to accept the premise that this one particular individual suffers from a sickness and is being cured. She will have enough background information about other friends or family members to outweigh any tendency to attribute the rapist's motives to all members of that category (family member or friend). Casual acquaintances and relative strangers, however, cannot be avoided as easily as total strangers. One must assume that interactions with the postman or the paper boy or with neighbors will have to continue on some level. When the rape victim goes shopping, or to work, or to school, she will have to deal repeatedly with people whom she knows only casually (the problems facing the employed rape victim have already been discussed in chapter 4). In addition, she generally lacks the type of background information that enables her to particularize her feelings when raped by a friend or family member. There is no basis on which to distinguish the motives of other casual acquaintances or relative strangers from those of the rapist. The problems associated with this type of victim–offender relationship illustrate once again the notion of ambiguity as it relates to postrape adjustment. Casual acquaintances and relative strangers are part of one's everyday world. A rape perpetrated by such an individual is likely to continue to intrude on one's perception of the everyday world for a considerable length of time.

One year after the rape, the fact that one or more of the rapists was a casual acquaintance of the victim becomes of primary importance in predicting the likelihood and intensity of an increased fear of being home alone. In fact, this variable is even more strongly associated with this reaction than is the fact that the rape was committed within the victim's home. The danger in connection with being home alone involves, in part, the need for deciding who shall be permitted to enter one's home and who shall be denied entry. Whereas friends are admitted and total strangers can be refused entry as a matter of course, casual acquaintances present an ambiguous situation. One who has been raped by a casual acquaintance may have a great deal of trouble deciding exactly whom she can trust. She is likely to feel increasingly vulnerable while at home alone and may end up trusting no one.

In view of these findings with regard to victim-offender relationships and adjustment problems, it is hardly surprising that interracial rapes are found to present fewer adjustment difficulties than intraracial rapes. Immediately after the rape, the average intensity of increased negative feelings toward known men is almost twice as high for victims of intraracial rapes as it is for victims of interracial rapes. If it may be assumed that most everyday activities are intraracial, and that most known men are of the same race as the victim, the reason for this correlation becomes clear. A victim of interracial rape may increase her level of racial hatred, but she need not abandon or fear her everyday world, in which most men are of her own race.

Worsened family relations were found in 41.7% of those cases in which the rape involved a nuclear family member (parent or sibling), as opposed to only 16.1% of cases where no nuclear family member was involved. One factor contributing to this correlation may be the guilt felt by the parent who was either unable or unwilling to protect the victim from an incestuous situation. For example, the mother of a victim may feel responsible for her child's victimization and may also feel guilty because of the relationship that she, herself, has with the offender. As is the case with the husbands of married rape victims, the natural tendency in such situations is to attempt to pass one's guilt onto the victim, that is, to blame her for her victimization. And, whereas a victim-blaming posture may be indefensible when a child victim is involved, a rapist-protecting stance may accomplish the same purpose. The victim is blamed not for her actual involvement in the incestuous incident but rather for disgracing the family by allowing the incident to come to the attention of others. To admit that the offender actually raped his young daughter or sister is to demean the self-esteem of every member of that family. The rape victim may thus find family members allied against her in an effort to keep the incident in the family or to shift their own guilt onto the victim if the incident does come to the attention of others. Even where family members do not actively take sides, their ambivalence is likely to put a severe strain on all victim-family interactions.

Location

In several instances, the location of the rape incident is found to have a significant effect upon the types of adjustment problems likely to confront the victim. For example, a victim who has been raped in her own home will be more than twice as likely to experience a subsequent increased fear of being home alone than a victim who was raped elsewhere (72.2% versus 34.4%). Furthermore, an adolescent raped in her own home will be considerably more likely to exhibit this reaction than will an adult raped elsewhere (64.7% versus 44.8%), a rare exception to the finding that adults face significantly greater adjustment difficulties than do younger victims (see chapter 4).

One year after the rape, a victim who was raped in the rapist's home or car is significantly more likely than other victims to experience increased negative feelings toward known men. In a rape that occurs in the rapist's own territory, the victim is likely to have her sense of trust in herself and others shattered. Since entering the rapist's home or car was a wrong judgment (provided it was done voluntarily), she may be reluctant to exercise her judgment concerning other people or other situations in the future. She can no longer assume that people will be honest in their dealings with her and may often assume the worst about them for the sake of her own safety. Since it is likely that the victim has placed the greater part of her trust in friends and acquaintances, it is with these individuals that her attitudes and behavior are most likely to change dramatically as a result of the rape. It should also be noted that the rape victim is unlikely to again enter the rapist's home or car, at least for a while. She will thus have no opportunity to relive the experience in a safer climate and thereby lessen her sensitivity to that particular location. Finally, one must bear in mind that rape in these settings is correlated with rape by men whom the victim knows casually or better. Problems associated with that relationship (see Victim–Offender Relationship) may be primarily responsible for these findings.

Over one-half (52.9%) of all adult victims who were raped inside the home of someone other than the rapist or the victim herself experienced worsened relations with their husbands or boyfriends immediately after the rape, as opposed to only 25.5% of those who were raped elsewhere. Once again, there is a high probability that the victim will be blamed for her involvement in the incident. Whether or not her attacker was previously known to her, a married woman who is raped in someone else's home will probably be subjected to a vigorous interrogation by her husband as to what she was doing there and why she was unable to avoid the assault.

A victim who is raped in an automobile or abandoned building will be more likely than other victims to experience worsened relations with her family immediately after the rape. Family members may demand to know what the victim was doing inside an abandoned building or why she accepted a ride from a stranger. The insinuation that "you got yourself into this" is likely to have a negative impact on victim–family relations. In some instances, a rape occurring in either of the above two locations may convince the victim's parents that they ought to monitor more closely their daughter's activities. However, the inner cities are filled with cars and pock-marked with numerous abandoned buildings and properties. Attempts to isolate the victim from these settings are likely to result in considerable tension and conflict between the victim and her parents.

Summary

Most rape incidents are characterized by the media in broad terms (for example, "brutal gang rape"). Very little attention is usually paid to the finer details of the incident. The criminal justice system does consider these details, but it fails to correctly interpret their significance within the context of postrape adjustment. The notion that a so-called less serious assault causes fewer adjustment problems has no basis in fact.

The victim of a brutal rape comes face to face with her own mortality. Aspects of the incident that represent a genuine threat to life (choking, presence of a weapon) often become more strongly associated with adjustment difficulties one year after the rape, since perhaps only then will a victim be able to rationally assess the actual threat to her life. Often her inability to "snap out of it" leads to difficulties with family members. However, the absence of rape violence may lead to equally serious adjustment problems. Here the victim is more likely to be blamed for failure to resist the assault or even for trying to cover up consensual sexual activity. Reinforced by the accusations of others, her own feelings of guilt or anger ("why didn't I struggle or run?") may begin to surface.

The sexual component of a rape incident is also likely to have a significant impact on the victim's postrape adjustment. "Completed" sex (penile-vaginal intercourse) sets the incident apart from other types of assault, and is more frequently associated with adjustment problems than is any other sex-related variable. Prior beliefs regarding sexuality and morality may contribute to serious adjustment difficulties in cases that involve deviant sex. However, variables like "fondling and caressing" that are not usually associated with sexual assault ("ambiguous" variables) may cause equally serious problems of another kind. Here, the victim may begin to confuse the tenderness of a lover with the mock tenderness of the rapist. In her mind, displays of tenderness may become permanently associated with the rape incident, with consequent feelings of anxiety likely to emerge during normal activities and interactions.

The finding that variables not normally associated with a forcible rape (for example, no roughness, fondling and caressing) are, in fact, correlated with serious adjustment problems is clearly illustrated in the case of victim-offender relationships. If the offender is a casual acquaintance or relative stranger, the victim will experience more severe adjustment difficulties than if he were a friend, family member, or total stranger. Whereas strangers can be avoided, and most friends and family members will not be mistrusted because of the actions of some other friend or family member, casual acquaintances and relative strangers make up a significant yet uncertain segment of one's everyday world. One cannot totally avoid the postman, or neighbors, or coworkers, yet there may be no basis on which to distinguish their motives from those of the rapist. A victim who is raped by a casual

acquaintance or relative stranger will have considerable difficulty in divorc-
ing the rape from her everyday world. Incestuous situations raise unique
problems for the victim because of a family's natural tendency to protect
the rapist by preventing the situation from coming to the attention of
others.

Finally, the location of a rape incident may affect the adjustment process in some instances. Victims raped in their own homes will fear being at
home alone. A rape that occurs in the rapist's home or car is likely to lead to
an increased fear of known men, probably because the victim no longer
trusts in her own judgment. If raped in the home of someone other than
herself or the rapist, there is a high probability that the victim will be
blamed by her husband or boyfriend for her involvement in the incident.
And, if raped in an automobile or abandoned building, the victim may
experience worsened family relations when family members attempt to limit
her activities to avoid a repetition of the incident.

6   Victim Adjustment: A Summary

The data described in the preceding chapters reinforce one central conclusion: Rape is a devastating phenomenon. It dramatically changes the way in which the victim perceives and interacts with other people, and it often changes the way in which she perceives herself. Its effects are not always short-lived.

For a considerable period of time following a rape, the victim fears the everyday world and restricts her activities within it. She has difficulty dealing with men, even men whom she has known and loved, and she sometimes fears that the rape has left her less attractive or sexually desirable. Occasionally, relations with her family deteriorate. More often, her normal eating and sleeping habits are seriously disrupted, and she is plagued by increasingly frequent nightmares. Rich or poor, black or white, assaulted by a stranger or attacked by a friend, a victim of rape is a study in psychic trauma.

Unfortunately, most approaches to rape and it's aftermath never go much beyond this rough sketch of the so-called typical rape victim. A distinction is invariably drawn between the adult victim and the child victim, but factors such as whether the victim is employed, or whether she has been choked during the course of the rape, are rarely viewed as being pertinent to the adjustment process. However, it is often these details that determine the course of a victim's postrape adjustment and thereby provide the means by which victim counselors could quickly identify and effectively defuse those adjustment problems most likely to develop in any given case.

In chapter 3, the authors described thirteen adjustment problems corresponding to a different aspect of the victim's everyday life. The least common problem, worsened relations with family, still occurs in one of every seven cases. Most of the problems discussed affect more than one rape victim in three. Table 6-1 summarizes the probability of each of the thirteen problems occurring immediately after the rape and 1 year later.

This study found that the likelihood of a particular problem emerging depends on specific data concerning the victim (for instance, age, marital status) and/or the details of the incident (for instance, choking, victim-offender relationship). The previous two chapters detailed these patterns. Interestingly, several variables appeared as significantly associated with a large number of adjustment problems. And, each time that they appeared,

Table 6–1
Summary of Adjustment Problems Immediately and 1 Year after the Rape
(*percent*)

Adjustment Problem	Immediately after the Rape	1 Year after the Rape
Increased fear of streets	65.9	54.1
Increased negative feelings toward unknown men	57.5	50.7
Decreased social activities	50.3	53.6
Change in sleeping patterns	49.9	43.0
Change in eating habits	47.3	43.0
Worsened sexual relations with partner[a]	46.6	39.1
Increased fear of being home alone	43.2	24.8
Worsened heterosexual relationships	40.2	26.2
Increased negative feelings toward known men	36.6	29.3
Increased nightmares	31.1	20.7
Worsened relations with husband or boyfriend[a]	26.9	26.0
Increased insecurities concerning sexual attractiveness	18.7	15.7
Worsened relations with family	17.0	15.2

[a]Only computed for appropriate age groupings.

they tended to affect the problem in the same way—if they tended to increase the likelihood of one problem, they also tended to increase the likelihood of others.

In the short run, adult victims are most likely to have adjustment problems, with adolescents less likely, and child victims least likely. However, adolescents are likely to face increased rape–related difficulties as they reach adulthood, and child victims are likely to have the most serious long–range adjustment problems. Living with mother, father, sister, or brother lessens the probability of adjustment problems; living with a husband increases adjustment difficulties. A rape victim who is employed will experience difficulties in adjusting to rape, and if the victim has a history of truancy or police trouble, adjustment problems will be significantly greater. If the victim has been previously assaulted or has received psychiatric assistance, adjustment will be more difficult, and having a high school education aggravates adjustment problems. In terms of violence, the more convinced a rape victim is, either during the rape or in retrospect, that her life was genuinely in danger, the more likely it is that adjustment problems will result, and rapes that involve penile–vaginal intercourse or deviant sex acts usually lead to adjustment problems. If the rapist's prior relationship with the victim is that of casual acquaintance or relative stranger, adjustment problems are more likely; if the rape took place in any of several locations, adjustment problems peculiar to that location are likely to result.

Clearly, the concept of a typical rape victim has no place within the context of postrape adjustment. The need for specificity is further underscored when the notion of ambiguity is introduced. With reference to this concept, qualifications should be noted in two areas: the absence of extensive violence or brutality also leads to serious adjustment problems, although of a different nature from those arising from violent, potentially life-endangering acts; and rapes that involve mock displays of tenderness (fondling and caressing), either instead of or in addition to other sex acts, will also lead to serious adjustment problems, although of a different nature from those arising from these other sex acts.

In short, the more that certain aspects of a rape resemble aspects of the victim's everyday world, the harder it will be for her to keep the rape incident from intruding on her normal activities. If raped by a casual acquaintance, all casual acquaintances become suspect in her eyes. If subjected to mock tenderness during the rape, all subsequent displays of normal love making may be viewed as rapelike. If signs of brutality are not in evidence, others may insist that the alleged rape was a part of, or arose out of, the victim's everyday activities.

The fact that other exceptions to these correlations do exist suggests that even paying close attention to the tendencies of specific variables may not be enough. For example, not being employed is associated with greater adjustment difficulties in the area of sexual relations with partner, and not having a high school education is associated with greater adjustment difficulties in the areas of worsened family relations and sexual relations with partner.

It is clear that the clinician cannot effectively counsel rape victims on the basis of general theories of adjustment. What is needed is a complete profile of the victim and as much detail as is possible regarding the incident itself. Even well-documented tendencies may not apply in specific problem areas, or they may be overshadowed by other, less obvious, correlations. When we find that whether or not a victim is likely to experience increased nightmares 1 year after being raped depends mostly on whether or not she is employed, or that the likelihood of increased negative feelings toward known men immediately after the rape depends primarily on whether the victim has suffered a previous sexual assault, it becomes obvious that our approach to counseling rape victims must be reassessed.

The sum total of these findings is that there is more than one kind of rape that is likely to have a devastating impact on the victim. Brutal rapes, rapes with weapons involved, rapes committed by strangers, all lead to a wide range of adjustment problems. But so do rapes between casual acquaintances involving limited physical force and displays of mock tenderness. Married victims face a series of potential problems regardless of other circumstances, whereas children, with few short-term problems, may be

Table 6–2

Independent Variables by Frequency of Appearance as Significantly Associated with Adjustment Problems

Variable	Total Mentions	Immediately after the Rape	1 Year after the Rape
Victim age	31	16	15
Victim–Offender are differential	23	11	12
Weapon involved	22	11	11
Brutal beating	20	13	7
Number of school years completed	18	15	3
Stranger(s) involved	18	14	4
Victim employed	18	13	5
Victim lives with mother	18	13	5
Nonphysical force	18	13	5
Physical force	18	10	8
Coercion	17	10	7
Penile–Vaginal intercourse completed	17	9	8
Marital status	14	13	1
Victim lives with sister	14	10	4
Victim lives with father	14	7	7
Previous nonsexual assault	13	11	2
Victim lives with brother	12	11	1
Victim has had prior police trouble	12	5	7
Friend(s)	9	7	2
Choking	9	5	4
Victim has had prior psychiatric assistance	8	8	0
Repeated intercourse	8	8	0
Location of incident	8	6	2
Extended family involved	7	6	1
Length of assault	7	3	4
Victim–offender racial class	7	3	4
Truancy history	7	2	5
Nuclear family involved	6	6	0
Contact without penetration	6	5	1
Fondling, caressing	6	4	2
Relative stranger(s) involved	6	4	2
Casual acquaintance(s) involved	6	1	5
Victim on public assistance	5	5	0
Roughness	5	3	2
Previous consenting relations with offender	5	3	2
Rectal intercourse	4	3	1
Fellatio	4	1	3
Nonbrutal beating	3	3	0
Previous sexual assault	3	3	0
Victim lives alone	3	2	1
Number of rapists	3	1	2
Intimidation	3	0	3
Cunnilingus	1	1	0
No sex act	1	1	0

Note: Maximum possible mentions were 52.

faced with far more severe adjustment problems years, even decades, in the future. Black women do not have significantly more problems than white women; rich women do not have fewer problems than poor women. Rape can affect nearly any facet of any female's life and can do so for extended periods of time.

The next several chapters deal with the consequences of a rape victim's involvement with the criminal justice system. To summarize before proceeding further, table 6-2 depicts all the variables found to be significantly associated with at least one adjustment problem, immediately after the rape and 1 year later. The number of times that a variable appears does not necessarily indicate its relative importance, since many variables disappear in the final analysis. However, each of these variables might profitably be considered in the counseling of victims of rape.

Part III
The Criminal Justice
Response

7

Introducing the Criminal Justice System

The response of the criminal justice system to cases of rape has been the focus of a great deal of media attention and criticism. In the fictional model aired on the two television movies "Cry Rape" and "A Case of Rape," police-victim interaction is unpleasant. Police question the victim harshly and intensively, asking a series of insulting questions of doubtful relevance. The victim's complaint, however, is recorded, founded (believed) and labeled rape, and a suspect is apprehended. There is a jury trial, and it is under brutal cross-examination by the defense that the victim is fully confronted with a variety of victim-blaming attitudes. She is put on trial; the defendant is found not guilty.

Nearly all the 1,401 victims in the current study experienced some degree of involvement with the criminal justice system in that virtually all these rapes were reported to police. The entry point for inclusion in the study was the emergency room at Philadelphia General Hospital (PGH), to which, at that time, police were to bring all women who made a complaint of rape and who agreed to treatment. When victims who had not yet reported to police arrived at PGH for treatment, police were typically notified.

The criminal justice system encountered by these victims does not, however, conform precisely to the model. In the first place, most cases never come to trial. Many cases are eliminated at the police stage via recording the complaint as no offense or marking the complaint as unfounded (disbelieving the victim) or unable to apprehend a suspect. Victims often withdraw cooperation after encountering police practices or courtroom procedures. For cases in which a trial does occur, it is more often a nonjury than a jury trial and only infrequently involves a defense of victim consent.

The chapters that follow explore the criminal justice process in response to rape, from initial police involvement through sentencing. The opening chapters focus on the role of police in general and the practices of the Philadelphia Police Department in particular. Procedures followed by Philadelphia police in responding to complaints of rape are examined vis-a-vis official departmental guidelines in effect during the study period. The police function in deciding which of a variety of charges to apply to complaints of sexual assault, the implications of this decision, and the charging strategies developed by police are discussed, including the use of nonoffense charges or labels (for example, "investigation of persons"). The process for marking a case as founded or unfounded is presented in a chapter in which types of cases that police tended to believe are compared to types of cases that police disbelieved. An examination of investigative procedures includes a discussion of the types of cases police solved, techniques of investigation employed, and the impact of departmental goals and procedures on the adjudication of cases that enter the court system. Chapter 19 summarizes findings in this important area.

Following a discussion of sources of data utilized and a brief description of the court system, a series of chapters examine the judicial process in relation to cases of rape and its impact on victims of rape. The chapter on the preliminary hearing includes a discussion of the phenomenon of withdrawal of cooperation by many victims at this stage. Cases in which the defendant pleads guilty are then described. Cases tried by jury are compared to those in which the right to jury trial has been waived, and the outcomes of each mode of trial are discussed. The types of cases that result in jail sentences are examined and, finally, the effects on victims of involvement in the court system are described. A conclusion summarizes findings relating to the response of the criminal justice system to rape and presents a frame of reference helpful to an interpretation of these findings.

Since nearly all the cases in this study involve reported rapes, one final area to be addressed is the proportion of all rapes that is under consideration here.

Most rape crisis centers and even the FBI assume that only a small percentage of rape victims comes to the attention of the authorities. An unreported to reported ratio of 10:1 is often quoted, but ratios as high as 100:1 are not unheard of. All these ratios share one trait: they are based on no evidence. They were pulled from the air or from the respondant's gut reaction.

The only available evidence is derived from victim studies, principally from the LEAA Bureau of the Census Surveys. In general, among the rape encounters that they uncover, slightly more than half were reported to the authorities.[1] There are, however, several serious problems with this finding. The interview schedule used to uncover rapes is awkwardly constructed, with questions only raised about sexual assaults once a respondent has reported a physical assault. And, it is by no means certain that a victim who will report to the police will report to a government survey.

In fact, in a survey conducted in San José among women who had made a report of rape to the police, only two-thirds of these known victims admitted their victimization.[2] If victims will not always respond to a survey even when they have reported to the police, it is likely that many victims who do not report to the police will also not confide to a census survey. The ratio of two rapes for every one reported, then, is certainly conservative.

An unsupported ratio of 10 to 1, however, is probably excessive.

Although there are many reasons for a victim not to report, a number of factors contribute to a rape becoming known to the authorities.

In the first place, the decision to report does not always rest in the victim's hands: for a child, the guardian must take steps to report and draw up a complaint. For adolescents and adults, well-meaning friends and/or family members may call the police without the victim's agreement. And, in some cases, a stranger or neighbor hearing a disturbance will dial the police. In these situations and many others, a victim has little choice in the matter. Table 7–1 details who contacted the police for 761 victims polled in the current study. The victim dialed the emergency police number only 23 percent of the time. Family members frequently call, as do other authorities. Of special interest are the victims referred by hospital authorities.

It was apparent during the course of the research that many victims report the rape to obtain medical treatment, comfort, and support. Of the 634 victims who were asked why they reported the rape, 241 (38%) stated that they reported because of a desire for help or comfort, whether physical, emotional, or medical. It is hypothesized that victims who have the resources or support to seek help and comfort privately (without relying on the public institutions) would be more likely to do so and not report to the police. Conversely, many victims of lower socioeconomic background are virtually forced to report to the police due to lack of alternatives for receiving care and assistance.

In sum, the best conclusion we can draw is that we do not know how many rapes go unreported. While a ratio of two unreported rapes to every

Table 7–1
Person Who Contacted Police to Report Rape ($N = 761$)

Source of Referral	Number	Percentage
Victim	175	23.0
Victim's mother/stepmother	168	22.1
Hospital authorities	93	12.2
Female friends	37	4.9
Sibling	33	4.3
Neighbor	30	3.9
Husband/boyfriend	27	3.5
Proactive police intervention	25	3.3
Stranger on the street or in a car	22	2.9
Father/stepfather	21	2.8
Male friend	18	2.4
School authority	11	1.4
Victim's child	8	1.1
Other relative	46	6.0
Other	47	6.2

reported rape is conservative, a 10 to 1 figure is probably exaggerated. A number of factors, including the intervention of family, strangers, medical authorities and so forth, increase the likelihood of a rape being reported and diminish the role of the victim in this process. As a result, whereas the findings presented in the criminal justice section relate only to victims of reported rapes, the findings can also be said to apply to a large proportion of all rape victims.

Notes

1. Law Enforcement Assistance Administration, *Criminal Victimization Surveys in the Nation's Five Largest Cities: National Crime Panel Surveys at Chicago, Detroit, Los Angeles, New York, and Philadelphia* (Washington, D.C.: U.S. Government Printing Office, 1975).

2. Law Enforcement Assistance Administration, "San Jose Methods Test of Known Crime Victims," Statistical Technical Report no. 1, National Institute of Law Enforcement and Criminal Justice, Statistics Division (Washington, D.C.: LEAA – NILECJ Publications STA-1, 1972).

8

The Police: An Introduction

This study focuses on the response of one police department (Philadelphia) to rape. Several studies with a national scope, however, indicate that the current findings reflect police practices that are widespread rather than unique. For example, two national studies report that in most police departments the rate of marking cases as unfounded is higher for rape than for other complaints and that rape victims are expected to meet a higher standard of conduct than is legally required.[1] In addition, a survey conducted by the Rand Corporation found that many departments have instituted procedures that maximize the quick solution of criminal complaints—often at the expense of the careful preparation necessary for successful prosecution of cases—and that little detective work is required in case solution.[2]

This chapter describes Philadelphia Police directives for responding to a report of rape during the period covered by this study. Data concerning actual police response to rape and victim evaluation of police treatment are also presented.

While in training prior to and during the onset of this study, all Philadelphia police received instruction that, for a charge of rape:

1. The carnal knowledge and penetration must be proven.

2. There must be force, actual or constructive.

3. There must be an absence of actual consent or the person attacked was incapable of giving legal consent.[3]

The requirement of penetration, however slight, is met by nearly all the cases in this study. Penile-vaginal intercourse is completed in 83.4% of the cases; another 5.6% have penile-labial contact. Many of the remaining cases could be classified as attempted rape. Others are automatically rape, because of the victim's age. Force and absence of consent, however, need to be tested.

Police directive 107 (5/14/71) outlined the police responsibility in rape cases for the study period and is appended to this chapter. Not only were police required to transport victims to Philadelphia General Hospital (unless the victim had sustained serious injuries, or two or more days had passed since the rape's occurrence) and to call for a detective, but several new requirements were instituted:

A policewoman was to be assigned to assist in obtaining a formal statement.

A juvenile aid officer was to be assigned when there was a juvenile suspect in custody.

The detective in charge was to gather a range of evidentiary material and to pursue a number of investigative procedures.

Special procedures were instituted for juvenile victims.

Supervisors were given certain audit requirements.

Below is a typical scenario describing what Philadelphia police are directed to do in initiating management of a rape complaint. The procedures are similar to those followed by police in other large cities; some are drawn from Jonathan Rubinstein's study of Philadelphia police practices, *City Police*.[4]

If someone dials the police emergency number, the call is automatically routed to the district from which the call is made. The person receiving the call, generally an experienced policeman, obtains the information and relays it to the dispatcher. The dispatcher assigns a district control number to the complaint and assigns the case. At the end of each tour, patrol officers must submit to their sergeant a triplicate form called a "48" for every assigned complaint. The assigned officer is clocked while on assignment.

If the call is a rape, or other felony, the dispatch is prefaced by an alarm bell. The information is announced first to alert all cars in the area, and then one car is given responsibility for the paperwork. In addition, a sergeant is required to respond to every emergency call.

Police can terminate the case at this stage, through the unfounding of a "48." The officer is not saying that there is a false report but that there is nothing to report; he found nothing when he investigated the complaint. However, for rape cases, this is rare.

Once an officer arrives, the instructions in directive 107 apply. The first officer at the scene attempts to apprehend the offender if he is in the immediate area, issues a description of the offender for general radio broadcast if he has fled, ensures that the crime scene is protected, and takes a preliminary statement from the victim. Before transporting her to the emergency room, providing she is not seriously injured, the officer may call for a mobile crime unit and must notify the supervisor of the detective division in order that a detective be assigned.

This is only the model, however. In real life, not all the victims in this study went directly to Philadelphia General Hospital, nor was a policewoman always assigned as specified by directive 107.

Police were present when a rape was in progress in very few cases. Less frequently still, police stumbled on a rape victim soon after the assault was completed. Mostly, police learned about a sexual assault from a telephone call. Only about one-fourth of the time did the victim herself report being raped. More often, a member of her family contacted the police, or the police were contacted by the hospital or by some authority, such as a security officer, or a friend or neighbor called the police, or a stranger who saw or heard the assault dialed the police emergency number.

Regardless of how the police were notified, they responded swiftly. In over three-fourths of all instances where police were called about a rape, they arrived at the scene in under 10 minutes. The victim's first contact with the police after calling them was her encounter with the patrol officer assigned. Most victims evaluations of this encounter were positive. Victims rated their treatment by police on a scale of 1 (poorest) to 4 (best). Only 5.8% of victims gave police the lowest rating, whereas 31.8% gave them the highest rating. Many more encounters are given a higher evaluation of 3 or 4 (79.3%) than are given a lower evaluation of one or two (20.7%).

About one-half the victims in this study (49.6%) were interrogated at police districts or detective divisions before being transported to the emergency room. According to directive 107, this was acceptable procedure only when the victim refused medical treatment or when two or more days had elapsed since the rape. Although it is also possible that some victims reported directly to the district, it seems unlikely that at least one of these conditions was present in so large a proportion of cases. Clearly, then, in many cases the police were conducting interrogations prior to treatment, despite guidelines to the contrary.

The pretreatment interrogations were often extremely long; for the cases involved, 25.9% of the victims spent between one and two hours, 15.1% spent two to three hours, and 14.3% spent more than three hours at the police station. Three-fifths of these interrogations occurred at the police district, the rest at the detective division.

Since so many victims were interrogated prior to emergency room treatment, it is possible that some cases may never have made it to the emergency room and may, therefore, have been eliminated by the police prior to inclusion in this study. Consequently, any estimate of case mortality by police is probably conservative.

Eventually, all victims in the current study arrived at the central emergency room. Victims tended to spend a long time there. Unless immediate surgical attention was required, victims waited. Although the examination procedure was short, over half of all victims waited an hour before being seen, about one-quarter waited more than two hours. During this period of time, a volunteer from Women Organized Against Rape was often available. A detective should have been available to begin interrogations, and he should have been accompanied by a policewoman to aid in obtaining a formal statement.

Only about half the time was a policewoman called in during the study period (55.7%). The remainder of the time, a detective conducted the interview alone. Nearly one-half of the victims interviewed claim they had no preference concerning the sex of the person who interviewed them (48.5%), and one in ten preferred a male (10.6%). However, the remainder claim they would have preferred a female (40.9%).

The detective formally began the process of assessing the victim's credibility, applying a crime label to her complaint, taking steps to apprehend her assailant, and gathering and consolidating evidence to substantiate her claim. In about one case in twenty-five, they requested the victim to take a lie detector test (4.3%). More often, detectives applied pressure on victims not to press charges (19.3%). In many of these instances, according to the victim, the police told her they thought she was lying (44.3%), that her case might be hard to press in court (26.5%), or that they might never find the offender (7.3%).

Among the study's sample, 13.2% of all victims reported they would never again report being raped, and an additional 7.4 percent stated they were not sure whether they would report. Exactly one-half of the victims who would not report again cited unpleasantness with the police as the reason. Yet most victims rated their treatment by detectives as good, although not as good as their treatment by the police officers who first responded to their call. Detectives were given the lowest rating in 13.4 percent of the cases versus the 31.4 percent receiving the highest rating. More encounters were given a high evaluation of 3 or 4 (68%) than were given a low evaluation of one or two (32%). A small number of victims even rated police personnel as the most supportive figures they met during the entire postrape experience (3.2%).

Victims were also asked to make a number of evaluations of detectives. Between two-thirds and three-fourths of victims found detectives fair, friendly, consistent, helpful, and understanding. On the other hand, between 9% and 17% of all victims rated detectives as harsh, tough, mean, malicious, indifferent, cold, unreasonable, unjust, and discourteous. About one-half thought detectives were warm, easygoing, and lenient, and one-third evaluated them as fatherly.

The next several chapters concentrate on the detective's decision to believe some cases and disbelieve others; on the decision to lodge a charge (the labeling decision); and on the extent of the activity in apprehending offenders, gathering evidence, and presenting it in court.

Notes

1. Battelle Human Affairs Research Centers, "Forcible Rape: A National Survey of the Response by Police" (Unpublished report, Law and Justice Center, Seattle, Wash., 1975), and Lisa Brodyaga et al., "Rape and Its Victims: A Report for Citizens Health Facility, and Criminal Justice Agency" (Unpublished report, National Institute of Law Enforcement and Criminal Justice, Washington, D.C., 1975).

2. Peter W. Greenwood and Joan Petersilia, *The Criminal Investigation Process,* vol. 1, *Summary and Policy Implications* (Santa Monica, Calif.: The Rand Corporation, 1975).

3. Philadelphia Police Department, "Training Manual," vol. 1, "Criminal Law," Pamphlet 6, "Rape" (rev. 1972).

4. Jonathan Rubinstein, *City Police* (New York: Ballantine Books, 1974).

Appendix 8A:
Philadelphia Police
Department Directive
107 (5/14/71)

SUBJECT: FORCIBLE RAPE

I. POLICY

A. Alleged forcible rape victims will be immediately transported to Philadelphia General Hospital for examination and/or treatment. (Exceptions: See Section II, A, 4, of this directive.)

II. THE INITIAL REPORT

A. The first officer/s arriving at the scene shall:
  1. Render first aid to the injured (if necessary).
  2. Ensure that the crime scene is protected.
  3. If the offender has fled, broadcast his full description, means and route of escape.
     a. The Hold–up Memorandum (75–130) shall be used as a "Priority Report" to give a description to Radio.
  4. Transport the victim to the Philadelphia General Hospital.
     a. If the victim has sustained serious bodily injuries, she shall be transported to nearest hospital and her family will be notified immediately by the transporting policeman.
       (1) Transporting policemen shall remain with the complainant until relieved by the assigned investigator or higher authority.
     b) If the victim refuses hospitalization, or, if two (2) or more days have passed since the time of occurrence, the complainant shall be taken to the Detective Division of occurrence.
  5. Notify by telephone (from the hospital), the supervisor of the Detective Division and district of occurrence.
  6. Prepare a Complaint or Incident Report (75–48)

III. RESPONSIBILITY FOR INVESTIGATION

A. Investigative jurisdiction shall be determined in this order:
  1. If known, the Detective Division wherein the crime was committed.
  2. If known, the division wherein the first contact was made with the victim.
  3. If none of the above, the division in which the report was made.

B. A detective shall investigate the crimes of rape or assault with the intent
to ravish.

  1. The Commanding Officer of the Juvenile Aid Division shall:

    a. Assign an investigator to assist the detective whenever a juvenile
suspect or offender is in custody.

    b. Assign a policewoman to assist in obtaining a "formal" state-
ment from the victim.

    c) Assign other personnel as required to assist in these investiga-
tions.

IV. INVESTIGATION

A. The assigned investigator shall:

  1. Interview the examining physician and attempt to obtain written
results of his examination.

  2. Personally interview the complainant.

    a. If the victim has suffered extensive bodily injuries, the investiga-
tion will be conducted at the hospital.

    b. The initial interview should be sufficient to determine all the
investigation steps to be taken and the scientific evidence sought.
(e.g., Whether or not to take fingernail scrapings, what to look
for at the crime scene, which pieces of clothing should be obtained as evidence, etc.)

  3. Secure the victim's clothing and ensure that suitable replacements
are provided.

    a. Outer clothing should be obtained because they may bear traces
of evidence that could establish contact with the defendant or
crime scene.

    (1) Each article of clothing should be placed in a separate bag.

    b. A property receipt must be issued for the clothing.

  4. Prepare a Search and Seizure Warrant to obtain the offender's
clothing if he has been located within a reasonable amount of time
(before he has had a chance to dispose of or launder his clothing)
after the crime was committed.

  5. As soon as possible, obtain additional evidence to support the
statement of the victim by:

    a. A careful crime scene search.

    (1) If the alleged rape occurred inside a vehicle, the search should
include the vehicle and the place where it was parked (if
known).

    (2) Attempts to secure all possible evidence from the scene (e.g.,
sheet, hair, fibers, secretions, blood, etc.)

      Note: If obtaining this type of evidence is not within the
capabilities of the investigator, the Mobile Crime
Detection Units shall be used.

   b. Detailed neighborhood inquiry.
      (1) Neighborhood investigation should include an interview with:
         (a) Residents
         (b) Persons present or known to have been in the area at the time of occurrence.
         (c) Those who pass through the area regularly (e.g., milkmen, salesmen, etc.).
6. Check with sex offender files to identify suspects who have previously offended in the same:
   a. Area
   b. Time of day
   c. Type of victim
   d. Method of crime
7. Ensure that the victim's complaint clearly indicated the elements of the crime. (e.g., penetration, force and absence of consent)
   a. Clear indication of the offense includes, but is not limited to actual resistance (e.g., torn clothing, physical abuse, etc.), outcry and prompt complaint.
8. Juvenile Victims
   a. All alleged rape victims under 18 years of age, even though they have been examined at the Philadelphia General Hospital, shall be referred to the Youth Study Center for Medical Examination. The assigned detective shall:
      (1) Give to the parent or guardian of the alleged victim a referral, addressed to "Examining Physician, Youth Study Center, Female Division."
         (a) The time for examination is between 8:00 AM and 8:30 AM.
         (b) No Examination Referrals are to be made to the Youth Study Center on weekends or holidays.
      (2) Include in the referral memorandum:
         (a) District complaint number.
         (b) Place of occurrence.
         (c) Complainant's name, address, date of birth, and race.
         (d) Alleged offender/s or suspect/s (if known). Insert name, address, age and race.
         (e) The last paragraph must indicate if a suspect has been arrested or if a warrant is requested.
         (f) If a warrant is requested note the charges on the "referral memorandum."
         (g) When a warrant is issued, it will be returned to the assigned investigator for service.
      (3) Be furnished the results of the medical examination by telephoning the "Special Intake Worker," Family Court, Youth

Study Center, MU–6–4815, between 1:30 PM and 4:00 PM, on the day of the examination or any other day of the same week during these hours.

(4) In the event that a procedural question arises, contact the "Special Intake Worker," Youth Study Center, between 9:00 AM to 4:00 PM, every day except weekends and holidays.

B. The Investigator's Supervisor shall:

1. Review and evaluate the investigator's findings.
2. When extenuating circumstances cause doubt as to what the specific charge should be, call and discuss the case with the duty Assistant District Attorney.

BY COMMAND OF THE POLICE COMMISSIONER

9 The Charging Decision

An answer to the question "What is rape?" is readily found in the criminal statutes of the various jurisdictions. However, when the police attempt to resolve the more immediate question "Is this rape?" or "What is this offense?" suitable authority on the subject is not always available to them. In most police departments, tacit understandings rather than formal guidelines determine the manner in which certain criminal complaints are labeled. And, as with statutes, labeling strategies may vary considerably from one jurisdiction to another.

Each of three studies of the charging strategies of police departments suggests a different motive for attaching a label of rape to some complaints of sexual assault and not to others: (1) deliberate statistical manipulation, (2) idiosyncratic departmental rules, and (3) detective case management. In the first study, Jerome Skolnick has isolated cases in which the labeling decision is used as a vehicle for deliberate statistical manipulation. As part of his excellent larger study of the police role in democratic societies, Skolnick compares the crime classification policies of the police departments of two jurisdictions. In one city, he found that police make extensive use of the "suspicious circumstances" label, whereas in the other city every complaint must be labeled as a chargeable offense.[1]

If a prostitute alleges rape in the first jurisdiction, her complaint is likely to be labeled "suspicious circumstances—rape." The complaint would not count in the rape statistics, nor would the assigned detective be required to apprehend the offender.

There are three advantages to a police department that uses extensively labels like suspicious circumstances. First, the complaint rate for rape is lowered; cases "legitimately" vanish from the final tally of rape complaints. Second, the clearance rate is likely to improve. On the one hand, if the police are able to use the suspicious circumstances label on cases in which the apprehension of suspects is unlikely, difficult cases are weeded out, and those complaints with the charge of rape are stacked in favor of the more "catchable" cases. On the other hand, any reduction in the number of cases requiring investigation increases the likelihood that the remaining cases will receive more attention, thereby increasing the probability of favorable outcomes. Finally, the police need not report these cases as unfounded, enabling the department to establish a record of believing more complainants than is actually the case.

A supervising officer in a jurisdiction that requires chargeable offense labeling commented on how his department would handle a prostitute's rape allegation:

> Well we're an honest police department. All those other departments that have these fancy clearance rates—we know damned well they're stacking the cards. It's easy to show a low crime rate when you have a category like suspicious circumstances to use as a wastebasket. Here, at least we know what's going on—everything is reported. Sure the prostitute could have been lying, and probably was. But the fact is that a prostitute can be raped and prostitutes sometimes are. After all, a prostitute has a right not to go to bed with somebody if she doesn't want to.[2]

In summary, the first study suggests that police may use alternative charges to improve their own public posture.

In the second study, Chappell et al. attempted to explain the marked difference in rape rate between Los Angeles and Boston.[3] The forcible rape rate for Los Angeles in 1967 was 35.4 per 100,000 population, versus only 7.7 per 100,000 population for Boston. Moreover, forcible rape accounts for about one-half of one percent of all index crimes in Boston, as opposed to more than one percent in Los Angeles, leading the authors to note: "The discrepant forcible rape rates, therefore, are not a function of different prevailing rates of crime in the two jurisdictions, but are specific to the offense itself."[4] The authors ultimately conclude that the rape rate is probably higher in Los Angeles, but they cannot rely on police evidence to confirm this suspicion. Comparisons are made only with great difficulty, primarily because each department has developed localized methods of determining which offenses warrant the label rape.

What differences do they note? It appears that in Los Angeles, the label rape is attached to a significantly larger category of offenses than is the case in Boston. Even cases of bottom-pinching turn up in the Los Angeles forcible rape files. The authors concluded:

> Instances such as the foregoing (bottom-pinching) never appear in the sample of forcible rapes in the files of the Boston Police Department although we may assume that similar kinds of activity go on there as well as in Los Angeles. For their part, the Boston Police include as forcible rape a number of cases in which very young females—girls of eight and nine—are molested in parks by equally immature boys. Sexual intercourse does not take place, and perhaps could not have taken place. Again, it seems likely that a number of such cases occur in Los Angeles, but the files on forcible rape there do not contain them, probably because they are handled by the juvenile division and classified under the more amorphous rubric of "delinquency."[5]

The Philadelphia data include a number of cases in which detectives used a seriousness-eroding charge—mostly denoting a lesser sexual offense—to handle a number of sexual assaults. Many of these cases might have been labeled rape by other police departments. Conversely, other complaints that were noted as rape in Philadelphia might have been given less serious charges elsewhere.

The Battelle Law and Justice Study Center Survey of 208 police departments found that 28% of all departments require penetration, force, and a weapon and/or resistance before a complaint can be classified as rape.[6] In jurisdictions where a weapon and/or resistance is required, the average number of recorded rapes is less than in comparable-size jurisdictions that do not hold rape victims to a higher standard of conduct than is required by FBI rules. Police departments were also asked: "In cases where a rape is reported, what charges other than 'rape' might be brought as the result of a sex act about which a complaint is made?" Sixty-two percent of those responding cited more general sex offenses (for example, "public indecency," "sexual misconduct"), 40% cited more specific sex offenses (for example, "indecent exposure"), and 36% cited other offenses (for example, robbery, burglary).[7] Many departments cited all three possibilities. In Philadelphia, as will be seen, most alternative charging takes the form of more specific sex offenses.

Finally, in the third study, Skolnick and Woodworth illustrate how different detectives on the same police force may use different labeling strategies. According to one detective:

> Are you learning about sex crimes? It's really pretty simple isn't it? You see, for each code section there is an escape section. We can charge a guy 314 (indecent exposure), and he has to register with the police department in whatever county he goes into. That's rough. So we can charge him with 650 1/2 (injury to public health or decency) and he doesn't have to register. (Do you decide what to charge?) Yes, I think a great deal about it, trying to decide whether to be rough or not. Guys I know like Alvin Moone (who had intercourse with a girl under 14), I don't charge hard. He was only after a little piece and is not a sex criminal. That damn guy (pointing to Frost's desk) will charge all of them 288 (child molesting). I never charge a 288 unless I'm sure that the guy is a sex criminal. It's a tough section. Not that I care if he has to register; but I hate to clutter up our files of pictures with those non-sex criminal guys.[8]

Although the current study does not concentrate on the variance in detectives' attitudes toward charging, a combination of deliberate manipulation, departmental idiosyncracies, and detective case management suggests that a rational decision-making model may not be appropriate for analyzing police charging strategies. This is because departmental idiosyncracies may develop over a period of time into a fixed set of habits of unknown origin. "Uncatchable" cases may nonetheless be given a rape charge as a result of these habits; very "catchable" complaints may be excluded. Similarly, detective case management may, in some instances, work against the rational pursuit of a perfect clearance by arrest rate. In short, many goals may be operative in the decision–making process in any given case. Quite often, these goals may conflict.

The remainder of this chapter details the manner in which Philadelphia Police employ seriousness–eroding charges when processing those cases that have not been disposed of by being marked as unfounded, not recorded, or given a nonoffense charge (strategies discussed in the following chapter).

Charging: The Philadelphia Data

Of 1,401 women in our sample, the police response is available in 1,397 cases (99.7%). The police reported no record in their files of 199 of these 1,397 cases (14.2%). Data from chapter 10 suggest that a portion of these missing cases may be attributed to deliberate nonrecording. Of the remaining 1,198 cases, police marked unfounded 218 complaints (18.2%).

The charging decision is available for all but one of the remaining 980 complaints. Table 9-1 compares the final case label in cases where a social worker research interview is available ($N = 377$). The following discussion deals exclusively with the former group. Note, however, that the relative proportion of cases falling into each category is remarkably similar.

Only those cases determined to be founded that are given a rape or attempted rape charge contribute to the total number of rape complaints reported by the Philadelphia Police Department to the FBI for inclusion in the *Uniform Crime Reports*. Of 1,401 women who were seen at Philadelphia General Hospital in connection with an alleged sexual assault, the police reported 747 "rapes" (53.8%) to the FBI. The variables associated with the use of seriousness–eroding charges to exclude cases are discussed below.

Seriousness–eroding Labels

The sexual aspects of the assault disappeared entirely in the charging of 14 (1.4%) of the 979 cases marked as founded. These complaints were labeled simple assault, aggravated assault, abduction–felonious restraint, robbery, theft, or burglary. Although eliminating the sexual component altogether is relatively rare, use of a lesser sexual offense charge is fairly common.

In all, 111 (11.3%) complaints were given the charge of statutory rape, sodomy, involuntary deviate sexual intercourse, voluntary deviate sexual intercourse, indecent assault, incest, corrupting the morals of a minor, or indecent exposure.

Table 9–1

Charge Listed for Alleged Sexual Assault Marked Founded by Availability of Social Worker Interview (*N* = 979)

Charge	Social Worker Interview Available	Percent	Social Worker Interview Unavailable	Percent	Total	Percent
Rape/attempted rape	454	75.3	293	77.7	747	76.4
Sex offenses [a]	75	12.5	36	9.5	111	11.3
Assault [b]	10	1.7	4	1.1	14	1.4
Nonrape-related charges [c]	63	10.5	44	11.7	107	10.9
Total	602	100.00	377	100.0	979	100.0

[a] Statutory rape, sodomy, involuntary deviate sexual intercourse, voluntary deviate sexual intercourse, indecent assault, incest, corrupting the morals of a minor, indecent exposure.

[b] Simple assault, aggravated assault, abduction–felonious restraint, robbery, theft, burglary.

[c] Investigation of persons, investigation of injuries, investigation of occupant of auto, missing persons, false police report, injury (hospital case), attempted suicide, runaway.

Clearly, use of a lesser sexual offense is often appropriate. For cases not involving penile–vaginal intercourse, the attempted rape charge may be used but so might a number of other charges. When only anal or oral intercourse was completed, Pennsylvania law at that time more easily supported the charge "involuntary deviate sexual intercourse." However, it is important to note that incidents that are not reported as rape in Philadelphia might be considered rape in other jurisdictions and contribute to that city's rape rate, and events that are considered to constitute rape in Philadelphia might be labeled something altogether different elsewhere.

The principal variable associated with the decision to use a lesser sex offense charge is age. Cases that involve victims who are 11 years old or younger often receive the lesser label, whereas those in which victims are older than 11 only receive such labels under special circumstances. Where the victim is 11 or younger, five variables are significantly associated with the decision to label the incident a lesser sexual offense:

1. Police are more likely to lodge the charges as a lesser sexual offense when a policewoman is not called in to take a statement or aid in the interrogation for the child victim (% lesser sexual offenses = 55.4 versus 19.2).

2. Police are more likely to lodge a lesser sexual offense charge on a child's complaint if the median income of the victim's census tract is over $9,000 a year (% lesser sexual offenses = 50.8 versus 26.6).

3. Police are more likely to lodge a lesser sexual offense charge on a child's complaint when anal intercourse is alleged (% lesser sexual offenses = 80.0 versus 34.6).

4. Police are more likely to lodge a lesser sexual offense charge on a child's complaint where the victim has had previous sexual relations with the offender (% lesser sexual offenses = 55.2 versus 32.1).

5. Police are more likely to lodge a lesser sexual offense charge on a child's complaint if penile–vaginal intercourse is not alleged (% lesser sexual offenses = 45.9 versus 26.2).

With victims who are 12 years old or older, only 5.5% of the complaints are given a lesser sexual offense charge. However, twelve variables are significantly associated with the decision to lodge a lesser sexual offense charge when the victim is in this age category:

1. Police are more likely to lodge a lesser sexual offense charge if the victim has been attacked by the offender before (% lesser sexual offenses = 35.0 versus 1.2).

2. Police are more likely to lodge a lesser sexual offense charge if the offender is a family member (% lesser sexual offenses = 58.3 versus 4.2).

3. Police are more likely to lodge a lesser sexual offense charge where the victim admits later to a social worker that there was no rape (% lesser sexual offenses = 45.5 versus 4.7).

4. Police are more likely to lodge a lesser sexual offense charge if penile–vaginal intercourse is not alleged (% lesser sexual offenses = 22.2 versus 3.6).

5. Police are more likely to lodge a lesser sexual offense charge if the assault episode lasts less than 15 minutes (% lesser sexual offenses = 12.4 versus 3.4).

6. Police are more likely to lodge a lesser sexual offense charge when no physical force is used (% lesser sexual offenses = 15.1 versus 4.1).

7. Police are more likely to lodge a lesser sexual offense charge if there is no weapon (% lesser sexual offenses = 8.4 versus 1.5).

8. Police are more likely to lodge a lesser sexual offense charge if the victim is a student (% lesser sexual offenses = 9.5 versus 2.6).

9. Police are more likely to lodge a lesser sexual offense charge if the offender is not a stranger to the victim (% lesser sexual offenses = 8.7 versus 2.8).

10. Police are more likely to lodge a lesser sexual offense charge where clear elements of coercion or intimidation are lacking (% lesser sexual offenses = 14.0 versus 4.5).

11. Police are more likely to lodge a lesser sexual offense charge if the offender is not rough with the victim (% lesser sexual offenses = 9.2 versus 3.9).

12. Police are more likely to lodge a lesser sexual offense charge when the victim is not employed (% lesser sexual offenses = 6.6 versus 1.0).

Again, all the variables are analyzed statistically as previously described. Figure 9–1 depicts the resulting branches, with nine terminal groups identified. These nine groups are arranged in descending order by percentage with lesser sex offense charges. Among the groupings where these lesser

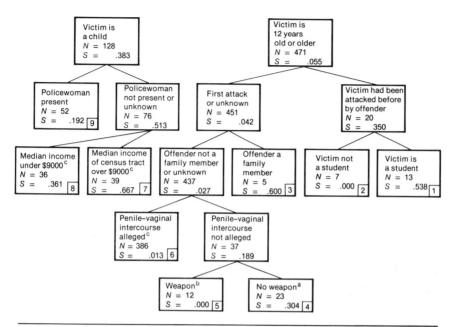

Group	Characteristics	Number of Cases	Percent Given Lesser Sex Offense Charges
7	Victim 11 or younger, policewoman absent, median income over $9,000	39	66.7
3	Victim 12 or older, first attack by offender, family member	5	60.0
1	Victim 11 or older, multiple attacks by offender, student	13	53.8
8	Victim 11 or younger, policewoman absent, median income under $9,000	36	36.1
4	Victim 12 or older, first attack, nonfamily offender, no penile–vaginal intercourse alleged, no weapon	23	30.4
9	Victim 11 or younger, policewoman present	52	19.2
6	Victim 12 or older, first attack, nonfamily offender, penile–vaginal intercourse alleged	386	1.3
2	Victim 12 or older, multiple attacks by offender, not a student	7	0.0
5	Victim 12 or older, first attack, nonfamily offender, no penile–vaginal intercourse alleged, weapon	12	0.0

S = Proportion given lesser sex offense labels

Note: N = 599 (3 cases where age is unknown were discarded initially); S = .125.

[a] 2 cases where the variable is unknown are discarded in final split.

[b] 14 cases where the variable is unknown are discarded in final split.

[c] 1 case where the variable is unknown is discarded in final split.

Figure 9–1. Interaction of Selected Variables According to the Proportion Labeled Lesser Sex Offenses.

sex offense charges are lodged more frequently, several interesting patterns emerge. Children from poor neighborhoods are raped; children from more affluent neighborhoods are more often "molested." Perhaps the police are more reluctant to apply the stigma–laden charge of rape when confronting more affluent parents or, for that matter, potentially more affluent offenders.

The fact that penile–vaginal intercourse is not alleged does not necessarily mean that a seriousness–eroding charge will be applied. Over one–half of all cases where penile–vaginal intercourse is not alleged resulted in a label of rape or attempted rape. In the immediate configuration, the critical element appears to be whether or not a weapon is present. With a weapon present, there is no use of less serious charges.

In conclusion, among cases marked as founded, about ten percent are given a lesser sexual offense charge. Although these cases may come to trial, the worst possible sentence is typically less than would be possible if the charge was rape, and these cases do not contribute to the number of cases reported as complaints of rape by the police. In other cities, many of these cases might be labeled with a rape charge. However, many cases to which Philadelphia Police give a rape charge might be given an alternate label. The best summation is that comparisons between cities will always be rough around the edges at best.

Notes

1. Jerome H. Skolnick, *Justice without Trial: Law Enforcement in a Democratic Society* (New York: John Wiley and Sons, 1966), pp. 172–173.

2. Ibid., p. 173.

3. Duncan Chappell et. al., "Forcible Rape: A Comparative Study of Offenses Known to the Police in Boston and Los Angeles," in *Studies in the Sociology of Sex,* ed. J.M,. Henslin (New York: Meredith Corporation, 1971), pp. 169–190.

4. Ibid., p. 178.

5. Ibid., p. 182.

6. Battelle Human Affairs Research Center, *Forcible Rape: A National Survey of the Response by Police* (Unpublished report, Law and Justice Center, Seattle, Wash., November 1975), p. 40.

7. Ibid., p. 48.

8. Jerome H. Skolnick and J. Richard Woodworth, "Bureaucracy, Information, and Social Control: A Study of a Morals Detail," in *The Police: Six Sociological Essays,* ed. David J. Bordua (New York: John Wiley and Sons, 1967), p. 114. Reprinted with permission.

10 Whom the Police Believe

The rape victim who reports the incident to the police is often not prepared for what follows. Media depictions usually focus on the phenomenon of rape victim as defendant, the victim of a crime being further victimized by the courts; little is ever said about the possibility of a case never even reaching the trial stage. Yet, for many rape victims, attempts at retribution are brought to a sudden and permanent halt at the police station. This may occur in spite of a victim's willingness to cooperate, and irrespective of the validity of her complaint.

The police must decide whether the event related by the victim meets a reasonable standard of credibility, and, if so, whether the event constitutes a crime. When the police believe that an act has occurred that does fit the legal definition of a crime, a case is marked founded as opposed to unfounded.

Whereas testing the validity of a victim's story is agreed to be a legitimate police function, the criteria by which validity is determined and the means employed by the police in so doing are both open to question.

From the standpoint of the police, a case that is marked unfounded is not included in the crime statistics, either as a rape or as any other offense, and it requires no other police attention. The complainant in an unfounded case, however, often finds herself in the unexpected and bewildering predicament of having come to the police for aid (depicted by the media as the courageous and correct course to take), only to have the door slammed firmly in her face.

The police may legitimately mark a case as unfounded only if "investigation shows that no offense occurred nor was attempted." Two cases drawn from Philadelphia Police files illustrate proper motives for unfounding a complaint:

> The complainant, an adolescent, originally reported being raped and beaten in the rear bedroom of a friend's house by a boy she could identify by name. On the next day, when she was to give a formal statement, she stated she was raped still in her friend's house, but in the middle bedroom and by four persons, each of whom she could now name. Originally, it was the first boy who was supposed to have removed her clothes. Now it was another boy. When confronted with her inconsistencies, the complainant refused to continue her story.

The complainant stated: "At about 11:15 P.M. he came back to the house and asked me again for a cup of coffee. I told him OK and he came into the house. When he got into the living room he tried to kiss me. I told him no and went to the kitchen to put the coffee on. He came back to the kitchen and tried to kiss me again. I again told him no and he picked me up and carried me to the dining room. He took my clothes off and laid me on the floor."

"I told him that I did not want to have intercourse with him and he put his hands between my legs. He told me to do something for him so I jerked him off. He did not climax at this time. He then picked me up and carried me to the couch. After putting me on the couch he did get down on me and ate me. I did enjoy this as I thought this was so far as he was going to go. I did climax and at this time Toni did pick me up again and carried me to the dining room. He laid me down and had relations with me. I climaxed again and Toni did also. I know this as he did tell me."

"I did not want to have relations with him as the word is out that he has something wrong with him."

"I left my husband about two months ago for about two weeks. The reason I left him was because he was working the cabs and when he came home at night he was too tired to have relations with me. I like to have relations every other night or every night. He just couldn't take care of me. After I lived in an apartment for the two weeks I realized this time my husband was taking care of my 10–month-old child."

"I was married when I was 17–years-old."

In the first of these cases, the detective did not believe the complainant's story. The details of the second case were all too believable, but the detective determined that the events described did not constitute a crime. Both his captain and an assistant district attorney concurred in this assessment, and the case was marked as unfounded.

Whereas obvious discrepencies or noncriminality of the event are legitimate bases for marking a case as unfounded, other factors have been described that influence this decision, both indirectly (in terms of police handling of the victim) and directly (when used as grounds for the decision).

To begin with, initial police assessments of victim credibility are likely to affect the tenor of the ensuing police–victim interaction. When a victim is assumed to be lying, and is either called a liar or is subjected to an intense grilling that focuses on such aspects as an absence of obvious injury or some delay in reporting the incident, she may understandably be upset and may withdraw cooperation.

Unfortunately, although the police estimate of victim veracity may not always be correct and bona fide victims may refuse further participation as a result of a hostile police response, lack of victim cooperation is itself considered sufficient grounds for marking a case as unfounded in most jurisdictions. The assumption is that victim withdrawal from the case indicates either that the victim is lying or that she realizes that the situation is not a police matter. A self-fulfilling mechanism seems to be involved here.

And certain characteristic abuses do, in fact, occur with respect to the criteria employed by police to measure victim veracity. In addition to the two legitimate bases for declaring a case to be unfounded discussed previously, three other motives have been proposed that are objectionable on substantive as well as procedural grounds.

In the first instance, the police have been accused of marking cases as unfounded when they simply do not like the victim or the subclass to which she belongs. Specifically, four groups of women have been identified in the literature as objects of this type of discrimination: the poor, minority females, prostitutes, and abusers of alcohol and drugs. Secondly, the police have been accused of declaring cases to be unfounded when they believe that the victim "asked for it," regardless of her credibility and the criminality of the events described. And, finally, the police have been accused of classifying as unfounded cases that they believe to be poor risk court cases, again regardless of credibility of victim and criminality of events. Their rationale seems to be: "No court will buy that story, so why bother with it at all?"

Of course, any given case may bring into play a number of the five motives for declaring a case to be unfounded (two that we have labeled legitimate, and three that we have labeled illegitimate), there being considerable overlap among these factors in certain instances. For example, rape complaints brought by prostitutes may be marked unfounded at a high rate, not only because they are prostitutes, but also because it is assumed that they are lying, that they ask for their victimization, that they don't stand a chance in court, and sometimes even because they don't understand the legal definition of rape. In addition, police procedures vary from victim to victim. Adolescent blacks might routinely receive a more intense grilling than adult whites. Slight injury might be viewed with more seriousness if the victim is white.

Several police reports have demonstrated that these sorts of criteria have been accorded considerable weight in the unfounding decision, providing examples of what amounts to: "Unfounded—drug addict," or "Unfounded—prostitute." The following excerpts from a police report illustrate this phenomenon:

> That at approximately 1:00 AM this morning she left her hotel room, leaving both her husband and a friend (no relation), and went down to the lobby, and into the bar. There she met two men, one black man, and one was white. She recalled that the black man's name was John. When the bar closed she left there with the two men and went to look for an after hours club, that was supposedly open. She stated that upon leaving the hotel, they turned right, and went about a block. Upon arriving at the club, they were refused entrance, because they could produce no membership cards.

At this time while standing there on the corner, a black man said hello to her, and she returned the greeting. They chatted for a few moments, and then she and the two men she had walked down with turned and went back toward the hotel, there the two men went inside, and she remained outside.

While she was standing there, the man who had greeted her outside of the private club, came walking upon the scene, and engaged her in conversation. He said that he was going to a party, and did she want to party. At this time a few of his friends joined him, and they also joined the conversation. She asked what did they have at the party, and they replied, "anything you want."

After walking along with them for awhile, she noticed the neighborhood was becoming a little deserted, and she wanted to turn back. They told her that they were being followed by the Police, and they ducked into an alley. They did this every time she indicated that she wanted to turn back.

Then they got to this big building, where they took her up to either the 5th or 6th floor, or maybe the 4th.

"When we got inside, all the lights were out. They started to take my clothes off. Then someone pushed me down off the couch." Then she was pulled to the floor, where one of the men had intercourse with her. After he was through, a second man had intercourse with her and then a third. At this time the lights went on and one of them handed her her clothes. She dressed and was walked down the steps. At the bottom of the steps, the man who went down with her then left her standing there.

She went to the corner and not knowing where she was, stopped the first car that went by and told the man what happened. He drove her to the first Police car he saw, and they took her to the hospital.

Without trying to locate the site of the alleged incident or apprehend the offenders, or even suggesting that the victim submit to a polygraph examination, the case was marked unfounded. The detective wrote:

a. Case Status, Unfounded
After interviewing complainant, many discrepancies were found to be present.
1. Complainant is an admitted Drug addict.
2. Complainant, also admits to going willingly with these men after a promise that drugs would be readily available at the alleged party.
3. Complainant states that she has been on a Methadone program in Wash., D.C. and that she attempted to "cold turkey" methadone about a week ago. (It is common knowledge that this is much more difficult than kicking Heroin.)
4. The presentation of an opportunity to get high (indicating drugs) to this complainant, influenced her decision to go with these men.
5. At this point it is the assigned Det. opinion that, anyone bartering for drugs, must of course realize that they must give something in return, and that the complainant realized this and when she did not get what she had been promised she then decided to report incident to Police.

It is alleged in the record that the case was marked unfounded because the victim was a liar as well as an addict. However, since many aspects of the victim's story that might have been subsequently verified were not even investigated, the principal motive here seems clear-cut: Unfounded—drug addict.

Menachem Amir, in a much criticized chapter of his book, *Patterns in Forcible Rape,* attempts to analytically identify those rapes where the victim "asked for it." He employs the following working definition of victim precipitation to guide his selections:

> The term "victim precipitation" describes those rape situations in which the victim actually, or so it was deemed, agreed to sexual relations but retracted before the actual act or did not react strongly enough when the suggestion was made by the offender(s). (The aspect of the vulnerable situation is not analyzed here but is assumed to operate in enhancing the offender's interpretation about the victim's availability as a sexual partner.) The term applies also to cases in risky situations marred with sexuality, especially when she uses what could be interpreted as indecency in language and gestures, or constitutes what could be taken as an invitation to sexual relations.[1]

Whereas this definition may be of some theoretical value, it is impossible to apply objectively in identifying genuine victim-precipitated cases, as Amir attempts to do. The fallacy in the definition is that it may encompass all cases or no cases, with every conceivable combination in between, depending on the decision-maker's attitudes toward men, women, their normal interactions, and what constitutes rape. If the police do, in fact, adopt an "assumption of risk" motive for classifying cases as unfounded (as some critics allege), then they may respond negatively to believable cases of legally defined rape. Detectives in this study have, in fact, admitted that they consider such aspects as whether the victim had dated the offender and willingly gone to his apartment and whether the victim was wearing a short skirt at the time of the incident, or a shirt without a bra underneath. If the logic of Amir's definition is adopted, factors such as these may be given considerable weight in the process by which cases are determined to be unfounded.

Not only is the victim precipitation reasoning objectionable, but the manner in which that determination is made is almost certain to be offensive to victims. It is unlikely that any rape victim would be inclined toward further cooperation with the police if confronted with questions like: "What do you expect wearing clothes like that?" "Why did you go out with him if you didn't want to get laid?" "Don't you know that only sluts hitchhike?"

The final category of illegitimate motives for classifying cases as unfounded comprises those cases that, although believable and within the legal definition of rape, are considered to be poor court cases. There is considerable overlap between this motive and assumption of risk, the latter type of case being viewed, perhaps correctly, as unwinnable in court. It has been suggested that prosecutors should not be allowed to participate in the founding decision, since they might tend to screen out any case that would give them a tough time in court, regardless of the validity of the complaint.[2] Theoretically, a case might make it past all other motives, both legitimate and illegitimate, yet still be marked as unfounded if the prosecutor feels that there is insufficient corroborating evidence for a conviction.

Most commentators would agree that the three illegitimate motives should be excluded from the founding decision: No victim should be turned away because the detective assigned to the case doesn't like her, or because he believes that she "asked for it" or that her case won't stand up in court. Even the two legitimate motives—clear fabrication, and failure to satisfy the legal requirements for rape—present real problems, however, with respect to the manner of report-taking. Principally, these problems involve the choice of suitable indicators for identifying false complaints.

The bottom line for police scrutiny of complaints of rape is that there is an appreciably higher rate of cases classified as unfounded for rape complaints than for any other crime. Table 10-1 details the proportion of cases determined to be unfounded by police in the nation's five largest cities for the years 1970 through 1974. Not only are the rates extremely high in certain jurisdictions, but there is also a significant variation among cities. Blackstone Associates surveyed more than fifty police departments in 1974 to analyze the police response to rape. The rate of marking cases as unfounded ranged from 1 to 25%, with most departments having a rate of about 10%.[3]

High rates for classifying cases as founded do not, in any case, necessarily indicate that the police believe rape victims. Marking cases as unfounded is not the only way to dispose of rape complaints. Questionable

Table 10-1
Percentage of Rape Complaints Marked Unfounded in the Five Largest Cities (1970-1974)

City	1970	1971	1972	1973	1974
Chicago	59.2	54.7	55.0	54.1	49.5
Detroit[a]		1.3	1.4	3.7	1.3
Los Angeles[a]		2.7	2.1	1.9	3.4
New York	8.4	5.7	10.5	13.9	19.0
Philadelphia	28.9	33.1	32.3	29.1	16.2

Source: Statistics provided by the director, Federal Bureau of Investigation, Uniform Crime Reporting Section (February 23, 1976).
[a]Statistics for 1970 were not available for the cities of Detroit and Los Angeles.

cases can be disposed of by not recording them in the first place; there may be a separate classification for cases that lack victim cooperation; and the use of case labels like "investigation of persons," "suspicious circumstances," or "unfounded radio runs" permit rape complaints to be converted into administrative matters that will not appear in the crime statistics.

In the following section, the Philadelphia Police Department's lodging of such nonoffense charges as a means of effectively removing cases from the system is examined. The possibility that the police in this manner actually dispose of a number of rape complaints is considered. Finally, those cases that the Philadelphia Police declare to be unfounded are critically examined in an effort to determine why the Philadelphia rate of determining cases to be unfounded is high in comparison to other jurisdictions and to understand the factors influencing these decisions.

Although the nationwide unfounded rate has been generally high, there are indications that it is decreasing. This may mean that some of the reasons traditionally used for disbelieving victims are finally being discarded. Susan Brownmiller argues that when women are in charge of rape investigations, these figures drop much further:

> A decade ago the FBI's *Uniform Crime Reports* noted that 20 percent of all rapes reported to the police "were determined by investigation to be unfounded." By 1973 the figure had dropped to 15 percent, while reported rape remained, in the FBI's words, "the most under-reported crime." A 15 percent figure for false accusations is undeniably high, yet when New York City instituted a special sex crimes analysis squad and put policewomen (instead of men) in charge of interviewing complainants, the number of false charges in New York dropped dramatically to 2 percent, a figure that corresponded exactly to the rate of false reports for other violent crimes. The lesson in the mystery of the vanishing statistic is obvious. Women believe the word of other women. Men do not.[4]

Indeed, the most striking finding in the current study is that the presence of a policewoman during interrogation of the complainant increases the probability that the complaint will be recorded, that the victim will be believed, and that the case will be given a rape charge. These findings emerge in spite of the fact that, in Philadelphia, the policewoman's role had merely been to record the victim's statement and was subordinate to that of the detective, who was male and in charge.

Nonoffense Charges

Police might as well classify a case as unfounded as include it in one of the "throw-away" categories like "investigation of persons." Both strategies succeed in deleting the case from the final tally of rapes or attempted rapes reported to the FBI for inclusion in the *Uniform Crime Reports*. Nor is there any pressure on the police to clear these cases, since they are not labeled as chargeable offenses.

However, there is an advantage to using a nonoffense charge rather than determining a case to be unfounded. Using these labels reduces not only the official tally of rape complaints but also the official tally of unfounded cases. Philadelphia Police reported to the FBI that they classified 16.2% of all rape complaints as unfounded in 1974. Adding cases given a nonoffense charge to cases that were actually marked as unfounded in the current study indicates that Philadelphia Police disbelieved and turned away over 27.2% of the women who alleged rape.

The variables associated with nonoffense labelling follow the logic involved in determining cases to be unfounded and in losing cases. As in those instances, the most significant variable is presence of a policewoman, which dramatically increases the probability that a victim will be believed and that an offense charge will be applied. The victim's interactions with the police then tend to be less of a confrontation and are more likely to provide her with the help and compassion that she is seeking in a time of desperate need.

Ten variables are significantly associated with a case being given a non-offense charge:

1. The police are more likely to use a nonoffense charge when a policewoman is not called in to take a statement or aid in the interrogation (% nonoffense = 16.6 versus 5.4).

2. The police are more likely to use a nonoffense charge if the alleged rape occurred at the offender's residence (% nonoffense = 18.8 versus 7.9).

3. The police are more likely to use a nonoffense charge for those victims judged by the Center for Rape Concern social workers to be heavy drinkers (% nonoffense = 22.9 versus 9.0).

4. The police are more likely to use a nonoffense charge when more than one offender is involved (% nonoffense = 16.0 versus 7.6).

5. The police are more likely to use a nonoffense charge if the victim has a history of truancy (% nonoffense = 18.3 versus 8.8).

6. The police are more likely to use a nonoffense charge where clear elements of coercion or intimidation are lacking (% nonoffense = 17.5 versus 8.2).

7. The police are more likely to use a nonoffense charge when no sexual act is completed or physically initiated (% nonoffense = 37.5 versus 9.4).

8. The police are more likely to use a nonoffense charge for those victims where the median income of the census tract in which they reside is under $9000 per year (% nonoffense = 13.5 versus 7.6).

9. The police are more likely to use a nonoffense charge if the victim has ever had prior trouble with the police. (% nonoffense = 17.6 versus 9.3).

10. The police are more likely to use a nonoffense charge if the victim has a history as a runaway (% nonoffense = 19.7 versus 9.2).

The ten variables are analyzed as described before. Figure 10–1 depicts the resulting branches, with seven terminal groups identified. These groups are arranged in descending order of percentage given a nonoffense charge.

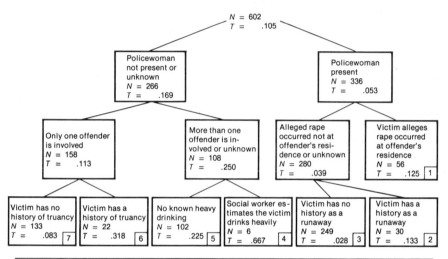

Group	Characteristics	Number of Cases	Percent Given Nonoffense Labels
4	Policewoman absent, group rape, victim a heavy drinker	6	66.7
6	Policewoman absent, single offender, truant	22	31.8
5	Policewoman absent, group rape, no heavy drinking pattern known	102	22.5
2	Policewoman present, rape not at offender's residence, runaway	30	13.3
1	Policewoman present, rape at offender's residence	56	12.5
7	Policewoman absent, single offender, no history of truancy	133	8.3
3	Policewoman present, rape not at offender's residence, no history of runaway	249	2.8

T = Proportion given a nonoffense label

Figure 10–1. Interaction of Selected Variables According to the Proportion Given a Nonoffense Charge

In general, extremely few cases result in a nonoffense charge when a policewoman is present at the victim's interrogation, unless the victim alleges that the rape occurred at the offender's residence or unless the victim has a history as a runaway. Even if a policewoman is absent, less than 10% of the cases are given nonoffense charges if only one offender is involved and the victim has no history of truancy.

The final configuration is the only one in this chapter to include the victim's drinking habits. The social worker interview does not include a determination as to whether or not the victim had been drinking immediately prior to the rape incident. Had this information been available, this variable might have appeared with greater frequency.

Also included in the final configuration is the number of alleged offenders (for a single incident). Of the "gang rapes" in the police files, 21% are marked as unfounded and, of rapes determined to be founded, 16% are given nonoffense charges. In sum, only about two-thirds of gang rape allegations are believed, allegations that are most often made by poor, black adolescents or young adults.

Perhaps the police attribute these allegations of group rape to the complainants' need for explaining away unaccounted-for time to the satisfaction of parents, boyfriends, or spouses. Or police may feel that the victim is at fault for peer relations that get out of hand and lead to group rape, often accompanied by the use of drugs or alcohol.

Lost Cases

As explained earlier, the Center for Rape Concern completed extensive home-visit interview schedules for 790 of 1,401 alleged rape victims seen at Philadelphia General Hospital between April 1, 1973 and June 30, 1974 (for child victims the period extended to June 30, 1975). For each victim, the Philadelphia Police Department agreed to provide the following information: Police district responsible for the case, district complaint number, major charge, and whether or not the case was determined to be founded.

The police made this information available in 709 of the 790 cases requested; the remaining 89 (10.3%) cases could not be located in police files. Some of these cases occurred out of their jurisdiction, and the absence of others might have been due to an inadequate search of records. Nonetheless, these 89 cases were analyzed to see if there was any evidence supporting the contention that the police had simply not reported a portion of these cases in the first place.

In spite of the high percentage of cases found in police files, as well as reasonable explanations for some of those that were not located, the current study does indicate that a portion of the missing cases probably disappeared because the police disposed of them by simply not recording them. Six variables were found to be significantly associated with these lost cases:

1. The police are less likely to find cases in their files where the victim admits later to a social worker that there was no rape (% lost = 37.5 versus 9.0).

2. The police are less likely to find cases in their files where the victim has had previous consenting sexual relations with the offender (% lost = 32.1 versus 9.4).

3. The police are less likely to find the cases in which the Center for Rape Concern social worker believes there are some elements in the victim's story that are not credible (% lost = 17.0 versus 7.0).

4. The police are less likely to find cases in their files where clear elements of coercion or intimidation are lacking (% lost = 16.9 versus 9.0).

5. The police are less likely to find cases in their files where no sexual act is completed or physically initiated (% lost = 33.3 versus 9.6).

6. The police are less likely to find cases in their files where a policewoman is not called in to take a statement or aid in victim interrogation (% lost = 10.0 versus 5.4).

The rating of victim credibility deserves some attention. Social workers were asked to evaluate the credibility of each victim's report of the incident on a scale of 1 to 4. A rating of 1 is not intended to indicate that the victim was probably not raped. Rather, it does indicate that several aspects of a victim's account are inconsistent and might raise questions as to the truthfulness of her story and are, as such, proper matters for courtroom scrutiny. Only 24 cases in which a victim stated to the social worker that no rape had occurred should have been unfounded outright. The police have reported no record of nine of these cases. Of the 577 cases for which social workers provided credibility evaluations, all but 73 cases (12.7%) received a high credibility rating of 3 or 4. For the purposes of this study, cases ranked 1 or 2 are called "partially incredible," and cases ranked 3 or 4 are labeled "credible."

The six variables most closely associated with case disappearance were analyzed. Figure 10-2 depicts the resulting branches. Five terminal groups are identified and arranged in descending order of percentage of cases not found in police files.

The isolation of groups 3, 5, and 6 strongly suggests the likelihood that some lost cases were not believed. All three groups are the sort that might be expected to contribute heavily to the unfounded totals or to the cases given a label like "investigation of persons." Instead, they seem to be weeded out at an earlier stage.

Several additional findings are worth noting. First, cases evaluated by social workers as partially incredible only disappear at a high rate where the victim's story does not include clear references to concrete elements of coer-

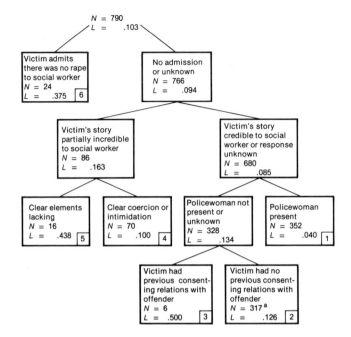

Group	Characteristics	Number of Cases	Percent Not Found in Police Files
3	No proof of fabrication, credible story, policewoman absent, prior consent	6	50.0
5	No proof of fabrication, partially credible story, clear coercion lacking	16	43.8
6	Proof of fabrication	24	37.5
2	No proof of fabrication, credible story, policewoman absent, no prior consent	317	12.6
4	No proof of fabrication, partially incredible story, clear coercion	70	10.0
1	No proof of fabrication, credible story, policewoman present	352	4.0

L = Proportion of cases not found

[a] 5 cases where the variable is unknown are discarded in final split.

Figure 10–2. Interaction of Selected Variables According to the Proportion Not Found by Police in Their Files.

cion or intimidation. Otherwise, poor credibility evaluations do not seem to keep cases out of the file system altogether. And secondly, the presence of a policewoman increases the likelihood that a case will subsequently find its way into the police files. In only 5.4% of all cases that disappear was a policewoman present.

To sum up, a portion of sexual assault complaints disappear. The evidence suggests that a portion of these lost cases may, in fact, be lost on purpose. And where cases have been lost, there are no arrests, no trials, and no convictions. Any tally of the cases not believed (determined to be unfounded) or given nonoffense charges should be identified as a conservative estimate of the total number of rape complaints that will not be included in the official statistics.

Cases Marked as Unfounded

Subtracting lost cases from the original total of 1,401 cases reported to PGH leaves a total of 1,198 rape complaints for the police to manage. Of these, the police determined 218 cases (18.2%) to be unfounded. Significantly more unfounded cases are among the 489 cases where there was no Center for Rape Concern social worker interview than among the remaining 709 cases where there was an interview (22.9% marked as unfounded versus 15% marked unfounded).

A number of indicators suggest that police–victim interactions are unpleasant when police mark the case as unfounded. Table 10–2 depicts police–victim interactions within the interviewed group when a police decision of unfounded is made. The data suggest that victims who have their complaints classified as unfounded are not likely to be amenable to further questioning concerning their allegations. They may have had enough.

Perhaps the most interesting finding in table 10–2 is the high proportion of unfounded cases when police detectives apply pressure on the victim to withdraw her complaint. The fact that in nearly one–fourth of all cases that are determined to be unfounded the police call complainants liars to their faces makes the remaining indicators of poor interactions readily cognizable.

The remaining discussion deals exclusively with the 709 cases for which there is a social worker interview, and focuses on the variables that contribute to the 15% rate at which cases are classified as unfounded. Once again, the most important variable is the presence or absence of a policewoman during the interrogation of the rape victim.

In all, thirteen variables are significantly associated with the decision to mark a case unfounded:

1. The police are more likely to mark cases as unfounded when a policewoman is not called in to take a statement or aid in victim interrogation (% unfounded = 21.9 versus 9.2).

2. The police are more likely to mark as unfounded cases that a social worker would evaluate as being partially incredible (% unfounded = 32.9 versus 13.7).

3. The police are more likely to mark as unfounded cases in which the victim reported to the CRC social worker that she had seen a psychiatrist prior to the alleged rape (% unfounded = 23.9 versus 11.8).

4. The police are more likely to mark cases unfounded if the victim is obese (% unfounded = 53.3 versus 14.2).

5. The police are more likely to mark as unfounded cases that a social worker would evaluate as victim-precipitated (% unfounded = 23.0 versus 12.3).

6. The police are more likely to mark cases as unfounded if the victim is 12 years old or older (% unfounded = 16.9 versus 6.6).

7. The police are more likely to mark cases as unfounded if the victim, herself, contacted the police (% unfounded = 21.8 versus 13.0).

8. The police are more likely to mark cases as unfounded if the victim alleges penile-vaginal intercourse was completed (% unfounded = 16.5 versus 7.0).

9. The police are more likely to mark as unfounded cases in which the victim exhibits demonstrable scratches (% unfounded = 25.3 versus 13.9).

10. The police are more likely to mark cases as unfounded if the victim has a history as a runaway (% unfounded = 24.1 versus 13.7).

11. The police are more likely to mark as unfounded cases in which the victim is a welfare recipient (% unfounded = 18.9 versus 11.9).

12. The police are more likely to mark as unfounded cases in which more than one offender is involved (% unfounded = 21.0 versus 13.9).

13. The police are more likely to mark cases as unfounded if the victim has ever had prior trouble with the police (% unfounded = 22.0 versus 13.9).

The thirteen variables are analyzed as before. Figure 10-3 depicts the resulting branches and identifies the seven terminal groups.

Credibility ratings have already been discussed. To reiterate, a social worker rating of partially incredible indicates only that the victim's story contains several questionable elements. These elements are matters properly reserved for courtroom scrutiny and do not constitute conclusive proof that no rape actually occurred. As previously noted, only twenty-four cases were identified in which the victim admitted that no rape had occurred. Over one-third of these twenty-four cases were not found in police files; three more were marked as unfounded. The fact that the police decision of unfounded is made for nearly one-third of all cases that social workers evaluate as "partially incredible" suggests that the police have usurped the

Table 10–2
Interactions between Interviewed Victims and Police by Whether Case Is Marked Founded

Interaction Variable	Percent among Cases Marked Unfounded	Percent among Cases Marked Founded
Victim perceives detective as:		
Fair	66.7	89.7
Friendly	69.3	87.3
Mean	36.9	13.1
Harsh	41.7	17.7
Fatherly	26.2	45.9
Malicious	32.9	11.9
Tough	37.6	23.5
Considerate	57.6	85.3
Indifferent	50.0	29.1
Warm	44.0	72.2
Helpful	56.5	84.8
Cold	46.4	24.4
Easygoing	54.6	71.5
Unreasonable	42.9	17.3
Unjust	42.8	16.8
Lenient	40.0	63.6
Understanding	60.0	85.9
Discourteous	35.7	14.6
Victim rating of a detective on a scale of 1 (poorest) to 4 (best):		
1	29.0	9.6
2	25.8	17.6
3	22.6	39.2
4	22.6	33.6
Police told victim they thought she was lying:	23.6	5.6
Police said the case would be hard to press in court	11.3	3.5
Total cases where police apply pressure to get the victim to withdraw her complaint	45.3	13.4
Total cases where the victim would not report rape again because of unpleasantness of police	13.2	4.3
Total cases where the most supportive person for a victim was a police officer or detective	0.0	3.5

courts' adjudicatory function and have eliminated cases altogether on the basis of their own doubts.

Social workers were also asked to evaluate victim precipitation. This highly subjective variable was loosely defined. Social workers were only

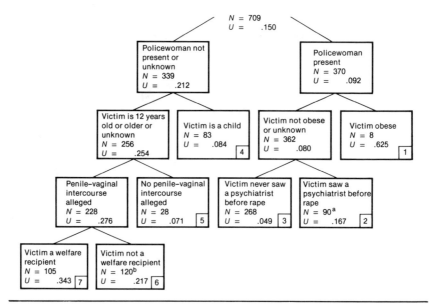

Group	Characteristics	Number of Cases	Percent Marked as Unfounded	Percent Evaluated Partially Incredible	Percent Evaluated Victim Precipitated
1	Policewoman present, victim obese	8	62.5	37.5	62.5
7	Policewoman absent, victim 12 or older, penile–vaginal intercourse alleged, victim a welfare recipient	105	34.3	20.2	31.7
6	Policewoman absent, victim 12 or older, penile–vaginal intercourse alleged, victim not a welfare recipient	120	21.7	15.7	24.6
2	Policewoman present, victim not obese, saw a psychiatrist precomplaint	90	16.7	4.8	40.9
4	Policewoman absent	83	8.4	12.4	4.3
5	Policewoman absent, victim 12 or older, no penile–vaginal intercourse alleged	28	7.1	25.0	18.5
3	Policewoman present, victim not obese, never saw a psychiatrist prerape	268	4.9	9.2	20.8

U = Proportion marked as unfounded

[a] 4 cases where the variable is unknown are discarded in final split.

[b] 3 cases where the variable is unknown are discarded in final split.

Figure 10–3. Interaction of Selected Variables According to the Proportion Marked Unfounded by Police.

told to rate all cases on the following scale: 0 = none, 1 = innocent, 2 = lack of discretion, 3 = some complicity, and 4 = victim arranged. The intent was not to blame victims; rather, the goal was to see if cases in which a social worker believes that other persons might accuse the victim of causing her own victimization were cases that also had poor adjustment or a negative criminal justice prognosis.

Cases rated 2, 3, or 4 are not necessarily victim precipitated. These ratings only indicate that social workers, using their own values, considered these cases to be at least in part victim precipitated. Certainly this judgment ought not to interfere with treatment of the victim or to minimize the offender's responsibility. The positive correlation between social worker rating and tendency of police to mark cases as unfounded suggests that the extralegal logic of victim precipitation is being used by the police to assess victim credibility.

The seven terminal groups presented in figure 10-3 are arranged in descending order of percentage marked as unfounded. Beside each group is the percentage evaluated by social workers as partially incredible, as well as the percentage thought by social workers to be victim precipitated.

In general, when a policewoman is present, the victim's complaint is determined to be founded unless the victim is obese or has seen a psychiatrist prior to the rape incident. An article in *Philadelphia Magazine* cites a case in which a Philadelphia detective assumed that a victim was lying because she was overweight and confronted her thus: "Number 1," he said, "you're pretty obese there and I just can't believe you've been raped."[5]

The variable "prior psychiatric contact" is particularly interesting because it increased fourfold the likelihood of a police decision of unfounded in the final "policewoman present" split (% marked as unfounded = 16.7 versus 4.9), yet it has never been determined whether or not police are actually aware of this contact. In addition, the final group of ninety woman with prior psychiatric contact received fewer partially incredible ratings than any other group. It would seem that any indication of prior psychiatric contact leads police officers to view with some skepticism an otherwise believable account, particularly if there is a suggestion of victim precipitation.

When a policewoman is not present, the police tend to believe children 11 years old or less and tend to disbelieve adolescents and adults, particularly if they allege penile-vaginal intercourse and are welfare recipients. If a victim does not allege penile-vaginal intercourse, police are not compelled to give the case a rape charge and consequently seem more willing to believe the victim's story. Conversely, the police tend to be more wary if they feel that a complaint cannot logically be given anything but a rape charge.

Whereas race of the victim is not significantly associated with the decision to mark a case as unfounded, socioeconomic status is. This would seem to indicate that police are focusing their doubts on the poorest complainants, most of whom are black, but not nearly so intensely on blacks of a higher socioeconomic class.

When the final seven groups are compared with respect to victim precipitation and victim credibility, a fascinating pattern emerges. Although victim story credibility is not significantly associated with victim precipitation, the correlation between a police decision of unfounded and credibility is significant, as is the correlation between a police decision of unfounded and victim precipitation. These findings reinforce the conclusion that the police determine a sizeable number of rape cases to be unfounded through the utilization of victim precipitation logic in the decision–making process. This conclusion is also consistent with the unpleasant interactions with police reported by victims who have had their cases classified as unfounded and with the unwillingness of many such victims to participate in any further interrogations.

Table 10–3 examines these variables (police decision of unfounded, credibility rating, and victim precipitation evaluation) from another angle. As can be seen from the data, police are most likely to declare a case to be unfounded when the victim's story is evaluated as partially incredible with some victim precipitation, and they are least likely to reach this conclusion when the story is evaluated as credible with no victim precipitation. However, in 50 cases among 395 complaints (12.7%), a social worker evaluated the victim's story as entirely believable with no suggestion of victim precipitation, yet these cases were marked as unfounded by the police. Apparently the variables mentioned earlier are being used to their fullest extent in removing these cases from the system. Presence of policewoman, obesity, prior psychiatric treatment, age, intercourse, and welfare status discriminate between those cases likely to be believed and those likely to be unfounded.

Summary

Police may declare a case to be unfounded only if "investigation shows that no offense occurred nor was attempted." According to social worker evaluations, only about three percent of all cases fall within this definition. Social workers were able to identify only 24 cases where the victim originally cried rape and later admitted that no rape had occurred.

The current investigation reveals that Philadelphia Police were not able to locate the records of about 14% of the victims treated at Philadelpha General Hospital during the study period. Although an unknown number of cases were not found because they were the responsibility of other jurisdictions, the evidence at hand suggests that a portion of these "lost" cases were disposed of as though they were considered to be unfounded.

Table 10–3
Cases Marked Unfounded by Credibility Rating and Vicim Precipitation

Credibility Evaluation	Some Victim Precipitation	No Victim Precipitation	Total
Partially incredible	N = 44	N = 29	N = 73
	P = 40.1	P = 20.7	P = 32.9
Credible	N = 108	N = 395	N = 503
	P = 17.6	P = 12.7	P = 13.7
Total	N = 152	N = 424	N = 576
	P = 24.3	P = 13.2	P = 16.1

Note: N = number of cases, P = percent unfounded, there were 133 missing cases.

Of the cases that the police were able to locate, 18.2% were marked as unfounded. The evidence suggests that the police sometimes usurp the courtroom function, discarding rape cases that contain several unlikely circumstances and, in effect, declaring the offender not guilty. Additionally, the police appear to endorse an extralegal victim precipitation logic, declaring unfounded those cases in which the circumstances of the victim-offender relationship are not wholly uncompromising. Using a nonoffense label in place of marking a case as unfounded reduces both the number of rape complaints and the number of cases marked as unfounded that are reported in the crime statistics.

Where a policewoman is present, even if only in the capacity of a secretary, cases disappear or receive nonoffense labels less often, and are marked as founded more often. Additional variables indicate that police tend to doubt the credibility of extremely obese women, women who have seen psychiatrists, women who are 12 years old or more, women who allege penile–vaginal intercourse, and women who receive welfare.

Not surprisingly, women who are not believed tend to have unpleasant interactions with the police they turned to for help.

Notes

1. Menachem Amir, *Patterns in Forcible Rape* (Chicago: University of Chicago Press, 1971), p. 266.
2. Comment, "Police Discretion and the Judgment That a Crime Has Been Committed—Rape in Philadelphia," *University of Pennsylvania Law Review* 117 (December 1968): 318.

3. Lisa Brodyaga et al., "Rape and Its Victims: A Report for Citizens, Health Facilities and Criminal Judicial Agencies" (Unpublished report, National Institute of Law Enforcement and Criminal Justice, Washington, D.C., November 1975).

4. Susan Brownmiller, *Against Our Will: Men, Women and Rape* (New York: Simon and Schuster, 1975), p. 387.

5. Arthur Spikol, "Thirty Rapes a Day," *Philadelphia Magazine* 16 (October 1973): 94.

11 Whom the Police Catch and How They Follow Through

Most mass media depictions of the police response to rape focus on the various misconceptions that intrude when the police ask the questions "Is this woman lying?" and "Is this rape?" While conceding that the police are legitimately responsible for weeding out false complaints (the decision concerning whether to mark a case as founded or unfounded and determining the crime category described by the complaint [the labeling decision]), many sources argue that the police set up impossible behavioral standards for victims to meet. These standards, which are based on misconceptions concerning the nature of women, of men, of their so-called normal interactions, and of what constitutes rape, are often insulting and humiliating to victims. An interrogation may culminate in the police in effect calling the victim a liar and not labeling the case rape. The women who weather these interrogations are, at least in the movies and on television, able to relax until the trial, when the onslaught begins anew.

Yet not every complaint that the police believe and list as a rape makes it to court. The police must apprehend and arrest at least one suspect. Police responsibility, of course, does not end with this arrest. Once in court, the case against the alleged rapist depends to a great extent on the value of the evidence collected by the police, as well as how competently the police, as witnesses, are able to present their evidence. The present chapter surveys one department's activities in this area.

This analysis uses an information resource different from the information described previously. Case histories are recorded by Philadelphia Police Detectives on a standard "investigation report" form. For each case, the police detail "origin and details of complaint," "interviews and interrogations," "action taken," "remarks," and "messages," in addition to required data items like age of complainant, race of complainant, charge classification, whether or not the case was marked as founded, and so forth. As new activity on a case occurs, additional investigation reports are completed.

The Philadelphia Police Department agreed to provide the Center for Rape Concern with complete sets of all rape investigation reports marked as founded and compiled over a fixed period of time. The reports were sufficiently dated that either an arrest had been made or there was not likely ever to be an arrest. Philadelphia Police reported to the FBI that there were 302 rape or attempted rape complaints marked as founded from October 1,

1970 through April 30, 1971. Files on 295 cases belonging to this group were located. Six files were incomplete, leaving 289 complaints or 96% of all cases that were marked as founded during the 7-month period available for analysis. These cases are the basis of this chapter's conclusions.

One of the 289 complaints was originally listed as an "investigation of persons." Once the police had apprehended a suspect, they decided that they were dealing with a rape after all and, therefore, listed the charge as forcible rape, marked it founded, and cleared it by arrest. On the other hand, seven of the sample cases that were originally marked as founded were later changed to unfounded. According to the investigation reports, most of these cases were newly marked unfounded because the complainant had freely admitted consent during subsequent interrogations. One complainant claimed that she had charged rape because she was afraid of how her husband might react to the true account. Another victim admitted to crying rape after a voluntary encounter because she had felt that it was the only way to get medical attention. Several adolescents confessed to using the rape complaint to explain their whereabouts to parents. Finally, there were cases where parents later revealed that the complainant was prone to sexual-assault story-telling.

Police did not pursue the seven cases now marked unfounded. Likewise, they ignored five additional cases where the victim withdrew her cooperation in the later stages of investigation. The police diverted their attention from these 12 cases to the 277 remaining cases classified as founded and retaining full victim cooperation.

This study defines a case as solved where police apprehend and arrest at least one suspect or where the police have positively identified a suspect who vanishes prior to an arrest being made. To meet the latter condition, the police must know the full name of the suspect, as well as an address at which he has lived and from which he has vanished. For purposes of this study, unless an arrest is made, or police are thwarted in their attempt to make an arrest only by the disappearance of a suspect whose name and last known address are known, the case remains classified as unsolved. This holds true even where the police know a nickname, or where a suspect works, or his general location or neighborhood.

Philadelphia Police solved 190 of the 277 sampled cases that they investigated (68.6%). Eighty-seven remain unsolved (31.4%). However, only 57.7% of all suspected offenders were arrested. This latter statistic is explained by the fact that the police need not arrest all suspected offenders to effect a case classification of *solved* in this study. In nine solved cases— eight cases of single offender rape and one case of pair rape—the suspects vanished before arrests could be made. As of this writing, all ten of these suspected offenders are still at large. Solved cases also include fifty-nine cases of multiple offender rape. Although at least one suspected offender

Table 11-1
Forcible Rapes Cleared by Arrest in Philadelphia, New York City, and All Cities with Population over 250,000 (1970-1972)

	1970	1971	1972
Philadelphia offenses	452	546	588
Philadelphia clearances	304	391	486
Percent cleared:			
Philadelphia [a]	67.3	71.6	82.7
New York City [b]	33.0	31.0	31.4
Cities over 250,000 [c]	56	55	57

[a] Annual Philadelphia Police Report (1972), p.4.

[b] D. Chappell and S. Singer, "Rape in New York City: A Study of Material in the Police Files and Its Meaning," p. 53.

[c] Federal Bureau of Investigation Uniform Crime Reports (1970), p. 14; (1971), p. 12; (1972), p. 14.

was arrested in each case, thirty-eight suspected offenders were never apprehended. The 87 unsolved cases yield 138 suspected offenders still at large. Adding these 138 offenders to the 48 offenders never arrested in the solved cases results in 186 offenders at large versus 254 suspects arrested in the 190 solved cases (57.7% of 440 suspected offenders apprehended and/or arrested).

In terms of clearance rate, the Philadelphia Police have an exemplary record. A case is defined as "cleared by arrest" if at least one suspect is arrested for a complaint (regardless of how many offenders might have been involved) or if any of a series of relatively unlikely "exceptional" conditions pertain. The most likely "exceptional" condition in a rape case is where the victim refuses to cooperate in the prosecution. As table 11-1 indicates, from 1970 to 1972 the Philadelphia Police, on average, cleared both a higher proportion of rape cases marked as founded than other cities of over 250,000 cleared and a far greater percentage than New York City reported.

The present chapter identifies what sort of rape events contribute to this high clearance rate, examines the methods employed to apprehend such a large percentage of suspects, questions whether or not the clearance rate is accompanied by good case preparation, and looks at how well the police fare in court.

Whom Police Apprehend

Where the offender is known to the victim, the police task becomes fairly straightforward. In one-third of the sample cases, the victim knew the offender by name prior to the incident. In the remainder of the sample, either the offender was unknown to the victim or, if seen before the incident, the victim had not interacted with him to the extent that she knew his name or address. Police almost always make an arrest when the victim is able to tell them exactly whom to arrest. However, as table 11-2 indicates, the police in Philadelphia also solve more than half of all cases where the offender was a stranger or relative stranger to the victim.

The time interval between the incident and the report is not helpful in predicting which cases will be solved among the group of stranger/relative stranger rapes. Admittedly, where the police arrive on the scene and interrupt the rape, they do get their man. However, as table 11-3 demonstrates, once the offender has fled it matters little whether or not the victim reports quickly. In fact, there is a weak but significant negative correlation between time interval prior to reporting and percentage solved. That is, it appears that the police make more arrests when the victim delays in reporting. However, this relationship is spurious, disappearing once cases are divided between single-offender rapes and multiple-offender rapes.

The study did identify four variables that are significantly associated with case solution where the offender is a stranger/relative stranger to the victim:

1. The police are more likely to solve cases of multiple rape than single rape (% solved = 69.6 versus 48.2).

2. The police are more likely to solve attempted than completed rapes (% solved = 67.4 versus 49.3).

3. The police are more likely to solve cases where the victim is black (% solved = 59.8 versus 45.6).

4. The police are more likely to solve cases where the offender did not force an entry into the victim's home or where she was staying (% solved = 58.0 versus 46.5).

The variable of forced entry requires some explanation. Nearly 40% of the sample cases where the offender was a stranger or relative stranger to the victim involved a violation of the victim's residential security. In 60% of these cases, the offense also included burglary or robbery. A case is categorized as a forced entry if the offender uses physical force, subterfuge, or an unlocked door or window to enter the victim's home or the place at which she is staying. Subterfuge may often be accompanied by force. For example, an offender rings the victim's doorbell and asks for a third person. The moment that the victim opens the door a crack, the offender shows a weapon and demands entry. Most forced entries involved physical force exclusively. In 26.8% of the forced entry cases, subturfuge was employed. In only 6.9% of the cases did the offender gain access through an unlocked door or window.

The four variables associated with case solution are analyzed as de-

Table 11–2

Type of Interpersonal Relationship between Victim and Principal Offender by Whether Case Is Solved by Police

Victim Offender Relationship	Cases Solved by Police	Percent Solved	Cases Not Solved by Police	Percent Not Solved	Total
Stranger/ relative stranger	98	53.6	85	46.4	183
Offender known to the victim (by name) prior to the incident	92	97.9	2	2.1	94
Total	190	68.6	87	31.4	277

Table 11–3

Time Interval Prior to Report to Police by Percentage Solved (Where the Offender is a Stranger/Relative Stranger)

Time Interval prior to Report of the Offense to Police	Percent Solved by Police	Number of Cases
Less than or equal to 30 minutes	46.0	100
More than 30 minutes, less than or equal to 1 hour	48.4	31
More than 1 hour, less than or equal to 4 hours	51.0	21
More than 4 hours	76.0	25

Note: Excluding 6 cases where police were at the scene, all solved

scribed in chapter 2. Figure 11–1 describes the resulting branches. Six terminal groups are identified and presented in descending order of percentage solved by the police.

According to these findings, the police are least successful where a single stranger forces entry into the home of the victim or the place at which she is staying, completes the rape, and leaves. On the other hand, police have considerable success where more than one offender is involved, even if the rape involves forced entry into the victim's residence. Table 11–4 compares single-offender and multiple-offender completed, forced entry rapes by percentage solved.

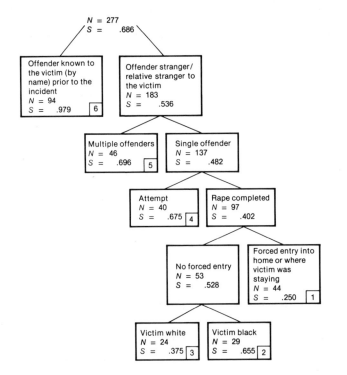

Group	Characteristics	Number of Cases	Percent Solved
6	Offender known	92	97.9
5	Stranger, multiple rape	46	69.6
4	Stranger, alone, attempt	40	67.5
2	Stranger, alone, completes rape, no forced entry, victim black	29	65.5
3	Stranger, alone, completes rape, no forced entry, victim white	24	37.5
1	Stranger, alone, completes rape, forced entry	44	25.0

S = Proportion solved by the police

Figure 11-1. Interaction of Selected Variables According to the Proportion Solved by Police

Police are much more successful in solving multiple-offender forced entry rapes. Why? First, since only one arrest is needed to clear a case, multiple offenders leaving multiple clues means a greater probability of arrests; the likelihood of subsequently apprehending one of the offenders increases as the number of offenders increases.

Table 11-4

Single Offender versus Multiple Offender, Forced Entry, Completed Rapes by Whether Case Is Solved by Police

Type of Forced Entry, Completed Rape	Cases Solved by Police	Percent Solved	Cases Not Solved by Police	Percent Not Solved	Total
Single offender	11	25.0	33	75.0	44
Multiple offender	14	87.5	2	12.5	16
Total	25	41.7	35	58.3	60

Second, since there are fewer incidents of multiple-offender forced entry rape than single-offender forced entry rape, patterns are more obvious. Within the sample cases, four rapes were part of a pattern of rapes all occurring within several blocks of each other in a "good" central city neighborhood over a 6-month period. All involved young adult white women who were raped and robbed by a group of three young adult black males. Despite a tremendous amount of time invested by the police, no progress was made until an anonymous phone call led to the apprehension of one suspect. Four rapes were thereby "solved." An additional three sample cases, each one a brutal robbery-rape, were solved when one of the offenders was subsequently arrested on another charge and identified by one of the victims during a line-up.

Finally, multiple-offender forced entry rapes are often more violent—involving great damage to both persons and property—than are similar single-offender rapes. Police may be more shocked by gangs invading private residences and therefore more determined to solve these cases.

It is easy to see why rape attempts (as opposed to completed rapes) are so easily solved. Clearly, if a rape is interrupted because police arrive at the scene, or if a friend, relative, or stranger interrupts the rape and holds the offender, apprehension is assured. In general, where a rape is incomplete it may signify that it was interrupted, that the chain of events did not occur as the offender had originally intended. This interruption may set into motion a new chain of events leading to the apprehension of the offender. The victim's screams may have been unexpected, considering the knife being held to her throat.

Two other groups are not so readily explicable. In both groups, a single offender who is a stranger to the victim completes a forcible rape at other than the victim's residence or where she is staying. In the group consisting of black victims, the police are fairly effective in solving cases ($S = .655$). Where the victim is white, the success rate is much lower ($S = .375$). In no other group does the variable of race enter into the final configuration. However, by examining the age of the offender, more explicable groupings are permitted to emerge.

Offender age is a tricky variable—when there is no arrest, the perceptions of the victim establish the category. In three cases, the victim stated that she had no idea as to the age of her attacker. These cases were discounted in testing this variable. Table 11-5 demonstrates that offender age splits the same branch that race split in figure 11-1. And the age split is more readily explicable: Young offenders are better known within their neighborhoods and are often already known to the police. All told, they are probably easier to identify.

Figure 11-2 reconstructs the final groupings (terminal groups 2 and 3). It reveals the study's answer to the question: "Whom do the police catch?" Note that the variable of race disappears from the final configuration.

This final solution also helps to explain, in part, why Philadelphia Police are more effective than New York City Police in making arrests for rape. Duncan Chappell and Susan Singer studied New York City police files and found a 35.7% clearance rate for 627 cases in their sample. They also found that their sample included 80.6% stranger rapes and 80.6% single-offender rapes, both of which exceed Philadelphia's statistics (66.1% and 73% respectively), and both of which represent groups that are less easily apprehended.[1]

In sum, there are noticeable differences in Philadelphia Police case solution for different sorts of rapes, ranging from a 97.9% solution rate where the offender is known to the victim by name to a 25% solution rate where the victim is raped by a stranger, acting alone, who forces an entry into her dwelling, and completes the rape.

Table 11-5
Age of Offender by Whether Case is Solved by Police in Stranger, Acting Alone, No Forced Entry, Completed Rapes

Age of Offender	Cases Solved by Police	Percent Solved	Cases not Solved by Police	Percent Not Solved	Total
Juvenile (under 18)	15	.750	5	.250	20
Adult	13	.433	17	.567	30
Total	28	.560	22	.440	50

Note: Excluding 3 cases where age could not be estimated.

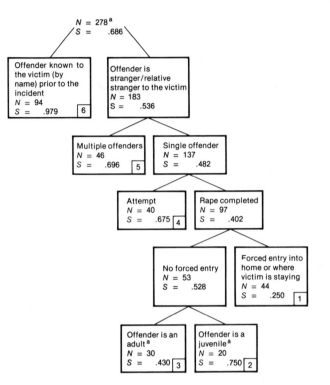

Group	Characteristics	Number of Cases	Percent Solved
6	Offender known	92	97.9
2	Stranger, alone, completed rape, no forced entry, juvenile offender	20	75.0
5	Stranger, multiple rape	46	69.6
4	Stranger, alone, attempt	40	67.5
3	Stranger, alone, completed rape, no forced entry, adult offender	30	43.3
1	Stranger, alone, completed rape, forced entry	44	25.0

S = Proportion solved by the police

[a] Three cases where age of offender cannot be obtained are discarded in final split.

Figure 11-2. Adjusted Terminal Groups According to the Proportion Solved by Police

How Police Apprehend Suspects

Very few of the elaborate mechanisms that are used to trap suspects on television police dramas are evident in real life. In 181 cases from the total sample, the police made an arrest. Table 11-6 illustrates the method of apprehension for the first suspect in each rape case. In 71.4% of all solved cases, someone told the police whom to arrest. In another 14% of solved

Table 11-6
Method of Apprehending First Suspect ($N = 179$]

Method of Apprehension	Number of Cases	Percent
Directly usable offender idenfification provided by the victim:		
at first police interrogation	96	53.9
after subsequently spotting or hearing from offender	10	5.6
victim provided license plate number	4	2.3
Total	110	61.8
Directly usable offender identification provided by another:		
anonymous phone call	7	3.9
others apprehend and hold suspect	2	1.1
others provide usable identification directly to police	8	4.5
Total	17	9.6
Police apprehend suspect at or near the scene:		
interrupt rape	15	8.4
apprehend offender in an immediate sweep of the area:	10	5.6
1. accompanied by victim	6	3.4
2. not accompanied by victim	4	2.2
Total	25	14.0
Offender identified from subsequent arrest or "mug shots":		
subsequent arrest matched with an unresolved rape; victim brought in to confirm identification	8	4.5
victim identifies detective division photograph or department slide	4	2.3
victim provides nickname, which police trace down in gang files and bring in victim to view photo	3	1.6
Total	15	8.4
Police solve the case:		
police see someone resembling wanted message or composite and apprehend suspect	9	5.1
other police investigation methods	2	1.1
Total	11	6.2

Note: Excluding 3 cases where method is unknown.

cases, the police were called quickly enough to make an arrest at the scene of the crime.

A recent Rand Corporation study of the criminal investigation process solicited information from 300 police jurisdictions, each having more than 150 full-time police employees or a 1970 population base of over 100,000. On the basis of 153 completed questionnaires and over twenty-five site visits, the study arrived at the following conclusions (among others):

> More then one-half of all serious cases eventually cleared are solved because (1) the offender is arrested at the scene, (2) the victim or other persons uniquely identify the offender, or, (3) unique evidence, like a licence plate or employee badge number, is provided by the victim or a witness.
>
> Most of the remaining cases are solved routinely by informant tips, review of mug shots, or fingerprint searches.[2]

These conclusions are supported by the present study of rape in Philadelphia, which finds that 93.8% of all solved rape cases are solved by the police utilizing one of these methods.

Criminologists Albert Reiss and David Bordua also suggest that victim identification of the offender is characteristic of most police solutions: "A majority of the cases that are cleared by arrest may be said to solve themselves in the sense that the violator is 'known' to the complainant or to the police at the time the crime initially comes to the attention of the police." The authors identify a second manner of solving cases: "Though good data are lacking on the matter, there is good reason to claim that the second largest proportion of all crimes cleared by arrest is 'solved' by arresting otherwise known violators."[3]

Of the cases just considered, 4.5% involved matching up a suspect arrested for another crime with the offender profile provided in a rape complaint. An additional 2.3% were identified by victims from detective division photos, and 1.7% by checking nicknames in police gang files. However, the focus has not been specifically on the types of persons arrested for rape.

Are rape cases that are solved by the police cases where the offender is already known to them through a number of prior interactions? Are offenders usually long-term residents of the community?

In answering these questions, the unit of analysis moves from rape cases to persons arrested for rape. For example, if one individual is suspected of having committed three reported rapes, three cases are cleared by that person's arrest. For this analysis, a study that concentrated on persons arrested was sought. The Treatment Alternatives to Street Crime (TASC) Program collected a great deal of information on all persons arrested in Philadelphia between April 1 and June 30, 1973.[4] This study included all persons arrested except those charged with drunkenness or any of several small categories of offenses (like federal fugitives) and for whom complete records could not be obtained. There were 7,644 arrests for this period, 844 of which involved multiple arrests of 703 persons, yielding a total of 6,800 individuals arrested.

Of these 6,800, 89 were charged with rape as their most serious offense. More than one-third of the persons arrested for rape had been arrested, as adults, by Philadelphia Police during the prior 12 months. Nearly two-thirds had been arrested at least once in their adult lives by Philadelphia Police. More than one-third had three or more prior adult arrests. This is of special interest when we consider that nearly half of those persons arrested for rape were twenty-one or younger at the time of arrest (47.2% of rapists were 21 or younger versus 25.1% 21 or younger for all 6,800 persons arrested). The younger arrestees only had between 1 and 4 years to accumulate these adult records, which begin at age 18. Looking back to their adolescent years, we find that 44.1% of those persons arrested for rape have a record of being adjudicated a delinquent in Philadelphia.

Table 11-7 describes the number of prior arrests for persons arrested during the study period, whereas table 11-8 examines the history of charges that at least 5% of rape arrestees have. Not only are most of those charged with rape already known to the police, but it seems that a number of them have already been identified by the police as violent offenders. Particularly noteworthy in table 11-8 is the frequency of prior arrests for weapons offenses, robbery, aggravated and simple assault, and rape and other sex offenses.

In addition to already being known by the police, persons charged with rape are, for the most part, long-term Philadelphia residents. Nearly all (95.4%) have lived in Philadelphia for more than 1 year, 92% for more than 3 years. Slightly over half (51.7%) of all adults arrested for rape still lived with their parents, 20% with spouses (including common-law spouses), and 10% with other relatives.

In sum, most rape cases that are solved are solved because someone tells the police whom to arrest. In addition, a relatively large proportion of those arrested are already known to the police. The method of capture rarely involves detective work in the conventional sense of that term.

Police Investigative Thoroughness

Since a majority of cases may be said to solve themselves, the real police work in the area of rape investigation is in case follow-through. The principal focus of interest, then, is the ability of the police to make their arrests stick.

Table 11-7
Comparison of prior Arrests for 89 Persons Charged with Rape and 6,800
Persons Charged with Any Offense from April 1 to June 30, 1973
in Philadelphia

Prior Arrests	Persons Charged with Rape	Percent	All Persons	Percent
0	33	37.1	2233	32.8
1 or 2	23	25.8	1637	24.1
3 or more	33	37.1	2930	43.1
Total	89	100.0	6800	100.0

Table 11-8
Most Serious Charges for which at Least 5 Percent of Persons Arrested for
Rape Have Previous Arrest

Most Serious Charge	Number Arrested for Charge Prior to Current Arrest for Rape	Percent	Percent of Persons Arrested Prior to Current Arrest (N = 6,800)
Weapons offenses	30	33.6	
Burglary	18	20.2	25.0
Robbery	15	16.9	13.0
Simple assault and resisting arrest	15	16.9	13.0
Larceny	14	15.7	22.0
Auto theft	12	13.5	13.0
Aggravated assault	10	11.2	14.0
Rape	7	7.9	
Liquor law violations	7	7.9	11.0
Sex offenses	6	6.7	
Disorderly conduct	6	6.7	13.0
Possession of a controlled substance	6	6.7	23.0

Note: Where there is no entry in column, figure represented less than 5 percent.

The Rand Corporation study cited earlier concluded that very few police departments "consistently and thoroughly document the key evidentiary facts that reasonably assure that the prosecutor can obtain a conviction on the most serious applicable charges."[5] The present study concludes that Philadelphia Police are more concerned with solving a case than with laying the basis for a well-grounded subsequent prosecution and that there is more and better evidence gathered when an arrest is not made. In addition, there are weak but significant findings to suggest that white victims generally receive better case preparation than black victims and, to a lesser extent, that cases with victims 21 or over receive greater investigative thoroughness than cases with younger victims.

Police investigative thoroughness is least evident where the victim knew her attacker. In about half of these cases, selected from the sample of police investigation reports, the police did not visit the scene of the crime to look for physical evidence. About three-quarters of the time they did not confiscate clothing, bedding, or any substance that might have confirmed the presence of sperm. In twenty-three cases the suspect, when confronted, admitted being at the scene of the crime but denied that any sexual relations took place. The police confiscated physical evidence to confirm the presence of sperm and did, in fact, refute this defense in only five of these cases. In less than one-tenth of the cases involving a known attacker did the police bother to call in a mobile crime lab to collect photographs and/or latent prints at the scene once the suspect was in custody. In fact, one investigation report records that a mobile crime lab was requested and refused because they were all being used elsewhere. Similarly, in three cases it was recorded by the first officer at the scene that the division refused to assign a detective to the case. In each of these instances, the officer making the request was told to handle the case himself. Formal identification procedures (like lineups) were conducted in less than one in twenty of these cases.

Philadelphia Police appear to gather more evidence in their investigation of cases where the victim reports being raped by a stranger. By splitting stranger rapes into solved cases ($N = 98$) and unsolved cases ($N = 85$), estimates can be obtained of investigative thoroughness in cases that go to court (the first group) as compared to the cases that police do not solve (the second group). Five variables were examined:

1. Whether or not police conduct a thorough search at the scene of the event for physical evidence.

2. Whether or not they confiscate the victim's underclothing or bedding or any object to be tested for presence of sperm.

3. Whether or not a mobile crime lab is called in for the purpose of making photographs or obtaining fingerprints or scrapings.

4. Whether or not police use their detective division photo files, their department's color slides, and/or their identification unit to create a composite drawing.

5. How many people they interview in their investigation.

In cases where the offender was a stranger to the victim, the police visited the scene 83.1% of the time, confiscated evidence 55.7% of the time, and called in a mobile crime lab in 42.1% of the cases. Detective division photos were shown 41.5% of the time, whereas color slides were shown and composites drawn in 19.1% and 13.1/% of the cases, respectively. Finally, police interviewed two or fewer people in 62.7% of the cases and more than two people in 37.2% of the cases.

Turning our attention to the solved cases, in only 39.8% of the cases was there confiscation of physical evidence to test for sperm, versus 55.7% of the unsolved cases. In seventeen cases the suspect, once apprehended, admitted that he was in the area at the time of the incident but denied that any sexual relations had taken place. Police confiscated physical evidence that might have refuted his statement in only seven cases.

There exists a weak but significant association in solved cases between race and evidence confiscated, with white victims more likely than black victims to have evidence collected by the police (51.4% versus 31.2%).

A mobile crime lab is brought in less frequently in solved cases than in unsolved cases (34% versus 50.6%). For solved cases, white victims are more likely to have a mobile crime lab called in than are black victims (44.4% versus 27.9%).

The only other significant relationship for solved cases exists with respect to the number of interviews taken. Police are more likely to interview more than two persons when the victim is white than when she is black (47.7% versus 24.6%).

With the unsolved cases, police are more likely to confiscate physical evidence to detect sperm when the victim is 20 or over (59.3% versus 32.3%), and they are more likely to call in a mobile crime unit (66.7% versus 22.3%). They are more likely to create a composite when the victim is white (25% versus 2.4%).

Generally, the police invest more time and effort in the cases they do not solve than in those that they do solve. The sole exception to this involves the collection of physical evidence for the purpose of detecting sperm, which is more common among solved cases. However, the other activities—looking for clues at the scene, calling in a crime lab, using photo, slide, and composite identification techniques, and interviewing witnesses—are all more prevalent among unsolved cases.

If the police are primarily interested in clearing cases, then evidence-gathering activities will be least common where the victim knew her attacker and less common among solved cases than unsolved cases within the category of stranger rapes. This pattern is statistically confirmed, leading to the conclusion that police are indeed more concerned with solving a case than with laying the basis for a well-grounded subsequent prosecution.

Police Courtroom Follow-through

Police case preparation need not be extensive if the arrested suspect freely admits his guilt. Unfortunately, this is not often the case. In nearly one-half of the cases in which a suspect is apprehended, the victim knows the offender by name. In about 40% of these cases, the suspect is someone with whom the victim has interacted to a great extent in the past and whom she presumably has trusted—a member of her family, a boyfriend or lover, or a close personal friend. In the remaining 60% of these cases, the offender is known to the victim by name but is neither friend nor family. In each case, police accepted the victim's story and actively sought the person that she had identified. And what was the suspect's reaction? In six cases, the suspect's reactions were not recorded, but of the remaining eighty cases there were only two instances of a suspect's corroborating the victim's story by confessing. As illustrated in table 11-9, many claimed either consent of the victim or no sexual contact at all.

It appears that victims who knew their attackers by name are quickly thrust into a courtroom setting where the victim's story is in conflict with the offender's story. Therefore, it is important for the police to identify and maintain ancillary corroborating physical evidence. Unfortunately, as demonstrated in the preceding section, cases where the victim knows her attacker traditionally receive the least investigative thoroughness.

Given the lack of any confession or ancillary corroborating evidence, and the presence of a prior victim–offender relationship, it is likely that these cases will experience considerable difficulty at the trial level. The Center for Rape Concern's court observer witnessed twenty-five rape trials between September, 1974 and June, 1975. A large part of her final report focused on police investigative thoroughness, which was considered critical to case outcome. One case that was observed, involving a victim who knew her attacker, serves as a case study of police neglect:

> In 1974, a young black welfare mother was allegedly raped by a member of the black mafia. The victim and the offender were acquaintances. Little force was used and no property was stolen. Perhaps more importantly, both the victim and the offender were lower class blacks. The police gave the case little attention. As was emphasized by the defense attorney later in the trial, the detective did a poor job of collecting physical evidence to corroborate the witness's story. No crime unit was dispatched to the scene. No fingerprints, bed sheets, clothing, or other physical evidence were collected. The detective was not present in court for the hearing. All in all, the detective made little effort on behalf of this case, and the witness's testimony stood alone in court, unbuttressed by other evidence the detective might easily have provided.[6]

The police gathered more evidence in their investigation of cases in which the victim reported being raped by a stranger. In addition, there were more confessions. In fourteen of ninety-eight cases of stranger rape, it is either not known what, if anything, the suspect stated when apprehended by police or there was no apprehension at all. As table 11-10 demonstrates, the suspect did confess in one-quarter of those cases where his reaction is known. However, the beginnings of a positive defense (consent/no sex/wrong man) were apparent in about one-third of these cases and in a

Table 11–9
Reaction of First Suspect Arrested When Victim Knew Suspect's Name prior to the Incident ($N = 80$)

Reaction	Number	Percent of Total
Suspect refuses to talk	34	42.5
Suspect agrees to talk:		
confesses	2	2.5
claims he was at the scene but that		
there was no sex	23	28.8
claims the event was consensual sex	13	16.2
claims the police have the wrong man	8	10.0
Total	46	57.5

Table 11–10
Reaction of First Suspect Arrested When Suspect Is Stranger/Relative Stranger to the Victim ($N = 84$)

Reaction	Number	Percent of Total
Suspect refuses to talk	33	39.3
Suspect agrees to talk:		
confesses	21	25.0
claims he was at the scene but that there		
was no sex	17	20.2
claims the event was consensual sex	5	6.0
claims the police have the wrong man	8	9.5
Total	51	60.7

large number of cases in which the suspect refused to talk. Under these circumstances, it is imperative that the police work at building a strong case.

On the basis of all available data, it appears that the police are more interested in solving a case than in developing a strong chain of evidence. Still, given the fair number of confessions, the lack of a prior victim-offender relationship, and the presence of more ancillary corroborating evidence than is available where the victim knows the suspect prior to the incident, it would seem that stranger rapes should fare reasonably well at the trial stage. However, several qualifications are in order. First, there is an expectation that cases involving black victims will have less police support in court than those involving white victims and, consequently, prognosis for these cases is less favorable. The Center for Rape Concern's court observer corroborated this view over a wide range of cases:

Observation indicated that the race of the victim affected the care taken in the collection of evidence. It is the observer's opinion that, in general, if the victim was black less effort was made by the police to return to the scene of the crime and to collect various items that could be useful later in linking the defendant to the crime. For example, in one black on black case, a woman was dragged off the street at the point of a gun, taken to an abandoned building, and raped by her assailant and another man. During the attack, the victim was able to grab the gun off the floor, throw it out the window, jump after it, and run to safety. Later, she returned to the scene of the crime with a police officer, who recovered her clothing and the gun. However, no fingerprint analysis of the gun was made by the police, nor was the interior of the house investigated for clothing, blood, or hair which might have been left by the assailant. The prosecution's case rested solely on her later identification of the man on the street. The case was dismissed because her identification was not strong enough, and there was no corroborating physical evidence such as fingerprints. This case was not an exception. There were other cases observed involving black victims where crucial steps in the evidence collection and the evaluation process had been overlooked.[7]

Secondly, when victim and offender are strangers, identification procedures must be conducted scrupulously, since they are subject to suppression in court if handled carelessly. Likewise, an improperly obtained confession may be of no value at all. Two sources have challenged the effectiveness of Philadelphia Police in these areas: the aforementioned court observer's report and a series of articles appearing in the Philadelphia Inquirer.

The court observer documents several cases of poor identification procedures, including this example:

Later, this detective brought the victim to police headquarters to attempt a photographic identification. She was asked to select the photo of her assailant from several hundred "mug shots." She was initially unable to identify the suspect and it was revealed later that the photograph depicted the suspect without glasses and twenty pounds heavier than he was at the time of the incident.

When the victim did not make the identification, the detective grabbed the suspect's photograph from the pile and waved it in front of her, crying, "See? That's the man who did it. And you can't even identify him." Although the woman later made unequivocally positive identification at a preliminary hearing by selecting the offender out of a large crowd, the case was nearly thrown out of court on grounds that the detective's angry comments had prejudiced her subsequent identification.[8]

In an award–winning series entitled "Crime and Injustice," Donald L. Barlett and James B. Steele of *The Philadelphia Inquirer* studied the outcome of 1,374 cases involving 1,034 defendants, all charged with violent crimes and tried in 1971.[9] Many of these cases were included in the current study's sample of Police Investigation reports. The previously cited series of four multiple-offender, forced entry rapes was part of a pattern of rapes occurring with a 6-month period in a "good neighborhood." As mentioned earlier, the police invested a considerable amount of time in their efforts to effect an arrest, but it was an anonymous tip that finally broke the case, leading to the quick arrests of three suspects. Barlett and Steele described the court outcome. All ten indictments returned against the first defendant were dropped by the district attorney's office when it was ruled that the victim's identification of the suspect had to be suppressed. A different judge suppressed both the second defendant's statement to the police and his identification by the victims. A motion for a directed verdict of not guilty was granted for his nine indictments. The third defendant, charged with nineteen separate indictments, entered into a plea bargain and received a 3-year sentence. In both cases of suppressed identifications, the defendant was placed in a lineup with older men. The statement taken from the one defendant was subsequently read to the victims to refresh their memory. The Barlett and Steele survey made the following observations: Rape cases in which the defendent and victim are strangers generally are prosecuted on the basis of a statement made to the police by the accused or a lineup identification made by the victim. Thus these are the cases most likely to be affected by the U.S. Supreme Court decisions of the 1960s, which defined the rights of a suspect. Also, there are a number of cases dismissed because police failed to abide by the high court guidelines. Sometimes, the survey found, the errors stem from overzealousness on the part of police, sometimes it is carelessness, and sometimes it is simply a matter of an investigator trying to see if he can get away with bending the rules.[10] Whatever the reason, the investigation showed that most of the procedural errors could have been avoided by closer cooperation between police and the district attorney's office.

Not only are ultimate case outcomes affected by improper identification and statement recording techniques but, in addition, the prosecutor's plea-bargaining position is often weakened. Where the police provide only insufficient or improperly obtained evidence, prosecutors will generally be more likely to bargain for a guilty plea, even if they are required to make substantial concessions. For this reason, the Rand Corporation study recommends that postarrest investigative responsibilities be taken away from the police and given to the prosecutor.[11] This recommendation is clearly based on the assumption that, as a rule, police departments fail to provide thorough evidence collection or proper identification technique and confession recording.

In the interests of completeness and accuracy, it should be pointed out that a general evaluation of police practice tends to obscure the many cases of exemplary performance of duty. Some Philadelphia Police bring considerable expertise to their investigation of rape complaints and are willing to invest substantial time and effort in solving these cases. Many more take their follow-through responsibilities quite seriously. The court observer cites the following example:

> One detective in particular, came to court every day during the trial of a case to which he was assigned, whether or not he was needed as a witness, to accompany the victim and to support her during the proceedings. He attended law classes at night to receive training to give better testimony. His testimony in this particular case was superbly prepared and legally airtight. At the completion of the case, the judge called the detective into his chambers to tell him that his work had been indispensable in the conviction of the offender. This detective was promoted to the homicide division shortly afterwards, probably as a direct result of his fine work in this case.[12]

However, the court observer is also quick to point out that cases that receive blue-ribbon treatment sometimes do so for political reasons. Cases that command extensive media exposure, that are particularly violent, that involve great damage to both persons and property, that are interracial, or that involve gaps in class or status tend to receive preferential police treatment.

Summary

Philadelphia Police succeed mostly in terms of the measure that they are most likely to publicize—their clearance rate. Admittedly, they do quite well in this regard. However, there are several categories of rape where the police are highly ineffective when it comes to apprehending a suspect. Cases where a stranger, alone, forces an entry into the victim's residence or the place in which she is staying and completes a rape—as well as cases where an adult stranger, alone, completes a rape away from the victim's dwelling—fare poorly in terms of percentage of cases solved.

Looking at the manner of case solution, it seems that most of the rape cases that are solved, solve themselves. In addition, the offenders apprehended are often those individuals already known to the police.

The cases that present the most difficulty for the victim in court—cases in which the victim and the offender know one another prior to the rape and the offender denies the rape—generally receive the least police support. Although stranger rapes receive more police support, they tend to turn on identity defenses that often allege improper identification procedures and statement taking. Two sources cite examples of police weakness in these areas. The best case preparation is found in cases where no suspect is apprehended. Finally, cases involving black victims tend to be investigated less thoroughly than cases involving white victims.

Using the Philadelphia Police as examples, the authors suggest that police are prone to parochialism in rape investigations. They strive for goals (such as a high clearance rate) that are, to a great extent, bureaucratically within their control, susceptible to their manipulations, and prone to create an impression of successful police handling of rape complaints. A closer examination, however, reveals a corresponding de-emphasis on the more valid but less publicized measure of police success: careful case preparation. The Rand study indicates that the presence of problems in this area (lack of investigative thoroughness, faulty identification procedures, improper statement-taking, and so forth) is not unique to rape complaints but is, rather, common to police department response to all complaints.

Notes

1. Duncan Chappell and Susan Singer, "Rape in New York City: A Study of Material in the Police Files and Its Meanings" (Research report submitted to the New York Police Department, 1973), p. 53.

2. Peter W. Greenwood and Joan Petersilia, *The Criminal Investigation Process*, vol. A, *Summary and Policy Implications* (Santa Monica, Calif.: The Rand Corporation, October 1975), p. 13.

3. Albert Reiss and David J. Bordua, "Environment and Organization: A Perspective on the Police," in *The Police: Six Sociological Essays*, ed. David J. Bordua (New York: John Wiley and Sons, 1967), p. 43.

4. Leonard A. Savitz, "Drug Use and Drug Users in an Arrestee Population: The Final Report of the Philadelphia TASC's Mass Urine Screening Process" (Research report submitted to the Philadelphia Treatment Alternatives to Street Crime Program, 1975).

5. Greenwood and Petersilia, *Criminal Investigation Process*, p. viii.

6. Anne Lawrence, "The Court Observer's Report" (Research report submitted to the Philadelphia Center for Rape Concern, 1975), pp. 27-28.

7. Ibid., p. 25.

8. Ibid., p. 12.

9. Donald L. Barlett and James B. Steele, "Crime and Injustice—A Series on the Breakdown of Criminal Justice—The Jailing of the Innocent, Freeing of the Guilty" (Reprints of series of articles prepared by *The Philadelphia Inquirer*, 1973), p. 18. Reprinted by permission of *The Philadelphia Inquirer*.

10. Ibid., p. 17.

11. 1973. Greenwood and Petersilia, *Criminal Investigation Process*, p. 30.

12. Lawrence, "Court Observer's Report," pp. 13-14.

12 The Police: A Summary

When asked if they had reported being raped to the police, slightly more than half of the women polled in an LEAA victimization study answered yes.[1] However, the ratio of rapes estimated by LEAA to have occurred in Philadelphia to the number of rapes actually reported by the Philadelphia Police is 3.36 to 1. This disparity indicates that the Philadelphia Police report only about one-half of the rape complaints that are reported to them.[2] Table 12-1 summarizes the findings of the current study with respect to the mortality of rape complaints, with the fall-off rate being given for each category of police involvement. It was found that the Philadelphia Police officially reported only 53.3% of the rape complaints that were reported to them.

Much of the data analysis in this study focused on the 790 cases where an extensive social worker interview was available. Many variables, singly and in combination, were determined to impact significantly upon case mortality. The congruity of the two sets of findings suggests that the 53.3%

Table 12-1
Summary Mortality through Case Labeling by Police by Occurrence of Social Worker Interview

	Cases with Interview	Percent Remaining	Cases with No Interview	Percent Remaining	Total	Percent Remaining
Victims at emergency room	790	100.0	611	100.0	1401	100.0
Not in police files or unknown	81	89.7	122	80.0	203	85.5
Unfounded	106	76.3	112	61.7	218	69.9
Nonoffense labels	64	68.2	44	54.5	108	62.2
Sex offense labels	75	58.7	36	48.6	111	54.3
Assault labels	10	57.4	4	47.9	14	53.3
Rape or attempted rape labels	454		293		747	

figure is probably a good ballpark estimate for the proportion of rape cases reported to Philadelphia Police that they, in turn, report in their crime statistics.

The LEAA study found that slightly more than one-half of all women who are raped report being raped to the police. Although the questionnaire used to elicit information about sexual victimization is suspect on a number of grounds and probably underestimates to some degree the number of rapes that actually occur, the reporting rate that study offers suggests that police decision-making eliminates about as many cases from the reported statistics as does the collective silence of nonreporting rape victims.

Further, the decision not to report a rape is likely to be related to the victim's expectations concerning the manner in which the police will handle her allegations. When asked if they would again report to the police in the event of another rape incident, about one-eighth of the interviewed victims said no; another one out of fifteen were uncertain. Approximately one-half of those answering in the negative cited their experiences with the police as the principal reason for their answers. Indeed, if it were left totally to the victim, probably fewer victims would report. In the studied population, only about one-quarter of the victims contacted the police themselves. Given the recent media depictions of shoddy police practices in rape investigations, it is likely that most victims at least have second thoughts before dialing the police.

If a victim calls the police, and if they believe her and apply the charge of rape or attempted rape, a suspect must be apprehended and tried before police-victim interactions can be terminated. Whereas police in this study did apprehend a large number of suspects, most rape cases were found to solve themselves. On the other hand, police evidence-gathering techniques, identification procedures, and in-court support are depicted as somewhat deficient. One inevitable conclusion is that the police view their job as finished as soon as a suspect is apprehended.

This study has focused on the three gates through which a complainant alleging rape must pass if she is to see her attacker stand trial for rape. First, she must be believed. According to this study, this means that her case will not be lost, marked as unfounded, or given a nonoffense charge. Second, the case must have the charge rape or attempted rape. And finally, a suspect must be apprehended and charged. Although success at these three gates does not insure a rape trial (for example, prosecution may be withdrawn), each gate must be passed as a necessary precondition to any rape trial.

In the present study, 27.2% of all rape complaints were not believed (omitting lost cases). Of the remainder, 14.3% were given lesser offense charges. Although there was not always an arrest, police solved 68.6% of a study sample of cases marked as founded that were given a rape charge. At each gate, differing combinations of variables increased or decreased the

Table 12-2
Variables That Impact on Outcome of Case

Variable	"Lost"	Unfounded	Nonoffense Label	Lesser Sex Offense	Solved
		Outcome Impacted			
Policewoman present	x	x	x	x	
Victim over 12		x		x	
Penile-vaginal Intercourse		x		x	
More than one offender			x		x
Social worker determines consent	x				
Partially incredible	x				
Previous consent	x				
Clear coercion/intimidation	x				
Victim obese		x			
Prior psychiatric contact		x			
Victim welfare recipient		x			
Rape at offender's residence			x		
History as runaway			x		
History of truancy			x		
Evaluated as heavy drinker			x		
Attacked before by offender				x	
Student				x	
Offender a family member				x	
Weapon used				x	
Median income of neighborhood under or over $9,000				x	
Victim can name offender					x
Attempt or completed rape					x
Forced entry into residence					x
Victim under 18					x

likelihood that a victim would pass through that gate successfully. Table 12-2 lists the variables that impacted on each decision point in the final configurations.

Using the twenty-four variables as story elements, scenarios were developed to illustrate the combined effect of all threshold points. Following are three hypothetical rape scenarios:

A 22-year-old social worker is attacked in her reasonably affluent center city apartment by a man she has never seen before. He breaks into her apartment in the middle of the night, robs and rapes her. Penile-vaginal intercourse is completed at gunpoint. The victim is of normal height and build but has been seeing a psychiatrist. She is interrogated by both a detective and a policewoman. A social worker subsequently evaluates her story as credible.

A mother, living on welfare, in a public housing project, calls the police to report that her 15-year-old daughter has been raped. The detective, unaccompanied by a policewoman, learns from the victim that she claims to have been invited into a girlfriend's house. After some drinking, the girlfriend's brother, whom she knows by name, began slapping her, removed her clothes by force, and completed penile-vaginal intercourse. The victim, who is tall but thin, admits that she has had previous consenting sex with her girlfriend's brother but claims that she was never before attacked by him. The victim, a student, has a history of truancy and has once been listed a runaway, but has never been a psychiatric patient. The victim does not admit consent to the social worker and the social worker who interviews her 5 days after the attack evaluates her story as credible.

A mother calls the police to report that her 7-year-old daughter has been raped by her babysitter's boyfriend. The family lives in an affluent section of town. The alleged attack occurred a fortnight in the past and was the only such attack, and the victim, along with her mother, is questioned by a police detective with no policewoman present. A social worker who later interviews the child evaluates her story as credible.

Each case is followed to its appropriate terminal groups at each decision point. The first victim's allegation is likely to be believed. There is a .96 probability that her case will not be given a nonoffense label. The net result is a .78 probability that her case will be believed. Had there been no history of prior psychiatric contact, the probability that this victim would be believed would increase to .89. If believed, her case would almost certainly be labeled rape. However, there is only a .25 probability that this case will be solved by the police.

Since the victim knows the offender by name in the other two scenarios, the police will almost surely apprehend a suspect, provided that they believe the victim's story. However, they may not charge the offender with rape. The second scenario will almost certainly not be believed by the police. This case has only a .22 probability of making it to the labeling decision. Most damaging to the victim's story, assuming that no policewoman is present, are the elements of previous consent, the seriousness of the charge combined with her welfare status, and her history of truancy. However, if she is believed, her case will be labeled rape and her attacker will be apprehended.

Finally, the child victim has a fair chance of being believed but, once believed, her case is likely to be labeled as a lesser sex offense. The case has a .73 probability of being believed and, if believed, a .67 probability of being given a lesser sex offense label.

In all three scenarios, it was assumed that a social worker interviewer would find the victim's story credible. Still, outcomes vary considerably. The following pages provide an examination of those variables that do not seem to impact on the final configurations.

The conclusions drawn in this study were derived from a wealth of data. Available for scrutiny were a detailed social worker interview given to a large number of rape victims, the results of emergency room observations, and a good deal of data from police files. A number of significant associations emerge providing a foundation for this report. However, there are many more variables that are not significantly associated with whether or not a case disappears, is marked as unfounded, is given a nonoffense or lesser sex offense charge, or is solved by the police. Some variables that were initially expected to be significant did not make it to the final configurations. Their absence merits some attempt at explication.

First among these curiously ineffective variables is race. The complaints of black victims are not disbelieved significantly more frequently, nor are their cases given lesser sex offense charges significantly more often than are white victims. Although cases with black victims are more likely to be solved, this distinction disappears from the final configuration. However, there are several race–related variables that do make a difference in case outcome. For example, it matters whether the victim is employed, whether she receives welfare, and how affluent a neighborhood she lives in. It seems that the posture assumed by police in their interactions with blacks depends mainly upon the socioeconomic status of each particular victim.

The police are as likely to believe a complaint where the offender is a friend or acquaintance of the victim as one where he is a stranger or relative stranger. However, they are most inclined to believe allegations of family and extended family rape. Apparently what matters most are past sexual relations and the details of the current allegation, such as where the rape occurred and how clearly the elements of coercion and intimidation are presented. Otherwise, it is not the victim's relationship to the offender that matters, but rather her own physical, psychological, and sociological characteristics. The tenor of police involvement is likely to depend upon whether the victim is fat, a truant, a runaway, a heavy drinker, or has formerly been to a psychiatrist.

Brutal rapes—those accompanied by violent beatings and/or choking— are not more readily believed than less violent rapes. Once again, attention is focused on victim characteristics to an arguably disproportionate degree.

Nor does it matter from which detective division the detective in charge is assigned. It seems that whatever pressures are applied in the decision to disbelieve a victim do not originate in any particular detective division or divisions. On the other hand, it does matter a great deal whether or not a policewoman is called into the investigation.

Much has already been said regarding the role of policewomen in rape interrogations. Although her level of involvement was generally not very significant in Philadelphia during the time of this study—very often she

served only as the recorder of information—her mere presence at the interrogation impacts materially on credibility of the victim's story and is often
largely determinative of the victim's reaction to the police encounter.
According to Susan Brownmiller, expanding the role of policewomen
increases even more dramatically the extent to which victims are believed.[3]

The next section shows how most departments already have begun to
use females in rape investigations and describes some of the innovations
recently begun.

Information concerning police innovations derive mainly from two
national surveys. Both were published by the Law Enforcement Assistance
Administration in November 1975. The first, "Forcible Rape: A National
Survey of the Response by Police," sampled 208 departments ranging from
agencies serving urban populations in excess of 500,000 to university police
agencies with manpower strengths exceeding sixty police employees. Police
officers with considerable experience in managing rape complaints were
asked to complete a questionnaire that concerned itself with classification
methods, factors involved with rape, processing criteria, procedures in
taking crime reports, victim services, investigative strategies, prosecutive
outcomes, training methods, and innovative activities.[4]

The second survey is part of a Law Enforcement Assistance Administration "Prescriptive Package." Fifty police departments known for their
innovations in rape cases management were surveyed. Thirteen sites were
visited, and studied in greater depth. Adding the findings of this survey to
the advice provided by a panel of detectives, police trainers, and others
experienced with rape cases, the "Prescriptive Package" includes a chapter,
"Suggested Guidelines for Police," which is that study's answer to the
question, "How should police manage rape complaints?"[5]

First among innovations generally presented is the formation of a specialized unit for the investigation of rape cases. Most departments have a
specialized homicide unit. Creation of a special unit for rape cases means,
first, that the department has decided rape is a crime sufficiently serious to
allocate special resources to its investigation. Second, is the recognition that
rape presents a variety of complex problems requiring skills that specialist
professionals can best provide.

Every police department visited by the "Prescriptive Package" team
had specialized to the extent of having special rape squads or combined
units handling rape and other violent crimes. In the other survey, when
asked "Are rape investigations handled by a special unit in your agency?"
91% of departments in cities of over 500,000 said yes whereas 66% of all
departments replied yes.[6]

However, these specialized units are not, exclusively, rape squads. For
cities over 500,000, in only 23% of departments do specialized persons or
members of special units routinely handle the initial response to the rape

complaint. More often, the most readily available patrol officer responds first. When special response systems are used, they are generally available 24 hours a day, and the first officer on the scene is responsible for conducting the follow-up 89% of the time, providing continuity to the police response.[7]

For large cities, about 14% of departments have special sex offense report forms, with an additional 5% using special rape report forms.[8]

Finally, of all special units surveyed, only 12% reported that at least 75% of investigators' time was spent on rape cases.[9] Consequently, the political decision to allocate more resources to rape investigations through the creation of a special unit poses a number of additional questions: Will it be an exclusive rape squad? Will it extend to initial contact with victims? Will there be separate forms? In addition, a number of procedural questions emerge about insuring coverage, handling overtime, and so forth. One question that always comes into play concerns the role that women will have in sex offense investigations.

This study concludes that women should always be available for victim interrogations but that interrogations need not be conducted solely by women. The national survey reveals that, in cities of over 500,000 with special units, 35% of the investigators are women.[10] However, once again, the decision to include women in rape investigation breaks down to a series of questions that determine how extensive their involvement should be. Should it stretch from patrol to suspect apprehension to courtroom testimony, or should it be limited to victim interrogations? This study advocates full and equal cooperation of male and female police officers throughout the investigation of rapes, as well as for every other crime.

The questions that deal with the creation of a specialized unit and the use of female officers tend to overshadow the many other issues that concern police management of rape complaints. Chief among these are the issues of evidence gathering, offender identification, informing the victim, interrogation techniques, training, information systems, audit trails, evaluations, and relations with hospital emergency rooms, victim counseling groups, other criminal justice agencies, and the general public. There has been concern expressed over physical setting. *The Wall Street Journal* reports that Sgt. Romero Yumul, head of the Seattle Police Department's morals details, has requested a new interviewing room: "He is hoping for a brightly painted room, complete with couches, coffee and women's magazines."[11]

The current study concludes that evidence-gathering procedures are not standard, that they are most lax when the victim knows the offender, by name, prior to the rape. A number of sources argue that rape victims have a difficult time in court, particularly when police do not provide any evidence to corroborate the victim's story. Any department serious about rape investigation should survey scientific investigative techniques currently available for sexual assault investigations and assure that each complaint of rape achieves standard evidence gathering. Mobile crime labs should be called in for most rapes and the procedures followed should be standard, even where the offender is known.

Pictures of known offenders, color slides, and methodologies for preparing composites all have been beefed up by various departments. Also, identification procedures have been improved. Many more departments are improving their photograph files. Some have even invested in computerized search systems. Identi-kits and photo-kits for making composites are increasingly used. New York's sex crimes analysis unit has microfilmed files, cross-referenced by name, nickname, modus operandi, unusual characteristics, and occupation, as well as a numerical identifier based on race, height, age, and hair color combinations. All these resources can be screened on a portable viewer for offender identification even in the privacy of the victim's home.[12]

New interrogation methods stress the use of crisis intervention techniques and the use of information gathering without victim-blaming slurs.[13] Evidence gathering, suspect identification, and interrogation techniques all relate to training of personnel involved. The national survey reports that statewide rape investigation schools are in operation in Texas, Massachusetts, and Arizona, and that new training curricula, both preservice and inservice, are being offered in many departments.[14] For large cities, 95% of departments offer preservice training, of which 93% include special evidence requirements; 90% include interviewing the rape victim; 73% discuss referral services; 58% talk about characteristics of offenders; 45% have a section on dealing with family and friends; and 38% deal with rape as a social problem.[15]

About one-half of the preservice training courses exceed eight instructional hours. Instructors for preservice training include medical personnel, behavioral scientists, rape counselors, and victims, 38%, 34%, 20%, and 6% of the time, respectively.[16] In addition, 90% of departments in large cities offer inservice training on similar issues.[17]

Most police departments recognize that victims generally have no idea of what is happening to them, what to expect, or why so many people are endlessly demanding information the victims consider personal, or appearances for purposes they do not understand. Many departments are devoting more attention to explaining to the victim what they are doing and why, at all stages. In some cases a guide for victims of sexual assault is available.

Information systems are well-publicized innovations for crime investigations. In Los Angeles, both the information that goes into their system, drawn from their reporting form, and the system that analyzes the information, the Pattern Recognition Information Correlation System (PATRIC), have been cited as exemplary both by the Csidas in their book, *Rape: How to Avoid It and What to Do About It if You Can't,*[18] and in the summary and recommendations of the National Rape Reduction Workshop.[19]

However, this study argues that, more important than a computerized modus operandi information system, is the establishment and maintenance of an audit trail that can trace all rape complaints from an incoming file through ultimate disposition. Only then could evaluations be efficient. Unfounded cases could be quickly pulled to see if they had been properly excluded, as could cases where the victim withdrew cooperation, to see what steps could be taken to enlist greater cooperation in the future. Moreover, such a system reinforces the notion that police responsibility extends from the moment a victim dials the police through ultimate disposition and does not fixate on the activities that affect the complaint rate and the clearance rate.

The national survey reports that 68% of agencies in large cities studied their management of rape complaints.[20] However, the "Prescriptive Package" concludes, "even in departments with recently established sex crimes units, little applied research is being conducted or encouraged by outside researchers."[21] Both studies conclude that research is needed, especially since so many new procedures are being instituted.

Finally, although more and more studies conclude that an interdisciplinary approach is needed in managing rape complaints, the "Prescriptive Package" team concludes that, even in the most innovative cities, cooperative arrangements have not been developed to their fullest potential.[22] Police do interact with emergency room staff, victim counselors, prosecutors, and a variety of other agencies. Yet, the analysis of findings concludes:

> It was beyond the scope of this study to explore the reasons for this state of affairs. It may be noted, nevertheless, that the inability of police and other organizations and groups to work together effectively is harmful both to the institutional self-interests of the agencies and to the victims of rape. Greater initiative by police officials to promote better working relationships and to devise innovative alternatives to the presently fragmented services for victims is sorely needed.[23]

In sum, most police departments have responded to pressures that they reevaluate their management of rape complaints. In one national study, 52% of departments polled claimed to have changed their rape case management practices in the past three years. Many claimed to have introduced new special training. Others hired more female rape investigators, while other departments improved investigative techniques. Many special rape units were formed, and women were placed on patrol. Another 31% of departments interviewed stated they intend to make changes in the near future. Intended changes parallel changes already completed in other jurisdictions.[24]

Despite these many changes, a second national survey warns against piecemeal innovation and notes that most departments are still parochial in their relations with outside agencies. There is a suspicion that much change is just window dressing.

Within the themes presented in this section, certain organizational imperatives emerge that are curiously familiar: standardize, professionalize, train, specialize, and follow through. Research and audit. Egalitarianism of the sexes is stressed in all aspects of investigation, and the exploitation of all technological resources available is advised. Finally, since new costs are being incurred, once again there are exhortations to spend money.

Emerging, both in concrete departmental changes and in study recommendations, are the classic American imperatives in problem solving. Conceding that many of the problems in the police response to rape can be solved by familiar methods raises new problems. Why haven't these solutions been adopted already? Using the Philadelphia Department as an example, we can hypothesize why innovations have not been quickly embraced.

Probably four factors combine to prevent the Philadelphia Police Department from rushing to well known solutions. First, rape is not viewed as problematical. It is a statistically infrequent crime, which police in Philadelphia feel is being managed effectively, given the restraints of budget and manpower and the leniency of the judges. Philadelphia Police often remind Philadelphia citizenry that they live in the safest of the ten largest cities, and that the clearance rate is high indeed.

Many of the problems associated with police management of alleged rapes might never have surfaced had not the emerging women's movement of the late sixties and early seventies focused on rape. To change now might be interpreted as though all were not well. Especially since many innovations might have the early effect of increasing the formally reported rape rate, assuming that change would probably increase the number of complainants believed, the number of complaints given the charge of rape, and possibly increase the confidence of Philadelphia women to the point where they might be more likely to report their victimizations. Besides, most victims who do report are satisfied by the police performance. Even Women Organized Against Rape, in Philadelphia, concede that many police officers do an exemplary job. The Center for Rape Concern court observer also cites a number of jobs well done. Although both sources note a number of problems, neither claims a blanket indictment. Why admit there is room for improvement and risk increased visibility?

Second, classic American problem-solving techniques are confronted by classic American bureaucratic dilemmas. Many social service agencies and criminal justice units are given impossible tasks. Drug programs are told to cure addiction. Police are told to enforce the law. Units like the police soon learn to develop measures that are somewhat within their control, that can be used to demonstrate that they are meeting their mission. Police tend to fixate on the reported crime rate and on their clearance rate. To effectively manage rape complaints, police must move beyond these parochial goals. To do a really good job, police must formally work with a number of outside agencies and accept their share of responsibility from the point a victim dials the police through ultimate disposition. They must be concerned with how they interact with victims, and should be committed to the victim's well-being and to building a strong case against her assailant. Parochial focus on reported rape rates freezes out responsibility for the quality of victim support and interaction. Parochial focus on clearing complaints freezes out responsibility for courtroom outcome. And, parochial bureaucratic subgoal specialization tends to be safe and self-serving.

Some Philadelphia police do go beyond a narrow perspective. They are ideologically committed to aid victims who turn to them for help, work closely with emergency room staff, volunteer and professional victim support services and the prosecutor's office, and are professionally committed not only to apprehending the victim's assailant, but also to gathering sufficient evidence and preparing strong testimony to insure a conviction. To move an entire department in the direction of its best officer's efforts, bureaucratically safe and self-serving measures must be sacrificed and police, as a unit, must widen boundaries. This, most departments are reluctant to do.

Third, innovations in rape management tend to raise the issue of women's involvement in police work. The present police establishment in Philadelphia is opposed to using women on patrol and as detectives. Raising the rape issue surfaces related concerns best kept quiet from the Philadelphia Police perspective.

Finally, innovation is expensive. Within all police departments, goals are politically determined. Various subunits compete for a share of the total action. Homicide units generally do well. They are specialized, with small caseloads and highly experienced investigators. However, other crimes have stiff competition in gaining attention. Specialized rape squads, robbery squads, or burglary squads could all be justified. Each crime is in crisis dimensions and all three would probably benefit from specialized attention. Yet, politics isn't always an even contest. Generally, it is easier to continue to be than to come into being. For example, it is more likely that a homicide squad will continue to exist than that a new burglary squad will come into being to supplant it. And, given a tight money market, innovations generally can only develop at the expense of preexisting arrangements.

In sum, police may be reluctant to commit expanded Department resources to rape investigation because it would threaten their publicly reiterated position that all is extremely well, because it would shake them out of the safety of bureaucratically controlled parochialism, because it would dramatically raise the issue of women's role in police operations, and because it would cost a great deal of money in a tight market. And, unless the Department is committed to a real opening up, piecemeal innovations would amount to little more than window dressing.

However, if any police departments were to internally elect to focus more resources on managing rape cases, they would be well advised to follow the lead of almost all other large jurisdictions by organizing a specialized squad and developing an entire new training regimen. They would have to face the question of the role of women in police operations head on. Their new rape squad would immediately have to address the issues of evidence gathering, coverage, offender identification, informing the victim, interrogation techniques, information systems, research and evaluation, and establishing real and meaningful relations with prosecutors, emergency room staff, and volunteer and professional victim support agencies. In addition, the current study recommends as an essential element of rape reform the establishment of an audit trail for all rape complaints from the time a victim dials the police through ultimate disposition. Constant inspection should isolate cases in which a victim's cooperation is lost or a victim is turned away because she is not believed, as well as cases in which a conviction is lost, so that causes can be identified, and, if necessary, reformative action taken. Only then can victims be liberated from the self–serving numbers game of a complacent police force, and only then can police, themselves, extend beyond safe, parochial goals.

Notes

1. Law Enforcement Assistance Administration, *Criminal Victimization Surveys in the Nation's Five Largest Cities: National Crime Panel Surveys of Chicago, Detroit, Los Angeles, New York, and Philadelphia* (Washington D.C.: U.S. Government Printing Office, April 1975).

2. The victim survey estimates 1,800 rapes occurred in Philadelphia in 1972 where the victim was 12 years old or older. Police report 588 rapes in Philadelphia during 1972. However, that figure includes some victims under 12. Using data described in chapter 11, an estimate can be made that, at a minimum 9% of the cases the police report—or 53 cases—involve victims 11 years old or younger. One might conclude that since more than three rapes occur for every one reported (1,800 rapes/535 reported = 3.36 rapes for every one reported), only one out of 3.36 women raped reported her victim-

ization. However, when asked, 55% of those victims surveyed by LEAA claimed they reported their rape victimization to the police. Therefore, the LEAA survey estimates that 990 victims reported being raped to the police (55% of 1,800), while Philadelphia Police report 535 women reporting to them. By this logic Police report 54% of the cases reported to them.

3. Susan Brownmiller, *Against Our Will: Men, Women, and Rape* (New York: Simon and Schuster, 1975), p. 387.

4. Battelle Human Affairs Research Center, "Forcible Rape: A National Survey of the Response by Police" (Unpublished report, Law and Justice Center, Seattle, Wash., November 1975).

5. Lisa Brodyaga et al., *Rape and Its Victims: A Report for Citizens, Health Facilities, and Criminal Justice Agencies* (Unpublished report, National Institute of Law Enforcement and Criminal Justice, Washington D.C.: November 1975).

6. Battelle Human Affairs Research Center, "Forcible Rape," p. 104.

7. Ibid., p. 89.

8. Ibid., p. 92.

9. Ibid., p. 105.

10. Ibid.

11. J. Simpson, "Rape Victim's Plight Gets Wide Attention from Police, Courts," *The Wall Street Journal,* 14 July 1975, p. 1.

12. Louis C. Cottell, "Rape: The Ultimate Invasion of Privacy," *FBI Law Enforcement Bulletin* 43 (May 1974): 2-6.

13. Morton Bard and Katherine Ellison, "Crisis Intervention and the Investigation of Forcible Rape," *The Police Chief* 41 (May 1974): 68-74.

14. Battelle Human Affairs Research Center, "Forcible Rape," p. 131.

15. Ibid., p. 132.

16. Ibid., p. 133.

17. Ibid., p. 134.

18. June Bundy Csida and Joseph Csida, *Rape: How to Avoid It and What to Do About It If You Can't* (Chatsworth, Calif.: Books for Better Living, 1974), p. 97.

19. Denver Anti-Crime Council, *Operation Rape Reduction: Proposed Program for Reduction, Rape Offenses in the City of Denver* (Unpublished report, Denver, Colo. May, 1973).

20. Battelle Human Affairs Research Center, "Forcible Rape," p. 140.

21. Lisa Brodyaga et al., *Rape and Its Victims,* p. 21.

22. Ibid., p. 23.

23. Ibid.

24. Battelle Human Affairs Research Center, "Forcible Rape," p. 141.

13 The Courts: An Introduction

The analysis of the judicial system response to rape cases in the chapters that follow draws principally on two sources of data. Of the original sample of 1,401 victims, cases marked as founded were processed through the court administrator's computer to determine which cases entered the adult justice system and to obtain the following information on each of those cases: whether a preliminary hearing was held, the outcome of the hearing (trial or dismissal of charges), the type of trial held (jury or nonjury), the verdict reached, and the sentence handed down.

Strict confidentiality laws prevented the gathering of any information on the juvenile court system. Some cases with juvenile offenders are included, however, in the present study; in Pennsylvania, the district attorney can initiate formal proceedings in the juvenile court to have an offender certified as an adult and tried in adult court.

In addition to the data obtained from the court administrator, twenty-five court cases were reported on by the Center for Rape Concern's non-participant observer. Notes were generally taken on the spot, on a range of topics, including police preformance at the trial, defense strategies, and so forth. An observation form was developed by the Center, designed to direct the observer's attention to several areas deemed significant, which allowed for an exploratory rather than a static approach.

Efforts were made to minimize the impact of observation on the proceedings. At the beginning of the trial, the observer would introduce herself to the judge, attorneys, and court clerks, and would briefly describe the Center for Rape Concern's research project. After this introduction, she would remove herself as much as possible from active participation. She was usually seated at the rear of the viewers' section, where she was least noticeable to participants in the trial. Notes were not taken in court when this seemed to distract the witnesses; in these cases observations were written immediately after court.

In effect, the judicial process is initiated after police have decided to believe a complaint of sexual assault (the decision to mark a case founded), have determined the criminal charges warranted by the event, and have apprehended the suspect.

When a less serious charge is applied to the offense (one that involves a maximum jail sentence of less than 5 years) the case may be tried in municipal (misdemeanor) court. In municipal court, the right to a jury trial is waived. The defendant can, however, appeal the decision of the judge to a higher court. The charges lodged for most cases of sexual assault are of a gravity that precludes trial in municipal court. Very few cases in the present sample were tried at this level.

In fact, almost all the cases marked founded required trial in felony court, which is called, in Pennsylvania, the Court of Common Pleas. There are, however, several procedures that antecede a trial in Common Pleas Court. The case may be terminated at any one of these preliminary steps. (It should also be noted that, in general, the court system is overburdened, and is plagued by delays at every stage in the judicial process).

In Pennsylvania, any person charged with a felony is guaranteed the right to a preliminary hearing on the charge(s) no sooner than three but no later than ten days after arrest. At the hearing, which is held under the municipal court jurisdiction, the judge determines whether a prima facie case exists, and, thus, whether a trial in Common Pleas Court is warranted. Identification of the alleged offender by the victim is essential to this process. Unfortunately, faulty notification procedures, expense, lack of prehearing briefing and support, and anxiety associated with giving public testimony all impact negatively on the rate of victim participation. As a result, many cases are terminated at this point.

Upon completion of a preliminary hearing, the defendant undergoes an arraignment, at which he is formally informed of the charges against him. The defense must decide whether or not to enter a plea at this time. A guilty plea at arraignment is almost always the result of plea bargaining. The defendant admits guilt, sparing the state the expense of a trial, and, in return, receives a reduced charge or a dismissal of some of the charges against him. The defendant gives up his right to trial and, in effect, his right to appeal. His reward is a reduced sentence.

If the defendant chooses not to enter a plea, or does not enter a plea of guilty at the arraignment, he states his intention either to exercise or to waive his right to a trial by jury. A jury or nonjury (waiver) trial is then scheduled.

In the period between arraignment and trial, the defense attorney has the option of filing motions that may call for suppression of some of the evidence obtained on a number of grounds. Pretrial motions generally focus on police procedures, frequently alleging improprieties in obtaining confessions, collecting evidence, conducting offender identification, and so forth. When the defense can demonstrate, to the satisfaction of the judge, police activity that fails to meet the standards established by law, the evidence may be suppressed. Often the evidence that is suppressed is so essential that the prosecutor will decline to prosecute, and the case will not go to trial. In any event, successful pretrial motions weaken the prosecutor's case.

For cases in which a Common Pleas Court trial does occur and in which the defendant is found guilty, the sentencing can range from a fine or probation to a prison term.

The chapters that follow examine in detail the preliminary hearing process, and the types of cases in which the offender pleads guilty and the victim is thereby spared the ordeal of a trial. In addition, cases that are tried by jury are compared to "waiver" cases, and the respective outcomes of each mode are discussed. The types of cases that result in a prison sentence are also delineated. Finally, the effects of the court process on the victim are described.

14 The Preliminary Hearing

Background

In Pennsylvania, a person suspected of a crime is guaranteed the right to a preliminary hearing on the charges brought against him in no less than 3 and no more than 10 days of arrest.[1] The defendant may waive his right to a preliminary hearing; the case will then automatically be held over for trial.

The purpose of the preliminary hearing is to determine if there is enough evidence to have the case bound over for trial. The judge must be satisfied that a prima facie case exists (that is, that there was a crime committed under the laws of the Commonwealth, and that the defendant is probably the perpetrator).

The establishment of a prima facie case requires a minimum of testimony, and the victim is usually the only witness called to the stand. The victim alleges that a crime occurred and identifies the defendant as the perpetrator. Medical evidence is not presented at most hearings.

In addition to serving as the basis on which the judge decides whether continuance to the trial stage is warranted, victim testimony at the hearing can have a significant bearing on the outcome of the trial. Statements made by the vicitim at the hearing that conflict with her subsequent testimony at the trial may be used by the defense to undermine her credibility. Although such inconsistencies are often only a matter of confusion over relatively minor details the following notes based on courtroom observation illustrate the impact that testimony from the hearing may have at the trial.

> In one case in which both the preliminary hearing and the trial were observed, the victim made one important change in her testimony between the two appearances. At the hearing she told the court that a man she had met in a coffee shop invited her to go to dinner with him after work. She accepted the invitation and got into his car. Instead of taking her to the restaurant, however, he pulled the car off the road and raped her at gunpoint. At the trial, however, she said that he had driven her to her apartment before they left for dinner so that she could freshen up before their date. The defense attorney used this discrepancy to argue that this victim was an unreliable witness. "She changes her story right and left!" he told the jury, "What can we believe?"

> The victim, however, told the jury, sobbing, that the reason she had failed to mention the stop-over earlier was that she was "too embarrassed to say

in front of all those people that I was so utterly stupid as to have gone back into the car with this monster after being safely in my own apartment. I couldn't believe that I had been such a fool to have been conned like this. I just couldn't bring myself to admit in public that I had been that stupid." [2]

Despite its narrowly-defined goal (case continuation decision making), the preliminary hearing process is beset with a number of problems that are directly related to the decision of many victims to withdraw cooperation at the hearing stage. And, nearly one case in five is terminated because the victim refuses to cooperate at this stage of the criminal justice process.

The Setting

During the period of this research the location of preliminary hearings in Philadelphia was changed primarily at the suggestion of the Center for Rape Concern and Women Organized Against Rape. Prior to April 1974, all preliminary hearings were held at the police districts rather than in the main courtrooms at City Hall. Since preliminary hearings can be heard by Magistrates, it is not legally necessary that the hearings occur at City Hall.

The locker-room atmosphere at the police districts, however, was considered to be detrimental to the well-being of the complainant. The surroundings were so informal that the complainant frequently was forced to give her testimony while standing within several feet or inches of the accused, his family, and his friends. In addition, all types of criminal cases were listed for hearing on the same day, in the same room, and before the same magistrate. Thus, rape cases were heard between cases of mugging, theft, and many petty offenses. The result, noted by the Center for Rape Concern's observer, was that "The victim often felt that her own moment of shame and humiliation was publicly displayed before gaping, unsympathetic and sometimes pruriently interested strangers." [3]

This location also did not encourage the most effective legal representation for either side. The most competent assistant district attorneys and defense attorneys could not spend all of their time at the precincts when important cases were taking place at City Hall. Therefore, the "second string" was present at the preliminary hearings. In addition, the magistrates were not required to have legal training.

Finally, in the spring of 1974, the procedure was changed. All preliminary hearings for rape cases were reassigned to one courtroom at City Hall on one day of each week. As a result, the treatment of the complainant improved, and the negative emotional impact of the hearing was reduced. The courtroom setting was more dignified and formal, and the judge was generally more sympathetic to the victim. Before taking the stand, the victim had an opportunity to observe the hearing of other rape complaints and become acquainted with the kind of questioning that she herself would undergo. However, problems were still evident. The brutal cross-examination of some victims, as well as the presence of numerous sensation-seekers in the courtroom, may have contributed to the decision of some victims to withdraw cooperation.

Prehearing Preparation

Without prior familiarity with courtroom proceedings, it may be difficult for a victim to present convincing testimony. For example, when the preliminary hearing is the first time that the victim has been to court or has been a witness, she may not be aware that, as a witness, she should only answer the questions asked of her. Consequently, the victim's responses may lack the focus necessary to establish her credibility as a witness. In addition, without any prior review of her testimony with the assistant district attorney, the victim may not be prepared to explicitly detail, in language suitable for the courtroom, the sexual acts to which she was subjected. General statements like "I was raped" or colloquialisms used to describe a variety of sexual acts are not admissable as evidence and may convey a discreditable image to the judge.

Unfortunately, during the time period covered by this research, most victims were not adequately prepared for even the minimal testimony required at the hearing. The assistant district attorney did not have time prior to the hearing to meet with each complainant to discuss her testimony and to explain courtroom procedures. The uninstructed younger victim, as well as the less educated and less sophisticated adult victim, is likely to have had the most difficulty in presenting herself and her story to the judge in a convincing manner. This may partially explain why the variables of victim age and victim receiving public assistance were significantly associated with the outcome of the preliminary hearing, as noted later.

A lack of pretrial preparation of victims may have had wider implications. Many victims require the moral support of the prosecutor to overcome an initial reluctance to cooperate with prosecution of the case. Victims who decide to proceed may withdraw after witnessing the confusion experienced by other victims on the stand.

Findings

The preliminary hearing is a critical first step for the case in the court system. The requirements for holding a case over for trial are easily met, especially if the police have done a thorough screening and careful investigation. The judge's decision rests almost entirely on the usually brief testimony of the victim. Rarely are other witnesses called to testify.

It was found that 81% ($N = 289$) of all cases were held for court. When data are analyzed for the sample of victims who had a social worker interview ($N = 165$, 84.8% held for trial) it is found that the use of nonphysical force, the victim's age, occurrence of penile–vaginal intercourse, the victim's financial status (as measured by her receiving public assistance funds), and who reported the incident to the police, are significantly associated with the outcome of the preliminary hearing (see table 14–1).

Further analysis to determine which combination of factors differentiates the cases into high success (held for court) and low success (not held for court) results in the configuration presented in figure 14–1. The variables listed provide the best predictive measure of success or failure at the preliminary hearing stage.

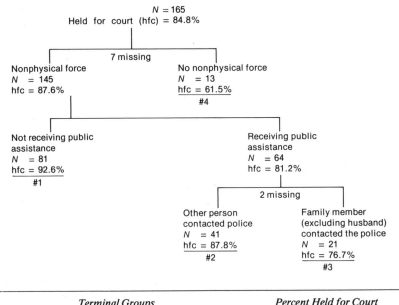

Terminal Groups	Percent Held for Court
1. Nonphysical force was used in the incident, and the victim is not receiving public assistance.	92.6
2. Nonphysical force was used, the victim is receiving public assistance, and someone other than a family member reported the incident to the police.	87.8
3. Nonphysical force was used, the victim is receiving public assistance, and a family member reported the incident (nonhusband).	67.7
4. No nonphysical force used.	61.5

Figure 14–1. Analysis of Preliminary Hearing

Table 14–1
Factors Associated with Preliminary Hearing Outcome

Variable	Response	Percent Held for Trial
Nonphysical force	no	61.5
	yes	87.6
Coercion	no	77.2
	yes	91.0
Fellatio	no	81.8
	yes	100.0
Victim's age	0–11 years	69.6
	12 + years	87.2
Victim on public assistance	yes	78.4
	no	90.0
Who contacted police to report the assault?	Family (nonhusband)	77.0
	other	89.1
Penile–vaginal intercourse	no	69.6
	yes	87.0
Physical pain reported by victim	no	76.1
	yes	88.0

Note: N = 165 cases, of which 140 were held for trial (84.8%) and 25 were not held for trial (15.2%).

Victim Participation in the Hearing

Failure of victims to appear in court is the most serious problem of the preliminary hearing process. As a clerk who handled the assignment of rape cases to individual courtrooms observed:

> Of all types of cases, rapes are always the most difficult to get going. And it's not for your usual reasons, either. With other cases, it's sometimes that you don't have the police officer present . . . or they forgot to bring the defendant down from Holmesburg or some other thing. But with rape cases, it's almost always the same thing, the victim failed to show up.[4]

Three nonappearances by the victim usually resulted in dismissal of the case. The lack of preparation or support, the prospect of speaking publicly (often for the first time) about a humiliating experience, and the necessity of confronting the offender may contribute to the high rate of victim absence at the preliminary hearing.

The age of the victim, whether she or someone else reported the rape, and whether the victim was receiving public assistance were significantly related to whether or not cases were held for court.

As is common for the entire court process, there are often endless delays at the preliminary hearing stage. During the period of this research and court observation, only about one in every five cases listed for preliminary hearing on a given day was actually heard. In addition, it is likely that when notified to appear in court, it may be too late, inconvenient, or costly for some victims to make arrangements for a babysitter and transportation to court. The delays and the lack of adequate notification would account for the association of the variable of receiving public assistance with failure of the case to be held for court. Many of these women were single, heads of households, and often unable to afford the expense of continuing with the case.

Furthermore, the age of the victim may be related to her ability to decide to participate, and to get to the court on her own. This correlation would account for the higher percentage of cases held for court for adult women.

The significance of who reported the rape to the police provides further explanation of these findings. It was found that disproportionately fewer cases in which a family member (excluding husband) reported the rape to the police were held for court than were those in which someone other than a family member reported the incident. Many of the cases where a family member reported the incident to the police involved children as victims. The motive for reporting rape in these instances is often a desire to obtain medical treatment rather than to make a commitment to prosecute the offender, especially if the latter is also a family member. On the other hand, in a majority of the cases in which someone other than a family member reported the incident, the victim herself contacted the police. In these cases, it is more likely that this is a decision made freely by the victim and that she intends to follow the case through to its disposition. When a family member reports the incident, however, this may have been against the desire of the victim and, at the time of the preliminary hearing, the victim may act on her wish not to become involved in the criminal justice system.

Of course, not all cases where a family member makes the initial report to the police involve a reluctant victim. In some instances, the victim may have asked a close family member to call the police or to speak for her because her degree of emotional upset would not permit her to communicate effectively. This, too, may have a negative impact on the outcome of the preliminary hearing because it has the effect of delaying the report to the police. It may be successfully argued by defense counsel that if someone is really the victim of a crime such as rape, that person would report to the police immediately.

It was hypothesized by the court observer that the victim's fear of offender retaliation might be related to withdrawal of cooperation at the preliminary hearing. The following dramatic case clearly supports this hypothesis:

The observer witnessed a preliminary hearing in 1975, which concerned the abduction, brutal beating, and rape of two young mothers by members of a notorious motorcycle gang. The brother of one of the victims was approached by one gang member who threatened retaliation against the women's children if they testified in court. The day of the hearing, the two defendants, both formidable and powerful men, came to court wearing black leather jackets and boots. They made loud, insolent, obscene comments throughout the proceedings. Other gang members prowled the halls outside the courtroom, dangling chains which rattled ominously from their waists. Both victims did manage to come to court and even to take the witness stand. When asked to identify the assailants in the court, however, both victims broke down and began weeping uncontrollably. They said they feared for their lives and those of their children, and they refused to answer the questions. The court offered to provide around-the-clock police protection for the duration of the court case. The victims, however, still refused to testify, and the case had to be dismissed.[5]

According to the court observer, this was not an isolated incident. Although most cases are not so dramatic, she hypothesized that many women fail to appear for the preliminary hearing because they have been subjected to threats from the defendant or his associates. Women have even been threatened in the preliminary hearing room itself while waiting to testify.

The research data, however, do not support this hypothesis. There is no statistically significant association between the victim's fear of offender retaliation and the preliminary hearing outcome. Where the fear is so strong as to potentially interfere with the prosecution, it seems likely that, in most cases, the victim did not even report the assault to the police. It is at the preliminary hearing, however, that the victim must face her attacker, usually for the first time since the incident. This prospect must certainly inhibit some victims from testifying.

Elements of the Crime

The variables that were most strongly associated with preliminary hearing outcome (nonphysical force and coercion) are clearly related to the process of establishing whether or not a crime (forcible rape) has occurred. When the judge is convinced that a forcible rape has occurred, the case is more likely to be held for court.

At the preliminary hearing stage it is not necessary that there be actual evidence of physical force. Since medical evidence is usually not presented and only victim testimony is given, the presence or absence of nonphysical force (verbal threats or intimidation) is found to have the most impact on the preliminary hearing outcome. When the victim reports that the defendant verbally threatened her, the judge is apt to question the victim for details. If the victim can respond explicitly, "he said take off your clothes or I'll kill you," in most cases the judge will decide that continuance to the trial stage is warranted. Further, the absence of such nonphysical force apparently works against the likelihood of the case being held over for trial. It is also possible that victims of assaults in which elements of nonphysical force are not present withdraw cooperation when they realize how much importance is attached to this at the preliminary hearing.

Although the sample size is too small to be significant, it is interesting to note that in every instance of victim hospitalization as a result of rape, the case was held for court by the preliminary hearing judge.

Identification of the Offender

No variables associated with victim–offender relationship were found to be statistically significantly related to disposition at the preliminary hearing stage. This finding is surprising because victim–offender relationship would seem logically related to the victim's ability to identify the offender, and this identification is critical to the case's proceeding beyond the preliminary hearing. That no association between victim–offender relationship and hearing outcome was found is an indication that the police are effectively screening cases so that only those cases where a positive identification has been made make it to the preliminary hearing.

Summary

The preliminary hearing is, in fact, a very small step in the entire criminal proceedings in a rape case. All that is necessary to hold the case over is the testimony of the victim in which she alleges that a crime was committed and identifies the offender. The preliminary hearing is, however, often frightening to the victim because she must face her attacker, usually for the first time since the rape, and she may also have to face his family or friends. In addition, she must testify before strangers about specific details of a forced sexual encounter. This is often the first time that the victim has ever spoken publicly, into a microphone, for any reason. In addition, the preliminary hearing transcript will certainly be utilized in subsequent hearings to raise questions in regard to inconsistencies in testimony.

Several of the variables associated with successful outcome at this stage (coercion, force, pains) appear to be related to establishing the fact that a crime occurred and this, of course, is properly addressed by the judge at the preliminary hearing. However, the age of the victim and her status as a recipient of public assistance, which are associated with outcome at the preliminary hearing stage, bring into question the effectiveness of the preparation that the victim is given prior to the hearing. Preparation, if provided at all, may be best if given earlier than a day or two prior to the hearing, since many victims may need considerable support to even resolve to give testimony at the hearing.

The court observations indicate, and the data analyses confirm, that the socioeconomic status of the victim is related to the preliminary hearing outcome. The system requires the victim to be good at public speaking, able to afford a babysitter, knowledgeable about the legal system, and articulate and knowledgeable about specific sexual terminology. Victims receiving public assistance often cannot afford to participate in the hearing process, and they often cannot participate effectively without some preparation.

The preliminary hearing should be a simple stage to pass through in the prosecution of rape complaints. Yet, over 15% of all sexual assault cases are lost at this point. The question must be raised: Are these cases lost primarily because the elements of the crime are not present or because of the other extralegal reasons? The next several chapters further explore this question.

Notes

1. Pennsylvania Supreme Court, *Pennsylvania Rules of Criminal Procedure,* Rule 140, Preliminary Arraignment, Subsection F, Subparagraph 1, Revised 1978.

2. Anne Lawrence, *The Court Observer's Report* (Philadelphia: Center for Rape Concern, 1975), p. 36.

3. Ibid., p. 30.

4. Ibid., p. 31.

5. Ibid., p. 33.

15 Decisions Made prior to Trial

The culmination of the rape victim's interaction with the criminal justice system is, of course, the trial itself. It is here, under emotionally difficult conditions, that the victim will be asked to testify in public about the incident. She will be subjected to cross examination by the defense attorney and, ultimately, a judgment will be made as to the credibility of her account of the events. Before the trial begins, however, a series of decisions will be made by the defendant, his attorney, and other criminal justice personnel. The defendant will decide whether or not to waive the right to a jury trial. And, administrative officials will decide which judge and which district attorney will be assigned to the case. Although none of these decisions is in the control of the victim, and most of them are not decisions of which she will be informed, they all have significant bearing on judicial outcome and case mortality. They are also important in determining the emotional impact of the trial experience on the victim.

Who Pleads Guilty

The first major decision that must be made by the defendant and his attorney following the preliminary hearing (assuming that the case is held over for trial) is whether to enter a plea of guilty or to contest the charges in open court. Entering a guilty plea nearly always involves an agreement between the prosecution and the defense in regard to a reduction in charges and/or recommended sentence. This chapter does not discuss the various arguments for and against plea bargaining, which are extensively covered in the literature.[1] Instead it focuses on the types of rape cases most closely associated with guilty pleas.

Of the 278 sexual assault cases that were held over for trial in the Court of Common Pleas during the research period, 21.2% resulted in guilty pleas. Of the 171 such cases that yielded social worker interviews and were therefore included in this study, 43 (25.1%) resulted in guilty pleas. In Philadelphia, the percentage of sex offense cases that result in guilty pleas is significantly lower than the percentage of guilty pleas where either burglary (44.7% guilty pleas) or robbery (43% guilty pleas) is the major charge.[2]

Despite a significant number of bargained convictions, it is not possible to know with any certainty the factors underlying the decision of the

173

defense to enter a guilty plea. The plea-bargaining process is not public. The district attorneys and the defense attorneys both maintain that secrecy is of the utmost important in the negotiations. Sometimes the bargain involves a promise by the defendant that he will testify against, or give information about, other defendants. The district attorney does not want the other defendants to learn the terms of the bargain before it is accepted. Until the moment that the plea is accepted by the judge, the defendant has the right to rescind the decision and opt for a trial. There is nothing in the public record to indicate whether or not the guilty plea was entered as the result of concessions from the prosecution.

Although the plea-bargaining process is not accessible to the public and could not be observed directly, CRC's court observer did have the opportunity to observe two cases involving plea bargaining.[3] Both cases were scheduled for observation because they were originally listed for trial. The defendants in each case decided to plead guilty immediately before the jury trial was to begin.

In the first case, the observer arrived in the courtroom expecting to observe a trial. When she arrived, however, the jury selection process was not in progress and neither the defense attorney, the prosecutor, nor the judge was present. The defense attorney and the judge were in chambers, conferring about a possible guilty plea. Apparently, the defendant, who was already on parole as a result of a prior conviction, had decided at the last moment not to risk another long sentence; he wanted to negotiate a plea. The assistant district attorney soon arrived and also disappeared into the judge's chambers.

While they were in conference, the victim appeared, accompanied by her boyfriend and young son. The victim, too, thought that the trial was about to begin. After about an hour, the two attorneys and the judge emerged from chambers. The assistant district attorney approached the victim and informed her that the defendant had elected to enter a guilty plea. She looked surprised but was considerably relieved.

The defendant was brought to the bar, sworn in, and informed of his rights. The assistant district attorney briefly presented his case, which was principally based on a positive identification of the assailant by the victim and her son, who had been present during the attack. The defendant agreed to plead guilty to rape and robbery counts in exchange for a 2-year sentence on each charge, to be served concurrently.

Victims in such cases often express considerable relief at being spared the ordeal of a trial. The victim in this case was also relieved that her young son, the corroborating witness, did not have to be subjected to what she felt would be for him a traumatic experience. The leniency of the imposed sentence was, she said "OK—it was worth it to me that my son and I were spared the experience of having to testify."[4]

The second case of plea bargaining that was observed involved the rape of an 18-year-old white woman by a group of white boys. One of the defendants had been a friend of the victim's boyfriend. The boyfriend had invited the group of boys into the victim's apartment. Later, when the boyfriend left, the remaining boys attacked and raped the young woman. The case was complicated by the presence of drugs in the house, the fact that the young victim was a runaway, and the fact that at the time of the incident the victim was 8-weeks pregnant with the child of her boyfriend. According to the assistant district attorney, the prosecution's case was also weakened by the fact that the victim was predicted to be a poor witness, someone who would seem "flighty, distracted and vague" on the stand.[5]

The defense intially proceeded as if it intended to go ahead with a full jury trial. Defense motions were presented challenging the admissability of certain portions of the prosecution's evidence. Shortly after the presentation of several pretrial motions, however, the defense abruptly announced the decision of all defendants to plead guilty. A conference was held with the judge. The sentence was several years on probation, with a stipulation that all offenders receive psychiatric counseling.

Both the victim and the prosecuting attorney were satisfied with the sentence, despite its leniency. A jury trial would clearly have been traumatic to the victim. The evidence of her unwanted pregnancy, her involvement with drugs, and the broken relationship with her parents would have been heavily emphasized by the defense. The assistant district attorney also felt that there was a good chance that the prosecution would have lost at trial, given the anticipated inadequacy of the victim as a witness and her vulnerability on matters of personal history.

According to the head of the Philadelphia district attorney's recently formed rape unit, several factors influence the posture of the district attorney's office regarding a possible plea bargain in any given case. If the victim is likely to have a difficult time presenting credible testimony in open court, if the ordeal of testifying is likely to cause the victim significant emotional trauma, or if little physical evidence is available to corroborate the victim's testimony, then the prosecution will be more amenable to a plea bargain. Whereas neither the district attorney's rape unit nor an explicit prosecution policy regarding plea bargaining was in existence during the time of this research, it is likely that the factors outlined above significantly influenced the plea-bargaining process at that time.

When one recognizes the factors considered in plea bargaining, the fact that "tempting the victim" and "choking the victim" were the only variables significantly related to the occurrence of guilty pleas (see table 15-1 and figure 15-1) becomes somewhat easier to comprehend. For purposes of this study, tempting was defined as the offender's use of promises of reward, either physical or emotional, to obtain access to the victim for the

Table 15–1
Factors Associated with a Guilty Plea

Variable	Response	Percent Entering Plea
Tempting used in incident	yes	35.1
	no	20.2
Choking used in incident	yes	36.6
	no	22.0

Note: $N = 171$; 25.1% pleaded guilty.

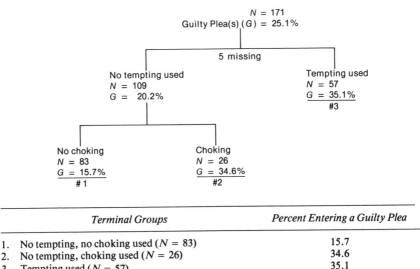

Terminal Groups	Percent Entering a Guilty Plea
1. No tempting, no choking used ($N = 83$)	15.7
2. No tempting, choking used ($N = 26$)	34.6
3. Tempting used ($N = 57$)	35.1

Figure 15–1. Analysis of Guilty Pleas

purpose of sexual assault. Tempting was primarily used with child victims but was also noted in cases involving particularly naive or dependent adult victims. These victims are likely to be viewed as potentially poor prosecution witnesses. In some cases (particularly those involving young children), whether the victim is legally competent to testify may be at issue. In addition, it is often extremely difficult for these victims to recount, in front of a crowded courtroom, how they were "fooled" by their assailants. Faced with this situation, the prosecutor may have little choice but to seek a negotiated plea.

The relationship of choking the victim to the likelihood of the defendant's entering a guilty plea is somewhat more difficult to interpret. The Center for Rape Concern's research into factors influencing victim adjustment revealed that choking frequently results in long-term adjustment problems. Why, then, would a prosecutor be especially willing to strike a bargain with the defense in so serious a case? The problem for the prosecutor would appear to be evidentiary in nature—in cases where choking is the only means of physical force used by the defendant to accomplish a sexual assault, a prosecutor may have little or no concrete evidence of rape violence to present at trial. In fact, there was little medical evidence of trauma from choking recorded in victims' hospital records, perhaps because the examining doctors were not consistently looking for this type of injury. In addition, a victim who is experiencing the extensive adjustment difficulties likely to result from a rape that involved choking may not be able to provide convincing courtroom testimony or even to show up for trial. In such cases, the resolve of the prosecutor to take the case to a jury trial may be weakened. In addition, the defense may be more willing to negotiate a plea out of fear that the victim's description of being choked would influence the jury.

Both the court observer and the current chief of the district attorney's rape unit argue that a negotiated plea may be more beneficial to the victim than an actual trial, even though any sentence imposed as the result of a plea is likely to be significantly lower than the probable sentence following conviction by a jury or a judge. In most cases where a guilty plea is entered, the victim is spared a considerable amount of emotional trauma. However, it is critical that the victim be involved, to the greatest extent possible, in the decision-making process. Some victims may prefer to go through the ordeal of a trial—even risking a real possibility of acquittal in a close case—rather than see their assailants get off with relatively light sentences.

Jury versus Waiver Trials

All states recognize some form of jury waiver. The choice as to whether or not to waive his right to a jury trial rests with the defendant (and his attorney), although the prosecution has the right to insist on a jury trial in any case. Because of the enormous caseload that must be managed by most court systems, the prosecution will nearly always accede to the defendant's preference for a bench (nonjury) trial.

In their study of the American jury, Kalven and Zeisel state that "to some extent, motivations leading to a guilty plea are similar to those leading to a waiver."[6] Lighter sentences are generally anticipated in waiver trials, and there is some evidence that this does, in fact, occur. The decision to waive a jury trial is also calculated, at least in part, on the basis of the assigned judge's sentencing reputation. In one case that was observed, a defendant had elected to have his case heard by a jury and received his courtroom and judge assignment. One week before his case was scheduled for trial, however, a convicted rapist was sentenced by the assigned judge to 10 to 20 years in prison, the maximum term for the offense. Learning of this sentence, the defendant abruptly changed his mind and waived his right to a jury trial. By doing so, the defendant was put on another calendar, guaranteeing that, in the event of a conviction, he would be sentenced by a different judge.

A countervailing consideration in the waiver decision is the commonly shared belief among defense lawyers that is is significantly more difficult to get twelve persons to agree on guilt beyond a reasonable doubt than it is to get only one person (the waiver judge) to make such a finding. In these cases, however, the defense generally relies on ambiguities in the facts of the case to confuse the jury. Where the defendant's case rests instead on one or more points of law, it is a waiver judge, and not a jury, who is deemed more likely to seize on the importance of these points in reaching a verdict.

The research findings indicate that certain types of cases are significantly associated with either a bench trial or a jury trial (see tables 15–2 through 15–4). For example, when a sexual assault involves a child or adolescent victim, a jury is assumed to be likely to take the side of the victim from the start, regardless of the strength of her testimony. If the incident allegedly involved extreme brutality, the defendant's chances for an acquittal by a jury may be deemed even more remote. Furthermore, a bench trial is more likely than a jury trial to result in a compromise verdict, such as a reduction of the charge to statutory rape when evidence of force is not available. With an adult victim, however, the defense has at its disposal a number of strategies for raising a reasonable doubt in the mind of at least one juror. For example, a previous victim–offender relationship or questionable aspects of the victim's reputation may open the door to defense claims of victim precipitation, assumption of risk, or consent.

Similarly, a history of previous nonsexual assaults against the victim may lend credence to the defense's contention that the victim has a habit of "crying wolf" and therefore should not be taken seriously or that she is "assault prone" and the criminal responsibility of the defendant ought to be reduced accordingly. Since a jury may be willing to accept this sort of logic in some cases, and a judge is assumed unlikely to do so, it is not surprising that cases where the victim has a history of assault go to jury trials.

It is also not surprising that interracial rapes (black offender/white victim) more often go to jury trials. A defendant in this type of case may feel that his only chance for acquittal rests in his successfully convincing a

Table 15–2
Factors Associated with Bench Trials (Waiver)

Variable	Response	Percent Waiving Jury Trial
Victim's age	12–17 years	64.1
	other ages	45.3
Victim lives with mother	yes	63.6
	no	36.6
Victim has had truancy problems	yes	71.4
	no	48.9
Victim has been previously nonsexually assaulted	no	57.4
	yes	20.0
Victim/offender racial class	intraracial rape	54.7
	interracial rape	27.8
External trauma or tenderness noted on medical exam	yes	88.9
	no	50.6

Note: $N = 171$; 90 (52.6%) waived jury trial.

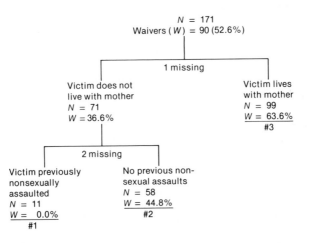

Terminal Groups	Percent Waiving Jury Trial
1. Victim does not live with mother and has had previous nonsexual assaults ($N = 11$)	0.0
2. Victim does not live with mother and has had no previous nonsexual assaults ($N = 58$).	44.8
3. Victim lives with mother ($N = 99$).	63.6

Figure 15–2. Analysis of Bench Trials (Waiver)

Table 15–3
Factors Associated with Jury Trials

Variables	Response	Percent Going to Jury Trial
Victim's age	18 years or older	25.6
	17 years or younger	6.0
Victim previously nonsexually assaulted	yes	40.0
	no	12.2
Lab saline wash for sperm	no evidence	7.4
	evidence	28.3
Victim/offender racial class	interracial rape	38.9
	intraracial rape	13.3
Victim lives with mother	no	23.9
	yes	10.1
Lab smear vagina for sperm	no evidence	7.8
	evidence	21.6
Lab smear vulva for sperm	no evidence	8.6
	evidence	22.3
Lab smear cervix for sperm	no evidence	7.5
	evidence	21.6
Victim/offender age differential	offender is more than 10 years younger	35.7
	offender is older than victim or within 10 years of her age	14.3
Schooling completed by victim	high school graduate	25.7
	not high school graduate	11.8
Victim employed	yes	28.1
	no	13.7
Victim raped by strangers	yes	23.1
	no	11.7

Note: N = 171; 27(15.8%) had jury trials.

racially mixed jury that it is he who is being victimized by a racist system of justice or a racist complainant. Since a defense of consent is often not feasible in such cases, a defendant may base his case on mistaken identity, arguing that all blacks look the same to a white woman. Again, it is reasoned that a jury is more likely than a judge is to be persuaded by this argument.

Finally, the findings reveal that it is more likely that the defendant will opt for a bench trial in cases where there is no medical evidence of the presence of sperm. The lack of evidence may be viewed as more likely to have an impact on a judge and to be overlooked by a jury.

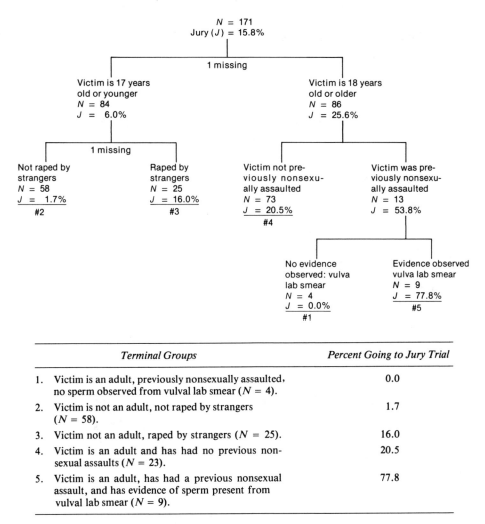

Terminal Groups	Percent Going to Jury Trial
1. Victim is an adult, previously nonsexually assaulted, no sperm observed from vulval lab smear ($N = 4$).	0.0
2. Victim is not an adult, not raped by strangers ($N = 58$).	1.7
3. Victim not an adult, raped by strangers ($N = 25$).	16.0
4. Victim is an adult and has had no previous non-sexual assaults ($N = 23$).	20.5
5. Victim is an adult, has had a previous nonsexual assault, and has evidence of sperm present from vulval lab smear ($N = 9$).	77.8

Figure 15–3. Analysis of Jury Trials.

The importance of choosing the correct trial forum for the defendant was illustrated clearly at a trial attended by the court observer. This particular case involved a mentally retarded adolescent who was abducted and then brutally abused by the defendant. The details of the case, if brought out in open court, could not have failed to arouse the jury's sympathy for the victim. Despite a great deal of evidence against the defendant, however, one element of the prosecution's case could not be established. The defense

Table 15–4
Jury/Bench Trials Comparison

Variable		Percent Jury Trials
Previous nonsexual assaults	yes	66.7
	no	17.5
Victim's age	adult 18+	35
	0–17	9.3
Victim lives with mother	no	39.5
	yes	13.7
Victim/offender racial class	interracial	58.3
	intraracial	19.6
Saline wash	sperm	33.3
	no sperm	11.1
Victim/offender age differential	younger offender	55.6
	Same age or older	21.0
Victim's marital status	divorced, widow, or separated	43.8
	single/married	19.1
Truancy history	no	26.4
	yes	4.8
School years completed	high school graduate	37.5
	not a high school graduate	17.4
Victim employed	yes	39.1
	no	19.0
Lab smear cervix	sperm	29.2
	no sperm	11.8
Strangers	yes	33.3
	no	17.4
Lab smear vulva	sperm	29.6
	no sperm	13.6

Note: N = 117; 27 (23.1%) were jury trials, 90 (76.9%) were bench trials.

chose to waive a jury trial on the theory that a judge could be trusted to weigh the case solely on its legal merits. The defendant was, in fact, acquitted of the charge of rape, although the judge later wrote in his opinion that he personally believed that the defendant had committed the alleged acts.

In summary, cases that are generally perceived as more serious—those incidents involving assaults on adult women by young, usually black, unknown defendants, and including concrete medical evidence of sexual assault—are most likely to be tried before a jury. Perhaps these defendants calculate that a severe sentence is likely to be imposed, regardless of whether they are convicted by a judge or by a jury. If a guilty plea is also not likely to increase the probability of a lighter sentence (for example, because of a prior criminal record), the only alternative may be for defendants in these

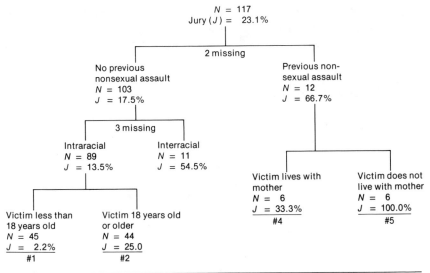

Figure 15–4. Analysis of Jury Trial

Terminal Groups	Percent Jury Trial
1. No previous nonsexual assault, intraracial rape, not an adult ($N = 45$)	2.2
2. No previous nonsexual assault, intraracial rape, victim an adult ($N = 44$)	25.0
3. Previously nonsexually assaulted and lives with mother ($N = 6$)	33.3
4. No previous nonsexual assaults and interracial rape ($N = 11$)	54.5
5. Previous nonsexual assault and does not live with mother ($N = 6$)	100.0

cases to raise enough ancillary issues (for example, the victim's having been previously assaulted) to cloud the issue of guilt or innocence. And, it is in a jury trial that such tactics are more likely to succeed. The following chapters examine the effects of these defense decisions on trial outcome and sentencing.

Notes

1. See, for example, Marvin Marcus, *Plea Bargaining, A Selected Bibliography* (Washington, D.C.: L.E.A.A., February 1976), and M.

Heumann, *Plea Bargaining—The Experience of Prosecutors, Judges and Defense Attorneys* (Chicago: University of Chicago Press, 1978).

2. Philadelphia Common Pleas and Municipal Courts, *Annual Report*, 1976.

3. Anne Lawrence, *The Court Observer's Report* (Philadelphia: Center for Rape Concern, 1975), pp. 42–46.

4. Ibid., p. 43.

5. Ibid., p. 44.

6. Harry Kalven and Hans Zeisel, *The American Jury* (Boston: Little, Brown, 1966), p. 26.

16 Convictions

This chapter reports the outcomes of those cases that go to trial. After an introduction on defense arguments, the variables related to disposition (conviction or acquittal) for the total court sample are discussed. Following this analysis, a closer look is taken at the outcomes of jury and bench trials.

Defense Arguments

Three major arguments are available to the defendant in a sexual assault case. They can be briefly summarized as follows:

1. Identity: the assault may indeed have occurred, but this defendant was not involved.
2. Consent: this defendant may indeed have had sexual relations with the complainant, but such relations were consented to by the complainant.
3. Fabrication: the alleged incident never took place.

Whereas in most cases the defense is based on any one of these three arguments, the use of one argument does not necessarily exclude the use of others. For example, a defense lawyer may base his case upon a claim of mistaken identity, but may add, *arguendo,* that this woman is the type of victim who would be likely to cry rape even if she were not victimized. While not actually asserting a second defense, a lawyer may succeed in putting additional doubts as to the victim's credibility into the minds of several jurors. Most defense arguments rely to some extent on myths about men, women, and rape.

As discussed in chapter 2, stereotypes as to what constitutes typical female behavior are marshalled to discredit the testimony of the complaining witness. The defense brings forward myths about how women are supposed to act in certain situations, compares them to the way a particular victim responded, and thereby "proves" that her behavior under the circumstances should be viewed as suspect. This method of argument is exceedingly difficult to rebut because it proceeds from myths, not facts.

Myths Supportive of the Identity Defense

One myth marshalled to bolster an identity defense is the notion that women become hysterical during rape incidents and are in no condition to remember the details of the incident and identify the attacker. A clever defense attorney will, at first, establish his sympathy for the victim and draw out from her the admission that the rape was indeed very traumatic. The attorney will then, however, turn this fact against the victim. If the defendant was a stranger, the defense may successfully argue that the victims recollection of the attacker's appearance can not be relied on beyond a reasonable doubt. Prosecutors are sometimes able to successfully counter this argument by putting forth the notion that pain may heighten, rather than obscure, sensory perception. "'Yes she was terrified,' one assistant district attorney argued during his summation . . . 'that's precisely why she did remember. That incident was so horrifying that it is burned into her memory so that she'll never forget it as long as she lives.' "[1]

Victims at trial find themselves caught in a "catch 22" because, as the following discussion indicates, lack of emotional response or hysteria may be used by the defense to corroborate the consent defense.

Myths Supportive of the Consent Defense

Of all the myths of female sexual behavior supportive of the consent defense, certainly the most prevalent is the assumption that once a woman has consented to one man, she will thereafter consent to any man: "Yes to one is yes to all." The court observation cases contain numerous instances where the defense attorney challenged a victim's story on the grounds of her prior sexual activity. Although this question is occasionally brought up directly, the defense usually prefers to make this suggestion by innuendo. This tactic undermines the effectiveness of the recent changes in state statutes that forbid the introduction of direct evidence of the victim's previous sexual experience (with anyone other than the offender).[2] In one case reported by the court observer, a white victim had been married several times, most recently to a black man, had had her first child out of wedlock at age 16, and was on welfare. During cross examination, the defense brought these facts out to suggest to the jury that the victim would consent to intercourse with anyone, even when attacked in the middle of the night at gunpoint. In another instance, the defense made use of the fact that, at the time of the assault, the victim was naked and asleep in a double bed with her boyfriend. The court observer reports this line of interrogation: "What? You mean you weren't wearing any nightgown?" the attorney demanded of her in a mocking, incredulous tone at the trial. "You mean you were actually sharing a bed with this man?"

By suggesting to a jury that there is an aura of promiscuity and immorality about a victim, the defense implies that the victim would freely participate in sexual activity with anyone under any circumstances. The defense may imply that, although the woman protested, she secretly desired the forcible encounter and perhaps invited it.

The defense attorney may argue that the complainant is promiscuous and that she was, therefore, likely to have consented in this instance as well. In one case that was observed, the defense argued that all young females during the late 1960s and early 1970s were promiscuous. The rape, which had occurred 3 years prior to the trial, involved a young woman who had allowed a group of unknown men—alleging to be friends of her husband—into her apartment and was then raped by them. The defense counsel told the jurors that they should remember that this incident took place in 1971. "That was the age of hippy free love. We go through historical epochs, you know. People then went around saying, 'My body, what is that?' "[4] The defendant was eventually acquitted.

Another consent defense, part of the "Catch 22," is that for the victim to have maintained composure during an attack is considered to be abnormal and provides grounds for casting doubt on the veracity of her rape allegation. One victim testified in court that, although she was terrified, she struggled to remain calm and rational throughout the attack. She wanted to remember every detail of the event for the police. She was even sufficiently self-possessed to arrange for a date with her attacker for the following week, planning to be waiting for him with the police.

When she was dropped off at her home by the rapist, she finally broke down. "It was like I had been holding all my feelings inside me during the incident," she said. "By the time I got home, I was just letting it all pour out." The victim testified that she could remember very little that occurred during the hour or so after she returned home. "I was so upset," she recalled, "that I can't remember anything about what I told my parents or anything."[5]

This victim's rationality during the incident, the defense suggested, could only be explained by the fact that her sexual relations were consensual. Further, it was argued, the complainant had later become hysterical only due to fear of parental retribution for her sexual "acting out." No other explanation, the defense argued, could adequately reconcile the fact that she had been "cool-headed enough to plot to see him again" during the encounter, yet later "so hysterical that she was unable to remember anything."[6]

Myths Used to Support the Fabrication Defense

Attorneys sometimes attempt to utilize the myth that an older or unattractive victim invented a charge of rape to attract attention or to make herself appear to be desirable.

In one case that was observed, the defense argued to the jury that the victim "really isn't very pretty. I'll bet she invented the story of rape to attract attention to herself, or perhaps she even consented out of loneliness." Then, dropping his voice and speaking specifically to the men in the jury, he added, "I'm sure you've all heard women lie through their teeth when they're lonely." In the same case, as further proof, the defense asked the wife of the defendant, a very attractive young woman, to parade before the jury, while he commented, "She is really more attractive than the complaining witness. Why would he need to rape this homely girl anyway with a wife like this?"[7]

As part of a defense based on a claim of fabrication, defense attorneys may argue that women are naturally spiteful. This argument is based upon the notion that a vindictive woman will avenge herself by crying rape. In court this defense most frequently takes the form of, "We were going together, and I broke up with her, and so she cried rape."[8]

In one such case, the complainant testified that the defendant, whom she knew as her sister's friend, came to her house one evening with two friends and proceeded to drag her upstairs and rape her. The assailant allegedly told her that he was being initiated into the black mafia and was undergoing his rites of admission while his two sponsors observed.

Later in the trial, however, the defendant took the stand and testified that he and the complaining witness had been having an affair for several months prior to the alleged incident. When he decided to leave her to return to his former wife, she became distraught and threatened to "get even" with him. The next thing he knew, he told the court, he was being arrested on charges of rape. At the time of his arrest, he said that he had not had sexual relations with the complainant for several weeks. "She was cornered and beaten," the defense said during summation. "And how did she respond? By alleging sexual misconduct as a form of revenge."[9]

Standards for Conviction or Acquittal

The prosecution must prove the defendant's guilt beyond a reasonable doubt. In his instructions to the jury the judge usually reviews this standard in detail. Beyond a reasonable doubt does not mean beyond a scintilla of a doubt, but many jurors will nevertheless apply this standard. As is the case in all trials, the fact finders must determine the credibility of all witnesses, including the complainant, and, where accounts conflict, decide whom to believe. The arguments that are often utilized to raise questions about the rape victim's credibility and the veracity of her account have been discussed. In addition to these arguments, however, Kalven and Zeisel contend that juries often attach substantial weight to the notion of a victim being contributorily negligent. According to their study of the American jury,[10] jurors tend to go considerably beyond the issue of consent or lack thereof in harshly scrutinizing the complainant's behavior.[11] If the victim has placed herself in a dangerous situation (by hitchhiking, traveling alone or at night, or returning to her home with someone whom she has just met at a party, for example) Kalven and Zeisel have found that juries tend to apply the notion of "assumption of risk" and relieve the defendant of any criminal liability for his part in the assault.[12] Further, the notion of *de minimis non curat lex* (the law does not concern itself with trifles) may be applicable in this context.[13] If the injury to the victim is slight, if the victim is reluctant to prosecute (and, therefore, is assumed not to be outraged), and if the victim is injured but her injury is not of concern to the jury ("she brought it on herself" or "she's as despicable as the defendant is"), then the jury may, according to Kalven and Zeisel, decide to acquit the defendant.

The notion of victim precipitation may play a significant role in the fact finders' determinations of assumption of risk by the complainant. An earlier study of rape in Philadelphia by Amir was the first to apply this notion of victim precipitation to rape cases in a systematic fashion.[14] Utilizing the concept of victim precipitation as developed by Wolfgang in his study of criminal homicide,[15] Amir analyzed over 600 rape complaints for elements of victim precipitation. According to Amir,

> In the sexual sphere, a man can interpret verbal and nonverbal behavior on the part of a woman in such a way that she will be placed in the category of a sexually available female. Thus, wrongly or rightly, a woman's behavior, if passive may be seen as worthy to suit action, and if active it may be taken as an actual promise of her access for one's sexual intentions. The offender then will react as seems appropriate toward such a woman.[16]

As Wood points out, "the effect of this theory is to make the victim partly responsible for the crime having occurred, thereby mitigating the guilt of the assailant."[17]

This concept (victim precipitation) has been the focus of much criticism. It is not intended that the veracity of psychiatric theories concerning victims consciously or unconsciously setting up a rape for either pleasurable or liberating experiences be debated here. The concept of victim precipitation is applicable to this research, however, because jurors do not limit themselves to the legitimate issue of consent at the moment of intercourse. According to Kalven and Zeisel, "it (the jury) closely, and often harshly, scrutinizes the female complainant and is moved to be lenient with the defendant whenever there are suggestions of contributory behavior on her part."[18] Slovenko notes that this is not the purpose of the law, and "it is the aggressor, who acts out his feelings against an available subject, (who is) legally at fault."[19]

To determine the relationship between victim behavior preceding the rape and case disposition, ratings of victim precipitation were made by the social workers interviewing the victims included in this study. For purposes of this research, the term "victim precipitation" was applied to cases where alleged sexual contact arose, in part, from the victim's naivete, lack of discretion, or complicity with the defendant. A victim-precipitated rape could range from one where a victim accepted a ride from a stranger or allowed a repairman into her home while dressed in a bathrobe, to a situation where a victim agreed to have sexual relations with the offender but then changed her mind and made this fact known to the offender prior to the alleged rape. The fact that the social worker rated the incident as victim precipitated does not mean that the social worker doubted the veracity of the account or placed blame on the victim, but rather that notions of victim precipitation, as developed by Amir, could be applied to the case. How the notion of victim precipitation influences the disposition of cases is discussed in the following examination of the findings.

Case Dispositions

Of 171 cases referred to the Court of Common Pleas for trial, 101 (59.1%) resulted in a conviction (on at least one of the charges lodged for one of the defendants) and 70 resulted in acquittal for all charges and all defendants (40.9%). Table 16-1 and figure 16-1 present the variables associated with these outcomes.

Table 16-1
Court of Common Pleas Outcome—Summary of Factors Associated with Conviction

Variable	Response	Percentage Convictions
Victim precipitation	none	71.4
	some	44.7
Intimidation with an object = weapon	yes	74.6
	no	50.5
Victim's age	0–11 years	75.0
	12–17	65.6
	18 +	51.2
Other sexual acts perpetrated	yes	81.8
	no	56.2
Scratches observed	yes	80.0
	no	55.7
Roughness used	yes	65.0
	no	49.0
Location of incident	other location	63.9
	rapist's home	47.8
Victim lives with brother	yes	66.7
	no	52.8

Note: $N = 171$; convictions = 101 (59.1 %), no conviction = 70 (40.9 %).

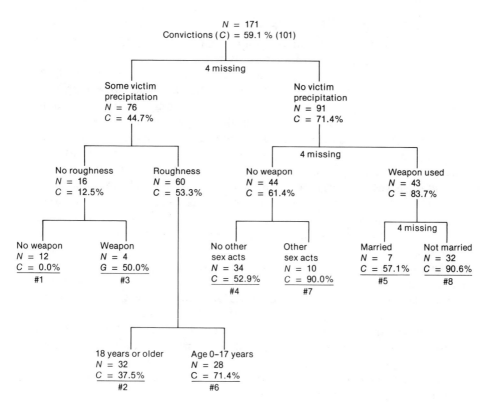

Terminal Groups	Percent Convicted
1. Some victim precipitation, no roughness, no weapon ($N = 12$)	0.0
2. Some victim precipitation, roughness, victim is adult ($N = 32$)	37.5
3. Some victim precipitation, no roughness, weapon present ($N = 4$)	50.0
4. No victim precipitation, no weapon present, no other sex acts ($N = 34$)	52.9
5. No victim precipitation, weapon used, victim married ($N = 7$)	57.1
6. Some victim precipitation, roughness, child or adolescent ($N = 28$)	71.4
7. No victim precipitation, no weapon present, other sex acts ($N = 10$)	90.0
8. No victim precipitation, weapon present, victim not married ($N = 32$)	90.6

Figure 16-1. Analysis of Common Pleas Court Outcomes for All Cases.

It is found that variables concerning the victim's behavior immediately preceding the incident are, indeed, more strongly associated with trial outcome than are other tested variables. Whereas the overall conviction rate was 59%, for the 91 cases that included no evidence of victim precipitation, 71.4% resulted in a guilty verdict. For the 76 cases that were judged to involve some elements of victim precipitation, only 44.7% resulted in conviction. In fact, all the variables that appear in the breakdown of terminal groups for case outcome in Common Pleas Court (figure 16-1) are related to the issue of victim precipitation or consent. Specifically, the presence of a weapon or evidence of physical roughness decreases the likelihood of successfully arguing victim precipitation. If the victim is under 18, she will probably not be viewed as being as much in control of the situation as would an older victim. As an extreme example, one is highly unlikely to accuse a 5-year-old child of precipitating sexual contact with an older man under any circumstances. Table 16-2 illustrates that, in cases where there is no weapon to corroborate a social worker's finding of no victim precipitation, case outcome is strongly influenced by whether or not other sexual acts (for example, fellatio, cunnilingus, rectal intercourse) were involved in the assault (terminal groups 4 and 7). Where the victim was, in fact, subjected to such acts, there is a 90% conviction rate (as compared to 52.9% where no other sex acts are alleged). This may be one instance in which traditional notions regarding female sexuality, which often hurt a rape victim's case, might very possibly help the case (for example, the notion that no woman wants to engage in deviant sex acts).

The findings indicate, therefore, that the notion of victim precipitation is paramount in the decision-making process for all cases that go to trial (jury or bench). Whereas it is obvious that the research social worker's opinion of victim precipitation was not brought before the court, it is clear that judgments of this nature can be, and presumably are, made by fact finders based on the accounts of the victim. These judgments of victim precipitation are bolstered or discredited depending on other elements of the crime (presence of a weapon, age of the victim, sex acts performed). The ratings of a social worker on victim precipitation, in conjunction with these elements, provide a good predictor of case disposition.

Jury versus Waiver Trials

The court observer noted that there was a considerable difference between the proceedings and personnel in bench trials and those in jury trials.[20] The observer reported that the judges in waiver trials generally appeared to be inferior in training, experience, and competence to those who presided over jury trials. The opposite might have been expected, since a waiver judge is responsible for determining both the facts and the law in cases before him.

One staff of assistant district attorneys was assigned to prosecute waiver cases and another to prosecute in jury trials. The more experienced assistant district attorneys were assigned to jury cases, the less experienced to the waiver cases. Perhaps this reflects the notion that more skills are required for a jury trial than for a trial before a judge. Waiver cases may be viewed by the prosecutor's office as training or preparation for jury cases.

The observer also reported that the list rooms—where trials without juries were held—differed greatly from the jury rooms. Generally, list rooms were much smaller than jury rooms because they did not have to accommodate a jury. The jury rooms tended to be decorated in an ornamental, baroque style, complete with pillars, marble sidings, oil paintings, carpets, and large chandeliers hanging from the high ceilings. The list rooms, more often than not, had linoleum floors, bare electric bulbs in the ceiling, and plastic paneling on the walls. Some list rooms were not air conditioned and became unbearably hot during the summer.

The meting out of justice in the list room is a long, tedious, and confused process. The observer reported that at around 9:30 a.m. the list room began to fill up with police officers, civilian witnesses, reporters, and friends and relatives of the parties involved. Soon the small room was crowded and overheated. People became restless. Around 10:00 a.m. the judge would arrive and take his place on the bench. Then, one by one, the clerk would begin calling the cases off the list, using the name of the defendant as identification. As each case was called, the witnesses in that case approached the bench and the process of determining if the case is ready began. The prosecutor consulted his witnesses. The defense attorney did the same. After much confusion it was decided whether or not the case could go forward.

More often than not, the case was not ready to proceed. For example, the defendant was in custody, and no one remembered to transport him from the detention center; or the detective on the case had gone on vacation; or the complainant was in the hospital; or the eyewitness's mother was sick and therefore that witness could not make it. The assistant district attorney would then consult with all witnesses to determine when they could be available again. He would then recommend to the court a postponement to an acceptable date. When another date had been agreed on, the case was listed as continued and the new date for trial scheduled.[21]

At one point during the research, the observer counted the proportion of waiver cases that were continued. A random week was selected. There were twenty cases scheduled. During that week, every sex offense case was tracked down. Of the twenty cases, none went to trial. In two cases, defense motions were presented and heard by the court, but otherwise, only one waiver case involving a sex offense was heard in City Hall. Ironically, the case that was heard did not appear on the master list because it had been originally listed as a jury trial. At the last moment, this case was changed to a waiver trial at the request of the defendant.

The number of continuances for jury trials is also high but not so high as for waiver cases. The critical factor may be that the assistant district attorney has more time to prepare for a jury trial than for a waiver. In a jury trial, the prosecutor will have contacted all his witnesses before the trial is scheduled to begin and made sure they are available. In a waiver case, however, the only notice a witness will receive is a subpoena in the mail. Such notification is undoubtedly much less effective.

The assistant district attorneys in the list rooms appeared to be overworked and overburdened. They arrived in the morning carrying massive folders containing all the cases that might be tried that day. Until a few minutes before trial, the assistant district attorney cannot know with any certainty which cases will actually proceed and which will be continued. If he has the time, he can only briefly review all the cases before arriving in court that morning. Thus, the observer found that he was often poorly prepared for the cases that did go to trial. Cases were poorly presented. Questions were asked inaccurately. Witnesses were confused and unprepared. Ultimately, many cases were lost. In contrast to this, the assistant district attorney in a jury trial usually has the time to prepare his case because he knows in advance which case or cases he will be responsible for on a given day.

The tone of proceeding in the two different kinds of trials is also distinct. In jury trials, a seriousness prevails. The interactions between the two attorneys, the witnesses, the jury, and the judge are formal. In waiver trials, the lawyers and judges interact in a less formal fashion, which the court observer characterized as flippant and often disrespectful.[22]

In one waiver trial observed, for example, the prosecuting attorney apparently had not reviewed the facts before the trial began. His questions wandered. At the summation, he stood up and ingloriously spilled the contents of his briefcase on the floor.

In another case, the judge greeted one of his friends who wandered into the courtroom just as the victim was testifying about a particularly upsetting aspect of the rape. The judge recessed the case and motioned his acquaintance into chambers. The judge then chatted with his friend for 20 minutes without closing the door, audible to those waiting inside the courtroom. When he returned to resume the trial, there was no apology to anyone.

As further evidence of the unusual tone of the waiver case, in one case the lawyers engaged in a heated argument on an issue concerning evidence. The judge let them continue shouting in an unrestrained, undignified way for several minutes before interrupting them. Finally, he called them into his chambers where the melee continued.[23]

During waiver trials, others often appear in the courtroom holding their subpoenas, wondering where they are to go. Often they have come to the wrong courtroom, or they have arrived at the wrong time. It was not unusual for the judge to interrupt the witness, peer over the bench, and address the person who has just arrived, such as: "Hey, who are you looking for?" "Well, sir, my slip here says I'm supposed to come down to City Hall today on the Jones case." "Let me take a look at that." Then, after some distracting discussion, the person is sent on his way. Meanwhile, the complaining witness has been kept waiting on the witness stand, trying to keep her composure and to remember the sequence of events about which she was testifying.

Procedurally, large parts of the legal process are bypassed in a waiver case. There is usually no summation at the close of testimony. Also, the attorneys often cite a case simply by name, rather than going through the entire argument and holding. The notion is that the judge, unlike the jury, can understand the arguments of counsel without having them spelled out in complete detail. However, these practices may also reflect the inexperience and lack of preparation of the attorneys involved. It is not always simply a matter of efficiency or legal shorthand.[24]

To some extent, the greater informality of the waiver trial is justified. Legal shortcuts are desirable because time spent in the courtroom has a high cost in both money and inconvenience. If the judge and the lawyers are able to communicate more efficiently in legal shorthand and the proceedings do go more quickly, the victim is the beneficiary. Certainly much of the highly formal ritual in a jury trial is not necessary and may even be detrimental to a just and efficient result.

It seemed to the observer, however, that much more than formality had been lost. Shortcuts excused sloppiness and lack of preparation. Informality turned into a lack of seriousness. Somehow, away from the watchful eyes of an impaneled jury, the judges and lawyers seemed to forget that they were trying cases in which people's personal feelings were significantly involved.[25]

Jury and Waiver Trial Outcomes

From the victim's standpoint, one compensating feature of a waiver trial is that it is more likely than a jury trial to result in a guilty verdict. These findings are reported in table 16-2 and figure 16-2. Of the ninety bench trials that were included in the research, slightly more than one-half (51.1%) resulted in a conviction, whereas only 44.4% of the twenty-seven jury trials were disposed of in this way. Whereas victim precipitation and credibility are significantly associated with case outcome in waiver trials,

Table 16–2
Bench Trial Outcome—Summary of Factors Associated with Conviction

Variable	Response	Percent Convicted
Intimidation with an object = weapon	yes	77.4
	no	36.8
Victim precipitation	no	67.4
	yes	35.6
Credibility rating	high	63.0
	low	32.1
Other sexual acts perpetrated	yes	81.8
	no	47.4
Victim lives with brother	yes	61.7
	no	40.5

Note: $N = 90$; convictions = 46 (51.1 %).

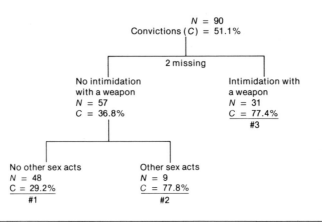

Terminal Groups	Percent Convicted
1. No intimidation with a weapon, no other sex acts ($N = 48$)	29.2
2. Intimidation with a weapon ($N = 31$)	77.4
3. No intimidation with a weapon, other sex acts ($N = 9$)	77.8

Figure 16–2. Analysis of Bench Trial Outcome.

the key factor in this decision appears to be the presence or absence of a weapon. In most cases, the presence of a weapon is likely to put an end to any serious inquiry into the issues of credibility and precipitation. If the victim were going to consent to sexual relations anyway, the defendant would have had no need to threaten her with a weapon. In 63% of the cases that went to a bench trial, however, there was no weapon involved. In these cases, the perpetration of other sex acts on the victim appears to be assigned the same probative value as the presence of a weapon in other cases (77.8% of the cases resulted in a conviction when no weapon was used but other sex acts were perpetrated, as compared to 77.4% of the cases resulting in a conviction when a weapon was used). The findings suggest that judges in waiver cases focus primarily on the issue of consent in determining the guilt or innocence of the defendants brought before them. Whether this reflects a significant correlation between the major defense argument (consent, identification, or fabrication) and the choice of forum (jury versus bench trial) cannot be determined from these data. However, the findings with regard to jury trial outcome suggest that there may exist such a correlation. Table 16–3 and figure 16–3 report the findings for jury trial outcome. No variable relating to victim precipitation, credibility, or previous sexual history emerges as significantly associated with jury trial outcome. Countless articles on rape laws and rape trials document the problems that have confronted the rape victim ever since Lord Hale's admonition made the victim's past sexuality a legitimate measure of credibility.[26] In a nationwide study of forcible rape and response to rape it was found that most prosecutors believe that evidence concerning the victim's sexual conduct is a major factor in jury deliberations.[27] The prosecutors agreed that the importance to the jury of the victim's credibility stems from the fact that the victim must generally prove the necessary element of lack of consent by herself—eyewitnesses are rare. As has already been noted, Kalven and Zeisel found that juries assess the rape victim's conduct on the basis of an assumption of risk factor.

Whereas an inquiry by a judge or defense attorney into past sexual conduct is likely to be a traumatic experience for any rape victim, the research findings indicate that evidence of victim precipitation may not be as important to a jury as is generally believed. In fact, it is found that juries

Table 16–3
Jury Trial Outcome—Summary of Factors Associated with Conviction

Variables		Percent Convicted
Physical pains from rape	no	83.3
	yes	33.3
Vaginal evidence of trauma discharge	yes	83.3
	no	33.3
Beating (nonbrutal/brutal) or choking	no	64.3
	yes	27.3

Note: $N = 27$; convictions = 44.4%.

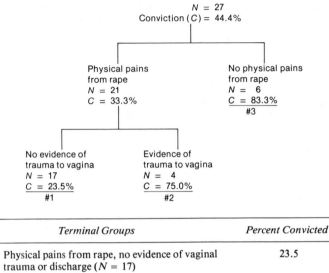

	Terminal Groups	Percent Convicted
1.	Physical pains from rape, no evidence of vaginal trauma or discharge ($N = 17$)	23.5
2.	Physical pains from rape, evidence of vaginal trauma or discharge ($N = 4$)	75.0
3.	No physical pains from rape ($N = 6$)	83.3

Figure 16–3. Analysis of Jury Trial Outcome.

are significantly more likely to return a guilty verdict in cases where there is no brutal beating or report of physical pains from the rape, unless there is some evidence of vaginal trauma. It is in these so-called nonserious cases that a defense of consent is most likely to be raised. The findings suggest that, unlike waiver judges, jurors are generally not amenable to this type of argument.

Ironically, it is the cases where the victim does suffer brutal beatings and physical pain that are most likely to result in the defendant's acquittal in a jury trial. Clearly, a defense of consent may not be feasible in a case of this nature. If the victim is able to substantiate her claims of extreme brutality (through photographs, scars, and so forth), then a defense of fabrication may be ruled out, too. The defense is therefore most likely to base its case on a claim of mistaken identity. It is hypothesized that juries may be reluctant to convict the wrong man in a case in which conviction is likely to result in a relatively stiff sentence. An identification defense in a less serious (less brutal) case—where the possible sentence is probably not as important a consideration in the minds of the jurors—is less likely to be effective in achieving acquittal.

The findings on jury trials must be considered preliminary in view of the small number of sampled cases that were decided by a jury. Analysis of all sampled court cases (jury and waiver trials) does indicate that efforts to explode the myths about women and rape might be better directed at judges and their areas of discretion (that is, bench trials), rather than at juries. The findings from this section and the results of the analysis of sentencing are taken up again in chapter 17.

Notes

1. Anne Lawrence, *The Court Observer's Report* (Philadelphia: Center for Rape Concern, 1975), p. 69.

2. See, for example, *Pennsylvania Consolidated Statutes,* chap. 31, sec. 31.04, Evidence of Victim's Sexual Conduct.

3. Lawrence, *Court Observer's Report,* p. 66.

4. Ibid., p. 67.

5. Ibid., p. 68.

6. Ibid.

7. Ibid., p. 67.

8. Ibid., p. 69.

9. Ibid., p. 70.

10. Harry J. Kalven and Hans Zeisel, *The American Jury* (Boston: Little, Brown, 1966).

11. Ibid., p. 249.

12. Ibid.

13. Ibid., p. 258.

14. Menachem Amir, *Patterns in Forcible Rape* (Chicago: University of Chicago Press, 1971), pp. 261–262.

15. Marvin E. Wolfgang, "Victim Precipitated Criminal Homicide," *Journal of Criminal Law, Criminology and Police Science* 48 (May–June 1957): 1–11.

16. Amir, *Patterns in Forcible Rape,* pp. 261–262.

17. Pamela Lakes Wood, "Note: The Victim in a Forcible Rape Case: A Feminist View," *The American Criminal Law Review* 11 (Winter 1973): 340.

18. Kalven and Zeisel, *American Jury,* p. 249.

19. R. Slovenko, ed., *Sexual Behavior and the Law* (Springfield, Ill.: Charles C. Thomas, 1965).

20. Lawrence, *Court Observer's Report,* p. 45.

21. Ibid., p. 49.

22. Ibid., p. 51.

23. Ibid.

24. Ibid., p. 52.

25. Ibid., p. 55.

26. Lord Hale's statement that "[Rape] is an accusation easily to be made and hard to be proved and harder to be defended by the party accused though never so innocent," I. Hale, *Pleas of the Crown,* 1778, is used by judges and attorneys to support the requirement for high standards of proof.

27. Battelle Law & Justice Center, *Forcible Rape: A National Survey of the Response by Prosecutors* (Seattle, Wash.: Battelle Research Center, November 1975).

17 Sentencing

The meting out of a sentence is a mechanism for powerful statements of social control, a statement of official action and reaction. The sentence is the critical outcome, particularly since numerous offenders plead guilty and sentencing moves the decision making back into the hands of the state.

Numerous studies have examined the relationship between sentencing patterns and the characteristics of individual judges and defendants. The fact that a defendant has a long record of prior criminal activity, or that he is sentenced by a "hanging judge," certainly cannot be ignored in any examination of sentencing patterns. Other studies can shed some light on the role that these factors may play.[1] It seems unlikely, however, that the inclusion of other factors would significantly alter the research findings presented in this chapter. It is assumed that certain types of victims are not any more likely to be assaulted by defendants with long criminal records than by others, or to have their cases tried before judges who are characteristically more severe or more lenient in their sentencing policies. In a truly random sample like the one used in this study, such differences do not distort the findings. Whether there are significant correlations among these variables (for example, prior criminal record of the defendant and characteristics of the victim) will have to await further research.

It has been suggested that certain classes of women are more readily viewed as "legitimate" victims of rape,[2] and that this factor is a significant one in the decision–making process. The notion that some women can legitimately be raped whereas others cannot has its beginnings in ancient history. Our modern sentencing structure can best be understood within this historical perspective.

Rape has always been generally viewed as a heineous offense, as witnessed by the severe punishments often imposed on rapists. It remains one of the few crimes in Western cultures that is punishable by death although no other life has been taken.

It is interesting to note, however, that all rapes are not viewed with the same seriousness and as warranting the same punishment. Early written laws, notably the code of Hammurabi and Hebrew laws set forth in the Old Testament, indicate revulsion in regard to the crime of rape. Both stipulated that the penalty for rape was death. These stipulations were, however, qualified. For example, Hammurabi's code stated that if the victim was betrothed and yet still living in her father's house and a virgin at the time of the incident, the penalty was death. Rape of a nonvirgin apparently did not warrant such a severe penalty.[3]

In Hebrew law, as well, several distinctions in penalty were made. Deuteronomy 22, v. 23–29 dictated that when a betrothed female was raped, the offender was to die. When the raped damsel was a virgin and not betrothed (that is, belonged only to her father), the offender was not to be put to death, but was instead forced to pay the father of the victim fifty shekels of silver. The victim became the rapist's wife, and he could never divorce her.

Many primitive cultures with no written laws maintained similar sanctions (for example, New Guinea).[4]

Early English common law held similar distinctions. The laws of Alfred the Great (c. 892 A.D.) stated:

> [If a man] seizes by the breast a young woman belonging to the commons . . . throws her down . . . lies with her, he shall pay 60 shillings compensation . . . if another man has previously lain with her, then the compensation shall be half this (sum). Also, if this is done to a woman of higher birth, the compensation to be paid shall increase.[5]

In the United States, too, there is a history of differing punishments depending on who is victimized. The briefs offered in *Furman* v. *Georgia* included a history of pre–Civil War punishments for rape in southern states and Washington, D.C.[6] Included were statutes for sixteen states, fifteen of which had separate penal codes for free persons and for slaves. In nine jurisdictions, rape committed by a white was not punishable by death, whereas in the case of rape or attempted rape of a white woman by a black man, the penalty was mandatory death. In Louisiana and Maryland, the crime of rape committed by whites was punishable by death or by life imprisonment, but when committed by blacks the death penalty was mandatory if the rape or attempted rape was upon a white woman. In thirteen jurisdictions, attempted rape of a white woman was punishable by death when committed by a slave, but a lesser penalty applied if the rapist was white. It should be noted that in every jurisdiction except the District of Columbia and Mississippi, the statutes imposing more severe penalties applied also to free persons of color. Rape was singled out as particularly offensive when committed by a black against a white.

Georgia reinforced the notion of reduced severity when rape was committed against a slave and stipulated that rape of a slave or free person of color was punishable by fine and imprisonment at the discretion of the court.

These statutes reflected the view of the law makers (white males) that there was not only differential harm when rape was committed by a white and when it was committed by a black, but that the crime of rape against a black female, if indeed it was considered a crime, was of less seriousness and harm to the individual victim and to the social order.

It is apparent from these early statutes that rape law has not offered equal protection to all. These early codifications indicate that the aim was not to protect women from sexual assault but to protect male interests.

In Hebrew law it was the father of the raped virgin who was compensated since no other male had proprietary interest in her.

The statutes of the southern United States prior to the Civil War and the response of white men to the rape of a white woman by a black exemplifies the white male's fear of a threat to his status due to a decrease in the value of his possession and/or loss of his possession to a black male.[7] For the white woman it was her chastity—the possession of white males—that was protected.

These early statutes recognized that it is the right of sole possession of a woman (which in turn promotes monogamy) that is violated by rape. It is this violation that is punished by law. Therefore, the law did and continues to discriminate between those victims who are chaste and the sexual property of a male and those who are viewed as unchaste and not belonging to any one person. The former are protected by rape laws and the latter are not.

Of special importance in this area is the study conducted by Wolfgang that examines the imposition of the death penalty on convicted rapists in eleven southern and border states. The study was sponsored by the NAACP Legal Defense Fund. The research findings were presented as evidence in six states to support petitioners' claims of racial discrimination in the administration of the death penalty.[8] The study demonstrates that blacks convicted of rape receive the death penalty with disproportionate frequency. When the race of the victim was taken into account, however, it was found more particularly that "a statistically significantly higher proportion of black defendants whose victims were white were sentenced to death." In fact, "black defendants whose victims were white were sentenced to death approximately eighteen times more frequently than defendants in any other racial combination of defendant and victim."[9] These findings have great significance not only in relation to the black defendant, but also they underline significantly the discrimination against the black victim of rape. When black men or white men rape black women, the crime, if indeed there is a conviction, is judged less severe. The implications, therefore, are that in attempting to determine the etiology of the disproportionate sentencing of black defendants to death in the crime of rape, we must examine not only the determinants relating to the defendant but also to the victim.

The fact that in all but three states in this country a husband cannot be found guilty (as principal) of raping his wife further supports this view.[10] Susan Griffin, in "The Politics of Rape," asks the rhetorical question,

"How can any man steal what already belongs to him?"[11] Indeed, rape has a history of being viewed as theft of another man's property.

The effect of the labeling of legitimate victims should, it is argued, be clearest in sentencing. In their report on sentencing guidelines, Leslie Wilkins et al., write "(it is) abundantly clear that when judges weigh the seriousness of the offense in determining sentence they are weighing the harm or loss suffered by the crime victim in what they perceive to be the 'real offense.' "[12] Carol Bohmer found that, whereas there are increased requests for psychiatric opinion by sentencing judges, they are powerless to use the reports properly and threatened by what they see as a corrosion of their power to make sentencing decisions.[13] The recommendations of psychiatrists are often unrealistic in terms of available options to the judge. These recommendations, however, do provide scenarios of the real offenses for judges to consider in the sentencing process and in measuring the seriousness of criminal incidents.

The research findings indicate that of the ten variables that are significantly associated with a prison sentence (table 17-1), only two relate to the

Table 17-1
All Convictions in Common Pleas Court—Variables Associated with a Prison Sentence

Variables	Response	Percent Imprisoned
Total strangers	yes	78.0
	no	47.5
Friends	no	68.6
	yes	25.0
Victim lives with sister	no	73.6
	yes	43.8
Previous sexual assault	no	63.6
	yes	25.0
Jury trial	yes	91.7
	no	55.1
School years completed	high school graduate	81.0
	not a high school graduate	53.3
Nonbrutal beating	no	64.6
	yes	36.8
Evidence from vagina	yes	75.0
	no	51.5
Lab saline wash shows presence of sperm	yes	70.0
	no	48.6
Choking	no	65.3
	yes	44.8

Note: $N = 101$; imprisoned = 60 (59.4 %), not imprisoned = 41 (40.6 %).

notion of the legitimate victim. If the victim has less than a high school education or has been sexually assaulted on a previous occasion, the probability of her assailant receiving a prison sentence in the event of conviction is significantly diminished. The notion of victim legitimacy emerges as somewhat more relevant in the decision as to the length of the imposed prison sentence. If the victim is unemployed or on welfare, her assailant is likely to receive a lighter prison sentence than in cases involving working victims. If the victim is white and her assailant is black, he will be punished more severely, if convicted, than an intraracial rapist under the same circumstances. Cases involving adolescent victims are least likely to result in prison sentences of two or more years.

Several other factors play an important role in the sentencing decision. If the offender was a stranger to the victim, he is more likely to be sentenced to prison, and also more likely to receive a term of 2 or more years. If he was a "friend" of the victim, his chances of receiving a prison term are slim, particularly if he waives a jury trial and there is no medical evidence of the presence of sperm (figure 17-1). Curiously, the degree of violence in a rape is found to have an inverse relationship to the severity of the sentence in certain instances. If the victim suffers what was defined as "nonbrutal beating" (that is, was choked, pushed, or slapped), it is less likely that her assailant will receive a prison sentence. This finding becomes more understandable when one considers that rapes involving less physical force than this are more likely to involve a weapon. And, when a weapon is present, an incarceration becomes more likely.

Predictably, a defendant found guilty in a jury trial is significantly more likely to be sentenced to prison than one found guilty in a bench trial (91.7% versus 55.1%). In addition, 75% of those convicted in jury trials were sentenced to 2 or more years in prison, whereas only 34.8% of those convicted by a judge were similarly sentenced.

It is worth noting that no black judge included in the research sample sentenced a convicted rapist to 2 or more years in prison, whereas white judges sentenced 77.8% of defendants found guilty in their courtrooms to prison terms of this length. Although the small size of this sample may make the degree of this distinction somewhat suspect, the distinction itself is statistically significant.

Sentencing can be viewed as an official statement about the seriousness with which the crime is viewed. The findings reported here do not include an analysis of the background, previous record, and so forth, of the defendant. However, these findings do demonstrate that the victim factors—whether she was white or she was raped by a stranger, or was employed, or was not an adolescent, or was not on public assistance—significantly influence the length of prison sentence imposed for the crime of rape. There is no indication that the rapes perpetrated against victims in

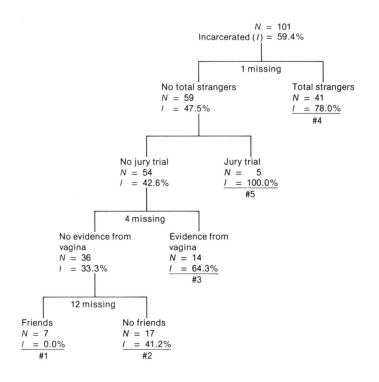

Terminal Groups	Percent Incarcerated
1. No total strangers, no jury trial, no evidence from vagina, rape includes friends ($N = 7$)	0.0
2. No total strangers, no jury trial, no evidence from vagina, no friends ($N = 17$)	41.2
3. No total strangers, no jury trial, evidence of vaginal trauma or discharge ($N = 14$)	64.3
4. Total strangers ($N = 41$)	78.0
5. No total strangers, jury trial ($N = 5$)	100.0

Figure 17-1. Analysis of Sentencing for All Court of Common Pleas Convictions.

these categories were more serious as measured by physical or emotional trauma (see chapters 3-6).

Overall, 60 of 101 convicted offenders (59.4%) were sentenced to prison, and 40 of these 60 (66.7%) were sentenced to prison terms of 2 or more years (table 17-2 and figure 17-2). When victims were asked by their social workers what they wanted to see happen to their attackers, 58.8%

Table 17–2
Variables Associated with Sentencing to a Prison Term of 2 or More Years

Variable	Response	Percent Imprisoned 2+ Years
Race of judge	white	77.8
	black	0.0
Who contacted police?	noninstitution	46.0
	institution (school or hospital)	0.0
Friends	no	48.6
	yes	8.3
Strangers	yes	56.1
	no	28.8
Victim's age	child and adult	50.8
	adolescent	23.8
Jury	yes	75.0
	no	34.8
Victim employed	yes	66.7
	no	35.4
Victim lives with sister	no	50.9
	yes	27.1
Victim/offender age differential	offender younger	77.8
	older or same	36.3
Victim on public assistance	no	48.4
	yes	24.3
Victim/offender class	interracial	72.7
	intraracial	36.0
Victim lives with brother	no	51.1
	yes	29.6
Pains from rape	no	58.3
	yes	34.2
Weapon used by defendant	yes	51.1
	no	30.8

Note: N = 101; imprisoned 2 + years = 40 (39.6 %), other sentence = 61 (60.4 %).

responded that they would like to see them jailed. However, less than 10% of the total number of cases in the study sample resulted in a jail term for at least one of the attackers. Although it is difficult to know the exact equation for ensuring the appropriateness of sentencing, it appears that present priorities are, for the most part, ill-conceived. If the characteristics of a particular victim are to be considered in the sentencing process, the focus should be on a realistic assessment of the likely social and psychological effects of the incident (rather than on notions as to how legitimate a victim she is). Rapes that are relatively nonbrutal can harm the victim as much, if

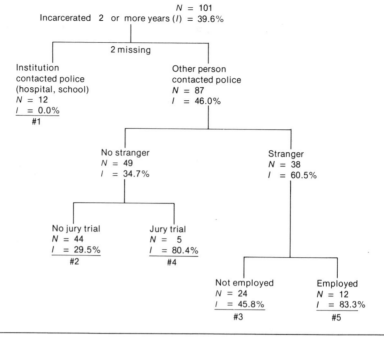

Figure 17-2. Analysis of Sentencing to 2 or More Years in Prison.

	Terminal Groups	Percent Imprisoned 2 or More Years
1.	Institution contacted the police to report the rape (hospital/police) ($N = 12$)	0.0
2.	Noninstitution contacted police, no strangers, no jury trial ($N = 44$)	29.5
3.	Noninstitution contacted police, stranger, victim not employed ($N = 24$)	45.8
4.	Noninstitution contacted police, no stranger, jury trial ($N = 5$)	80.0
5.	Noninstitution contacted police, stranger, victim employed ($N = 12$)	83.3

not more, than those that involve physical brutality or the presence of a weapon, and judges should consider this possibility in deciding on suitable punishment for the convicted assailant. Rapes by nonstrangers are often more emotionally traumatizing to the victim than those committed by strangers. The fact that the incident was reported to the police by a hospital or school rather than by the victim or some other individual does not necessarily indicate a less serious or less credible case. However, the convicted defendant in such a case is unlikely to go to prison for 2 or more years.

The terminal groups derived by predictive attribute analysis (figure 17-2) include no variables found to be statistically associated with seriousness of the incident for the victim (for example, physical trauma, raped by a casual acquaintance, presence of a weapon). States such as Michigan have revised their rape statutes to provide for degrees of rape, where degree of force and harm to the victim determine the range of sentencing possibilities. Perhaps such a system will provide for a less arbitrary, more rational sentencing policy attuned to the true seriousness of the crime.

Notes

1. See, for example, Edward Green, "An Analysis of Sentencing Practices of the Criminal Court Judges in Philadelphia" (Ph.D. diss., University of Pennsylvania Department of Sociology, 1959); Shari Diamond and Hans Zeisel, "Sentencing Councils: A Study of Sentence Disparity and Its Reduction," *University of Chicago Law Review* 43 (Fall 1975): 109; Edward Green, "Race and Sentencing," in *The Sociology of Punishment and Correction* eds. Norman Johnston, Leonard Savitz, and Marvin Wolfgang (New York: Wiley, 1970), pp. 248–261; and Stuart S. Nagel, "Judicial Backgrounds and Criminal Cases," in *The Sociology of Punishment and Corrections*, eds. Norman Johnston, Leonard Savitz, and Marvin Wolfgang (New York: Wiley, 1970), pp. 228–236.

2. Kurt Weis and Sandra Borges, "Victimology and Rape: The Case of the Legitimate Victim," *Issues in Criminology* 8. (Fall 1973): 71–115.

3. Cyril Smith, "History of Rape and Rape Laws," *Women Lawyers Journal* 60 (Fall 1974): 188.

4. Marilyn Strathern, *Preliminary Report on Questionnaire Relating to Sexual Offenses as Defined in the Criminal Code,* New Guinea Research Unit, Papua, New Guinea, October 1974.

5. Great Britain Laws, Statutes, etc., 445-1066, *The Laws of the Earliest English Kings,* trans. Frederick Levi Attenborough. (Cambridge, University Press, 1922), p. 256.

6. U.S. Supreme Court, *Briefs Amici Curiae Furman v. Georgia,* Criminal Law Series, vol 3., no. 33. Leroy Clark. 1971-1972.

7. See Lawrence Baughman, *Southern Rape Complex: A Hundred Year Psychosis* (Atlanta, Ga.: Pendulum, 1966).

8. Marvin E. Wolfgang and Marc Riedel, "Race, Judicial Discretion and the Death Penalty," *The Annals of the American Academy of Political and Social Science* 407 (May 1973): 119–133.

9. Ibid., p. 119.

10. This area of the law is rapidly changing. Delaware, Maryland, New Jersey, and Oregon have removed the spousal exclusion for all or part of the

subsections of their laws. See Leigh Bienen, "Rape III," forthcoming *Women's Right's Law Reporter* 1979, and H. Field and L. Bienen, *Jurors and Rape: A Psycho-Legal Investigation,* forthcoming, Lexington Books, Lexington, Mass., 1980.

11. Susan Griffin, "The Politics of Rape," *Ramparts* 10 (September 1971): p. 34.

12. Leslie T. Wilkins et al., *Sentencing Guidelines: Structuring Judicial Discretion: Report on the Feasibility Study* (Washington, D.C.: National Institute of Law Enforcement and Criminal Justice, U.S. Government Printing Office, #027-000-00583-7, February 1978).

13. C. Bohmer, *Judicial Use of Psychiatric Reports in the Sentencing of Sex Offenders* (Philadelphia: Center for Rape Concern, 1973). 13 pages.

18 The Impact of the Trial on the Victim

Most victims consider the rape trial a negative experience, but there is considerable variation in response to the courtroom experience. Some victims find the trial emotionally devastating, whereas other women find the court experience positively therapeutic. This chapter first presents the Center for Rape Concern court observer's findings regarding the cumulative effects of the court experience on the victim, reflecting elements of the trial such as the seriousness with which cases are treated, and the types of arguments employed by the defense.[a] The victim herself is an important element; her prerape personality, attitudes and social experience, are all found to influence her reaction to trial. The verdict is often less distressing to the victim than her experiences during the actual proceedings of the trial. Second, this chapter compares the adjustment reactions of victims whose cases go to trial with the reactions in cases where no trial is necessary (that is, where a guilty plea is entered).

The Public Trial

Many victims are upset by the discovery that they must publicly testify about something that is to them a very private matter. There is often standing room only in the section of seats reserved for the public in courtrooms where sex offenses are tried. The bulk of the observers in these cases are retired men, the unemployed, school children, and policemen in training. As one older man observed, many who come to see rape trials "just like to get out of the house." The trials in Common Pleas Court provide, and have provided over the years, a daily, free source of social activity.

During the period of this study, the number of regular courtroom observers soared. Most of the newcomers were young men who had recently become unemployed. A younger man, interviewed during the recess of a rape trial, said that he had been laid off from his job as a mechanic. It made him nervous to sit around the house all day with his wife and kids, so he had taken to coming to court. "I heard about this from an older guy on the block," he said, "and I've been coming down ever since. It's great entertainment."

The old people and the unemployed are not the only ones who frequent the courtrooms. Also present on occasion are large groups of school

---

[a] Anne Lawrence, *The Court Observer's Report* (Philadelphia: Center for Rape Concern, 1975).

children. The judge usually takes the opportunity of a recess to lecture the children on the American criminal justice system and to answer questions. Young rookies from the police academy also attend sessions to listen to experienced detectives give testimony in rape cases.

The issue of the presence of observers in a courtroom is a complex one. The defendant has the right to a public trial. Courts should be accessible to public scrutiny and criticism. Students and rookies receive valuable exposure to the criminal justice system, others have found an interesting and harmless way to spend some empty hours. However, the constant flow of people and the sea of shifting and unfamiliar faces can be extremely disruptive to the court procedure. It is also upsetting to witnesses, especially to rape victims.

When a 16-year-old rape victim gave testimony to a court packed with old men and a group of a local parochial junior high school students, her parents were confused and disturbed by the situation. They asked: "Who are all these people and why are they in here listening to this?" Another victim was angered by having to speak of her rape before a group of high school students. "I didn't want to have to speak of this experience in front of all those people," she told the observer.

The problem is familiar: Who is more important, the society or the individual? Since the interests of society clearly took precedence at the time of these observations, the victim had no choice but to testify publicly, regardless of the degree to which she was personally humiliated by the experience. However, since the time of these observations, the Pennsylvania Supreme Court ruled that it is within a judge's discretion to clear the courtroom during a victim's testimony.

Isolation in the Courtroom

One of the most difficult aspects of a rape trial for the victim is her loneliness, her sense of the uniqueness of her experience. Those persons closest to the woman, those potentially most capable of providing her with emotional support, are often witnesses in the case. They are, therefore, sequestered during those difficult moments when the victim actually gives her testimony. There is no spot in the courtroom more lonely than the witness box, facing the hostile defense attorney and defendant, as well as many strangers. The trial personnel are usually all men. There are relatively few female attorneys or judges. Although there is occasionally more than one defendant in a case, there is rarely more than one complainant. The victim must do without support and companionship.

An interesting exception to the usual solitary complainant would seem to vouch for the truth of this observation. In one case observed, a single offender sexually assaulted five women. Generally, such cases would be severed, and each case would be tried separately. In this case, however, the practice was not followed, and the cases were joined.

During the shared court appearances, the five victims in this case came to know each other intimately and seemed to develop a genuine esprit de corps. The five women came to court early each day of the trial to give each other moral support, went out to lunch together, and sat together during court recesses. After their attacker had been convicted, one of the women gave a party to celebrate their victory. The observer felt that the trial experiences of these five women were considerably less traumatic than that of almost any other victim observed during the study. The support group that these victims developed largely overcame the negative features of the court experience. The presence of support, particularly of other women who have shared similar experiences both inside and outside the courtroom, can go far to alleviate the loneliness and emotional trauma of the court experience.

Reliving the Rape Incident

If a long period of time has elapsed between the incident and the trial, the court experience can reopen the entire emotional incident for the victim. Not all victims react the same way, but a victim's reaction when she is forced to relive the incident in court can be a critical factor in her ability to emotionally survive the trial. In one case involving an emotionally fragile victim, the rape incident had taken place several days after the victim had moved to Philadelphia from the west coast with her boyfriend. While the woman was alone in the apartment, a man arrived at the door and identified himself as a friend of her boyfriend. He returned a few moments later with another man, and the two of them forced their way into the apartment at gunpoint. They were joined shortly thereafter by a third man. All three men raped and terrorized the woman for close to two hours.

The experience devastated the young victim. She testified that after the man left, she felt "very, very dirty" and sat in the bathtub for several hours, washing herself and "crying and crying." She was so upset by the incident that the couple was forced to move out of their new apartment immediately so that she would not be reminded of the incident.

After an investigation, all three assailants were picked up by the police. The three trials were severed through defense motions, and then various delays occurred. Over the course of the next 3 years, the victim was required to give testimony at no less than six different hearings in the case and to come to court on many other occasions when the case was continued. Two of the defendants were convicted and sent to prison. Each court case took its toll by continually reopening the incident for the victim.

Two years after the incident, the woman and her boyfriend, now her husband, decided to move back to California, primarily to escape the haunting memory of the attack. No sooner had they moved, however, than they were subpoenaed once again to testify in the third and final trial. The couple flew back to Philadelphia in the fall of 1974, at the state's expense, to give testimony. Nonetheless, the case resulted in a mistrial. In February 1975, the couple received another subpoena for the retrial of the third case.

According to the detective assigned to the case, when the victim received this final subpoena in the mail she became hysterical and had to be placed under the emergency care of a psychiatrist. On the basis of his treatment of the victim, the psychiatrist gave testimony in a California court on a motion to quash the subpoena on the grounds that returning to Philadelphia to give testimony would jeopardize the woman's emotional health and endanger her first pregnancy. The trial of the third offender subsequently took place with the testimony of the victim given in the form of a deposition based on her testimony at an earlier trial.

The experience of having to give testimony in court always threatens to be emotionally injurious to any victim. In this example, the ordinary strain of a rape trial was compounded by the fact that the victim had to testify repeatedly over a prolonged period of time, one trial for each of the three defendants and yet another trial because of the mistrial. Although an extreme example, this situation is by no means unique. In other cases observed, many victims reexperienced the attack while giving testimony, thereby disrupting whatever emotional recovery they had undergone since the incident.

Seriousness of Proceedings

One aspect of the trial that does not relate directly to the victim but that can affect her emotional reaction and well-being is the seriousness of treatment that her case receives in court. Seriousness is defined here as the formality and propriety of the environment surrounding the trial.

One case that was treated with a particular lack of seriousness involved the rape of a young black woman by one of her husband's friends. In this incident, the husband's friend had come by in the morning to pick up a package and had asked the victim to go out for a drink. She accepted, and they later took the bus to the defendant's home to listen to some records. Once in his home, the victim was attacked by the man and several of his friends. She jumped out of a window and fled on foot, partially unclothed. Shortly thereafter she reported the incident to the police. The court observation report expressed "shock at the degree to which none of the legal personnel took the case seriously. There seemed to be a general, unspoken consensus from the very beginning that among the judge and the attorneys this was a lost case. A serious effort to prosecute was not made.''

This lack of seriousness in court was clearly apparent to the victim. She later reported to a social worker that she felt that the outcome of the case had been planned in advance of the trial. She stated that ''[t]he two lawyers acted like buddies and I had a funny feeling that I was going to lose. The judge, she reported, ''was relaxed and smiling in his chair, just like he was in his home.'' Throughout the trial, she said that she experienced strong feelings of inadequacy and humiliation. ''They made me feel like an ass, like a fool,'' she reported. She felt enormous anger after the not-guilty verdict was announced, and she continued to experience this anger long after the completion of the trial. She referred to the criminal justice system as ''rotten,'' vowing that if she were raped again, she would certainly not report the incident to the police. More than any other single factor, the lack of seriousness with which her case was treated accounted for this victim's negative reaction to the trial experience.

Some other cases are treated more seriously, yet still result in a negative court experience for the victim. The level of seriousness or formality does not necessarily determine the victim's emotional reactions, but it is often one factor contributing to a victim's considerable emotional upset.

Defense Arguments—Myths about Women

Among the objective aspects of the rape trial that most strongly influence the response of the victim are the particular arguments used by the defense to cast doubt upon the rape allegation. One of the most striking aspects of defense arguments in sexual offense cases is the extent to which stereotypes of what constitutes typical female behavior are marshalled to discredit the testimony of the complaining witness. Myths about how women are supposed to act in certain situations are brought forward, compared unfavorably to the ways a particular victim responded, and used to ''prove'' that her behavior under the circumstances should be viewed as suspect. This is a highly insidious method of argument and one that is exceedingly difficult to rebut because it proceeds from myths, not facts.

The stereotypes that are seen in rape cases invariably portray a woman as degraded, oppressed, dependent, and victimized. There is no doubt that the use of such stereotypes by the defense during the trial is highly damaging to any victim's self-confidence and self-image. Such tactics strongly contribute to the victim's negative emotional reaction to the legal process. Many women emerge from the experience of testifying with their feelings of strength and self-reliance all but erased, an unfortunate result of the trial.

In general, cases that involve these types of defenses and focus substantially on the victim's own motives tend to be more emotionally destructive than cases in which the victim's behavior and motives are not in question. In a consent defense, the response of the victim, not the actions of the offender, becomes the issue. The focus is also on the victim's behavior in cases that allege that the woman fabricated the rape allegation for her own malicious purposes. Both these arguments focus the trial squarely on the behavior of the victim. She is made to feel that she is on trial. In an identification defense, by contrast, the act of rape is assumed to have occurred. The focus of the case is shifted to the circumstances surrounding the identification and the strength of supportive physical evidence. In this type of defense, the victim no longer feels on trial for her behavior. Only her ability to correctly identify her attacker is questioned.

Victims seem to react to the consent defense in one of two ways—either they get angry, or they lose self-confidence and become confused. In one case observed, a teenage girl was raped by a gang of youths in the elevator of a housing project. The defense attempted to put forward that this girl was so promiscuous she had decided to have sexual relations with an entire group of boys that she had never before seen. The defense attacked her credibility, her past sexual behavior, and her reason for being in the housing project in the first place. At first, the girl appeared to be incredulous at his suggestions. But, gradually, she began to appear more and more confused. She kept looking around her, as if to solicit help from others in the courtroom, such as the judge. She seemed to be asking the question with her eyes: "Can all this really be true about me?" At the end of the trial, the victim seemed not to feel anger as much as a loss of self-esteem and confidence.

Anger is probably a healthier response to these tactics, but not all women have the strength or ability to publicly vent their feelings of outrage. One example of an angry response is a case in which the defense established that, on the evening of the rape, the victim was wearing no nightclothes and had been asleep in bed with her boyfriend. The complainant was infuriated by the suggestion that she was promiscuous. She later told the social worker that the defense attorney had been "inhumane" to have implied that sexual relations with her boyfriend, with whom she had been involved for several years, were in any way related to the sexual attack from the intruding stranger. She expressed considerable anger and hostility towards the defense attorney for abusing her in this way on the stand. Through this expression of anger, she was able to maintain her self-esteem and sense of worth.

A woman who has been the victim of a sexual attack can later experience considerable guilt. She wonders if she resisted actively enough, if she used every possible avenue of escape, or if she cried out loudly enough. In these cases, the victim harbors doubts about the appropriateness of her behavior. She wonders if, perhaps, her behavior was tantamount to consent even though she had refused the encounter. Clever defense attorneys using a consent defense strategy can sometimes take advantage of these feelings of ambivalence and guilt to break down the victim on the stand, to destroy publicly whatever rationale she had constructed for her behavior under the circumstances.

One case illustrates the effect of a consent defense on the emotional well-being of a victim who felt highly ambivalent about her own behavior. The victim was an 18-year-old, black, high school student who had recently moved to Philadelphia from the South. She was living with her natural father in a housing development. At the time of the rape, she had been in the city for only 2 months.

On the day of the incident, she had gotten into an argument with her father about whether or not she could go out to a show that evening, it being a school night. She finally went to the show against her father's wishes and stayed out late. Her date for the evening was a boy whom she did not know and who did not accompany her home, although it was 3:00 a.m. when she was dropped off. The victim went to return to her father's apartment, but she found the elevator broken. Two young men were standing there, apparently also waiting for the elevator. They struck up a conversation with the victim. On this point, both the woman and the two men, who later testified in their own defense, agreed. They did not agree on what happened subsequently. According to her, one of the men pulled out a razor and told her to come with them to a vacant apartment in the adjoining project. The victim claimed that she was forced into the apartment and then raped by both men. The men, however, told the story differently. They said that the victim told them that she had been fighting with her father and did not want to go home that night. They told her that they knew of a vacant apartment where she could stay, and she accepted their offer. Later that night, they said, they had begun "messing around," resulting in their both having intercourse with her.

In the observer's opinion, this woman probably did go to the apartment willingly for a combination of reasons: desire for approval and affection from the two young men, anger at her father, possibly fear of her father's retaliation, and finally out of naivete. Once in the deserted apartment, however, the situation quickly got beyond the victim's control. The three probably engaged in some friendly sexual banter, which the two men interpreted as an invitation. First one, and then the other, forced himself on her. The case seemed convincing on the point that she did not consent to the actual intercourse because of evidence that her blouse was torn, which indicated a struggle at the time of the actual encounter. Also, she ran out into the street immediately after the attack and flagged down a patrol car to report that she had been attacked inside the building.

The defense questioning throughout this case elicited a confused response from the complaining witness on the issue of her consent. She alternately cried or acted with hostility during the questions. The cross-examination appeared to bring to the surface her own inner confusion about her behavior that evening, especially her own doubts about why she had initially gone with the men. The whole trial experience appeared to be highly upsetting to the victim. When the verdict of not guilty was announced, the victim screamed and then began to cry and wail uncontrollably. Eventually, she had to be physically carried from the courtroom by one of her young male companions. The assistant district attorney told the observer that this victim had called him several times during the week following the conclusion of the trial, to ask if there was anyway the case could be reopened.

Defense strategies of fabrication can be even more emotionally disturbing to the victim. The sample of cases observed in this study included only one fabrication defense, so a balanced view of the effect of this line of argument on the victim was not possible. Nevertheless, in the observed case the victim was absolutely devastated by the trial experience. Equipped with lengthy testimony from witnesses, the defense first attempted to establish that the victim had a motive for fabricating a story of rape; in this instance, that she had been involved in an affair with the defendant, which he had abruptly terminated to return to his former wife. Second, the defense attempted to show that the victim had a past history of acting in a malicious and spiteful manner towards others in order to establish the likelihood of her responding to being spurned by complaining to the authorities. Although she was not directly attacked as much as she might have been in a consent defense, the victim was greatly upset by these allegations. Sitting in the observer's section in the courtroom, she alternately wept and displayed anger throughout the entire presentation of the defense's case.

Cases focusing primarily on the issue of identity, in contrast, appear to be less devastating to the complainant. No one questions the fact that the victim was sexually attacked against her will. The question, rather, is whether or not the defendant is the man who was involved. The questioning focuses not on the victim's motives and responses to the incident, but rather on the attendant physical circumstances of the incident, her opportunity to observe the assailant, and any corroborative evidence that would tend to link the accused to the incident. In such cases, the principal witnesses are usually the police personnel charged with investigating the crime and conducting the identification procedures, not the victim.

In an identity case, the defense attorney often feels that it is to his strategic advantage to appear sympathetic to the complaining witness. ''I agree that (Mr.s X.) was attacked,'' one defense counsel told the jury in summation of a case involving a particularly grisly incident. ''This was a brutal, senseless, shocking crime. The man who would commit such an act should be severely punished. But not my client. He wasn't the man who did it.'' A defense counsel under such circumstances also attempts to express sympathy and concern to victims during cross–examination. ''I know this is difficult for you, so take your time,'' he might say, in marked contrast to his behavior when aggressively questioning a witness's sexual morality in a consent defense.

All defense strategies discredit the victim to some degree, either by twisting her own testimony or by introducing someone else's testimony to contradict hers. A defense attorney is only interested in creating sufficient doubt in the mind of either the judge or the jury so that his client will be acquitted, and is likely to use all available means.

Characteristics of the Victim

The effects of the trial on the victim are not only the result of objective aspects of the courtroom situation, but they also interact with the personality, attitudes, and experiences that the victim herself brings to the situation. In general, the trial tends to be a positive experience for those women who are able to verbalize their experiences, and for those who have sufficient exposure to the vocabulary and the procedures of a legal hearing to feel somewhat comfortable in court. For women who are less verbal or less familiar with legal procedures, the trial tends to be a more negative experience.

One woman who had a positive trial experience was a young, white social worker who was raped in the middle of the night by a stranger who broke in through her apartment window. At the time of the rape, she felt enormous anger toward her assailant. ''I was angry, very angry,'' the woman later testified at the trial. ''I thought, I'm going to do everything I can to get this man for doing this to me.'' She showed great determination in seeing the legal case through.

When the case finally came to trial, the victim entered into the prosecution with great enthusiasm. Her testimony from the witness stand became an opportunity for revenge against her attacker. Her testimony was so dramatic and effective that the defense attorney repeatedly interrupted her to object that her rendition was too ''subjective'' to be entertained by the jury. The high point of her testimony came when she was asked to point out her assailant to the jury. She rose to a fully upright position from the witness chair and pointed at the defendant, using her entire arm to make the motion as dramatic as possible. ''That is the man who raped me,'' she said with great feeling. The assistant district attorney told the observer that this woman was the best witness he had ever seen in a rape trial.

The defendant was subsequently found guilty. The victim later told the observer that when she learned of the verdict, she was positively ''overjoyed.'' Several factors contributed to the very positive feelings this victim had toward her trial. In part, her response was due to the fact that the defense was based primarily on identification. The focus of the case was not on her motives and behavior, but on the objective circumstances surrounding the assault. More important was the fact that she was able to express her anger in the courtroom. For her the trial served two therapeutic functions. First, it gave her a chance to ventilate the experience of the rape by relating it to the jury. Second, the trial provided her with an opportunity to direct her anger toward the assailant, to fulfill a desire for retribution in a constructive and purposeful manner. This experience brought her a satisfactory emotional release, a sense of ''joy'' and ''relief'' at the conclusion of the rape case.

For women who are less educated and articulate than this victim, the sophisticated legal terminology used by lawyers can be disorienting and can easily reinforce any feelings of inadequacy they already have. One victim, a young, black welfare mother, was unable to understand many of the questions asked by both lawyers because of the complex grammatical construction and sophisticated legal vocabulary that characterized the proceedings. For example, she could neither comprehend the meaning of a ''prior inconsistent statement,'' nor could she ''approximate in inches'' how wide she had opened the door to let the intruder enter. The witness responded to questions put to her by saying: ''I don't know,'' by asking that the questions be rephrased or repeated, or by not answering at all.

As the questioning continued, the victim became increasingly distraught. She began moaning plaintively, rocking back and forth on the witness stand. Finally, she broke down and began sobbing, wailing to the judge, ''But I'm trying so hard, trying so hard.'' In this case, the victim found the legal terminology and concepts so foreign that she became completely disoriented and confused. Her inability to comprehend the questions and to answer directly no doubt greatly contributed to her sense of inadequacy in the situation, producing a highly traumatizing court experience.

The more articulate a woman is, the better her chances of a more satisfying court experience. Her ability to speak, however, is not the only determinant. Her social milieu can also influence her response to the stress she experiences in court, especially when she is testifying. Women of different class, racial, and educational backgrounds express feelings of emotional distress differently in a trial situation. The observer noted that upper- and middle-class women are much more apt to verbalize their distress, to complain to the court when they feel victimized by the proceedings. Lifelong experience in receiving favorable treatment from social authorities has led them to expect their complaints to be heard with respect. On the other hand, lower class victims who have had the experience of receiving less than favorable treatment from the authorities more often adopt an attitude of withdrawn hostility and smoldering anger.

During the course of the study, the same defense attorney was observed in two separate cases. In both cases, the attorney asked the victim the identical question: "You really enjoyed having sex with the defendant, didn't you?" The first victim, an upper-middle-class white woman, immediately became highly indignant, refused to answer the question, and demanded of the assistant district attorney that he register an objection to defense counsel's question. The second victim, an 18-year-old, black high school dropout, responded by clamping her mouth shut and staring with intense hostility and anger at the defense attorney. More privileged women tend to assume that someone will come to their defense when attacked in this situation, and they therefore act accordingly; less privileged women do not make any such assumptions and, hence, tend to be less verbal about their anger.

Isolation from the Proceedings

Sometimes the rape trial becomes a negative experience for a victim simply because of a breakdown in communication. In one case, two young men were found guilty of an attack on a 16-year-old girl. They were convicted of corrupting the morals of a minor, involuntary deviate sexual intercourse, and other crimes. The judge, however, dismissed an original charge of rape on the grounds that not all technical elements of the crime had been proven by the prosecution. The two men were sentenced to a prison term. The judge commented after the trial that the complainant was "an extraordinarily credible witness, better than ninety-five percent I've seen."

Seemingly, all parties in the prosecution were highly pleased with the outcome of the case. All, that is, except the victim. No one explained to her after the completion of the case why the judge had found the men "not guilty" of rape. In her mind, she had defined the attack as a rape, and the other charges seemed incidental to her. Thus, her interpretation of the men's story—that she had engaged in intercourse with them consensually—had been believed.

Interviewed some weeks later by a social worker, the victim said that she had felt great anger and disappointment at the conclusion of the trial. "I always thought that if you told the truth things would work out. I told the truth but it didn't work out."

"The victim is very disturbed," the social worker noted on her report, "and feels that there was an implicit suggestion that she could have resisted and avoided the actual rape." In this case, the victim's perception of the court experience bore little relationship to the outcome. Unfortunately, because of the failure of the judge and district attorney's office to adequately inform her of the case's resolution, she had misinterpreted the verdict as a slight to her credibility. She felt that she had lost the case. In fact, she had been fully believed, and the case had resulted in a series of convictions on major charges. This instance indicates the importance of a post-trial session between the victim and the assistant district attorney or his representative, so that the verdict and its legal meaning can be explained and any possible misunderstanding avoided.

In sum, if the victim reaches the stage of a court trial, she usually has very little, if any, idea of what the procedures entail. Not only is she just a witness for the state, but once she begins testifying she can feel that she is being put on trial instead of the defendant. With little support, she faces a public courtroom and possible verbal harrassment from the defense attorney. Her emotional survival can be contingent on the reception of her case in court or solely on her personal abilities to understand and hold up under the process. The verdict is a significant factor, but its relative importance can vary depending on what the victim must endure at trial. Generally the reaction of victims to court trials will vary significantly depending on the factors mentioned.

Victim Adjustment and the Trial

Chapter 2 describes the methodology and goals of the Philadelphia Assault Victim Study. The focus of the research at the Center for Rape Concern was on the social and psychological effects of sexual assault on the victim. The data analysis reinforces one central conclusion: Rape is a devastating phenomenon. It dramatically changes the way in which the victim perceives herself. It's effects are not always short-lived.

The court observer noted the effects of the trial on the victim in the courtroom. What are the effects on the victim's adjustment in terms of factors studied by the Center for Rape Concern social workers, that is, the victim's relationships with family, friends, husband/boyfriend; her feelings about herself; her fears?

To examine this, the reactions of those victims whose cases were held for trial were compared to those whose cases were not held for trial. In addition, victim reaction in cases that actually went to trial were compared with the reactions of victims whose cases made it to the trial stage but who did not have to go through with the trial because either the charges were dropped or a guilty plea was entered by the defendant. Their postrape adjustment was measured utilizing the 1-year follow-up home-visit questionnaire.

Due to the small sample of victims who met these criteria (only forty-eight victims whose cases proceeded to trial stage also had a 1-year follow-up by the Center for Rape Concern), it was impossible to control for all intervening variables. Therefore, the findings must be considered preliminary. They do provide, however, additional corroboration of the notion that the trial itself, regardless of outcome, contributes to the negative adjustment of the victim.

The research into the effects of rape on the victim found that choking was significantly related to difficulties in adjustment in eighteen areas. Chapter 15 discusses how choking is associated with the decision to plead guilty. It would be logical to assume, therefore, that if going to trial has no impact on the victim, the victims who go to the trial stage but did not have to go through with the trial would have more adjustment difficulties, because they were more likely to have been choked during the rape. The findings indicate that exactly the opposite is true. Tables 18-1 to 18-4 depict the adjustment factors associated with the trial experience.

In table 18-1 it is interesting to note that, whereas the number of cases not held for court is as small, none of the victims whose cases did not proceed past the preliminary hearing was experiencing an increased fear of going out alone 1 year later as a result of the rape. This finding may be related to the fact that the rape was "resolved" at an early stage, and they did not fear offender retaliation.

Tables 18-2 and 18-3 indicate that going to trial is a devastating experience for the victim. Those victims whose cases went to trial were more likely to have increased nightmares, decreased social activities, and more dissatisfaction with heterosexual relationships than their counterparts who made it to the trial stage but did not have to testify.

Table 18-1
Adjustment Factors Associated with Preliminary Hearing Outcome ($N = 40$)

Fear of Going Out Alone 1 Year Later	Not Held for Court	Held for Court	Total
No fear	3	12	15
	(20)	(80)	
	(100)	(32.4)	(37.5)
Fear	0	25	25
		(100)	
		(67.6)	(62.5)
Total	3	37	40
	(7.5)	(92.5)	

Note: Figures in parentheses are percentages.

Table 18–2
Adjustment Factors Associated with Trial: Nightmares ($N = 48$)

	Trial Status		
Nightmares 1 year later	Victim Did Not Go to Trial	Victim Went to Trial	Total
No	16 (51.6) (84.2)	15 (48.4) (51.7)	31 (64.6)
Yes	3 (17.6) (15.8)	14 (82.4) (48.3)	17 (35.4)
Total	19 (39.6)	29 (60.4)	48 (100.0)

Note: Figures in parentheses are percentages.

Table 18–3
Adjustment Factors Associated with Trial: Level of Social Activities ($N = 48$)

	Trial Status		
Level of Social Activities 1 Year Later	Victim Did Not Go to Trial	Victim Went to Trial	Total
Less	4 (15.4) (33.3)	22 (84.6) (61.1)	26 (54.2)
No change	7 (46.7) (58.3)	8 (53.3) (22.2)	15 (31.3)
More	1 (14.3) (8.3)	6 (85.7) (16.7)	7 (14.6)
Total	12 (25.0)	36 (75.0)	48 (100.0)

Note: Figures in parentheses are percentages.

Discussion

It is clear from the description of trials provided at the beginning of this chapter that the trial meets all of Harold Garfinkel's conditions of successful degradation ceremonies.[1] This may be true for the defendant, but it is

Table 18-4
Adjustment Factors Associated with Trial: Quality of Heterosexual
Relationships (N = 48)

Quality of Hetero-sexual relationships 1 Year Later	Trial Status		
	Victim Did Not Go to Trial	Victim Went to Trial	Total
Worse	1 (5.9) (8.3)	16 (94.1) (44.4)	17 (35.4)
No change or better	11 (35.5) (91.7)	20 (64.5) (55.6)	31 (64.6)
Total	12 (25.0)	36 (75.0)	48 (100.0)

Note: Figures in parentheses are percentages.

more clearly applicable to the victim. She must testify (he need not) and thereby be confronted and transformed into something viewed as inferior in the local scheme of social types. Garfinkel states that, "the public denunciation effects such a transformation of essence by substituting another socially validated motivational scheme for the previously used to name and order the performances of the denounced."[2] Indeed, it is before many witnesses that the victim is denounced and her motives questioned. The victim's movements are carefully controlled, and she is transformed in the eyes of onlookers, friends, family, as well as in her own eyes.

In addition, the victim who goes to trial is forced to relive the experience on the witness stand. Fears and emotional turmoil that may have subsided earlier are once again aroused, and she may not be able to work through and control these feelings at a point in time far removed from their source. It is not surprising, therefore, to find that it is in the areas of nightmares, heterosexual relationships, and social activities that adjustment difficulties are likely to develop for the victim who has been to trial.

The trial process may increase the victim's feelings of guilt and may lead her to question her own motivation. This guilt and uncertainty may emerge in the form of nightmares, which represent the victim's attempt to regain some of the control that has been lost at the trial. Through nightmares, the victim is able to safely replay the situation over and over again until she feels that she is once more in command of her life.

The trial is associated with later difficulties in heterosexual relations, with normal functioning likely to be disrupted on two levels. First, the victim may feel that she is changed in men's eyes; that they look at her differently, and, in fact, they may. Public exposure of the fact that a woman's protector (her father or husband, for example) could not protect her is humiliating and guilt provoking for them and may seriously impair their subsequent relationships with the victim. Second, most of the individuals with whom the victim interacts at the trial are men—the judge, the lawyers, the doctors, and the police witnesses. She is humiliated either by them or before them and may be reluctant to relate to them or to any men in the future.

This withdrawal may also occur in regard to later social activities. If, in a successful degradation ceremony, the victim's sense of self-worth is diminished in her own eyes as well as in those of the community, it is likely that it will take longer for her to resume her social activities than it will for a victim who does not go through this "ritual" (the trial).

In conclusion, the data from this study support the contention that the trial can be extremely negative in terms of a rape victim's long-term adjustment. It will, at the least, delay the victim's return to prerape levels of functioning.

Notes

1. Harold Garfinkel, "Conditions of Successful Degradation Ceremonies" in *Prison within Society* ed. Laurence Hazelrigg (New York: Doubleday, 1968), pp. 68-77.

2. Ibid., p. 71.

19

The Criminal Justice System: A Summary

Not all rape incidents are reported to the police. Indeed, analysis of case dispositions for those rape cases that are reported to the police suggests that the initial decision to contact the police may be a mistake. Only a small percentage of victims ever see their attackers found guilty, and an even smaller percentage see their attackers sentenced to serve time. There are, however, a number of factors that argue in favor of notifying the police in all cases of sexual assault.

Table 19-1 summarizes case mortality at each stage of the criminal justice process. Although the study population comprised 1,401 rape victims, the police were unable to locate case files in 203 of these cases. Although there are several valid reasons to explain why a number of these files were not found,[1] the authors have detailed their own reasons for concluding that a portion of these cases were disposed of simply because the police had some doubts as to victim credibility. For the remaining 1,198 cases, there are data available with which to determine whether or not each case was marked as founded, in addition to the criminal charge attached by the police to each founded complaint.

In Philadelphia, the majority of cases that do proceed beyond police screening and into the court system are scheduled for trial in the Court of Common Pleas. Approximately one case in five, however, does not make it past the preliminary hearing. According to the Court of Common Pleas, the reason for this case mortality is withdrawal of victim cooperation—the victim does not show up for court or is otherwise unable to testify. However, Cannavale found that the label "lack of witness cooperation" was often inappropriately applied.[2] Determining the extent to which this actually occurs will require further research.

From tables 19-1, 19-2, and 19-3 the following observations can be made concerning the processing of rape cases during the study period:

1. More cases entered Common Pleas Court than completed a preliminary hearing. This is, in part, because any defendant may waive his right to a preliminary hearing. In addition, juveniles who are certified as adults proceed directly to the grand jury.

2. Among cases that entered the higher court, about 70% went to trial. For the remainder, prosecution was withdrawn or the defendant entered a guilty plea. Cases that do go to trial are three times as likely to be tried before a judge than by a jury.

Table 19-1
Rape Case Dispositions for 1,198 Rape Complaints in Philadelphia

Disposition	Total Number [a]	Percent of Original 1,198 Cases
Victims reporting rape	1198	100.0
Cases marked unfounded by police	218	18.2
Cases where no charge was recorded	108	9.0
Cases believed by police where a criminal charge was lodged:		
rape or attempted rape charged	747	62.4
lesser sex offense charged	111	9.3
assault charged	14	1.2
Total	872	72.8
Cases prosecuted in the adult justice system (560 cases resulted in no arrest, were prosecuted in the juvenile justice system, or were not in Philadelphia court files)	312	26.0
Cases tried at the municipal court level:		
prosecution withdrawn	8	0.7
acquitted	2	0.2
guilty plea	4	0.3
found guilty	6	0.5
transferred	3	0.3
Total	23	1.9
Cases not completing a preliminary hearing	55	4.6
Cases completing a preliminary hearing	234	19.5
Cases tried in common pleas court (includes cases completing a preliminary hearing, cases where a juvenile is certified an adult, and cases with no record of a preliminary hearing):		
prosecution withdrawn	23	1.9
guilty pleas	59	4.9
acquitted—nonjury trial	73	6.1
guilty—nonjury trial	76	6.3
acquitted—jury trial	22	1.8
guilty—jury trial	23	1.9
transferred cases	2	0.2
Total	278 [b]	23.2
Total cases from common pleas court with a guilty disposition:		
at least one defendant sentenced to state prison for over 2 years	70	5.8
at least one defendant sentenced to county jail for under 2 years	26	2.2
probation, suspended sentence, or fine	62	5.2
Total	158	13.2

[a] Excluding cases not found in the police files (203).

[b] The 278 cases involved 383 defendants, charged as in table 19-2.

Table 19–2
Summary of Charges for 383 Defendants

Charge	Defendants	Percent
Rape	302	78.9
Sexual assault and attempted rape	23	6.0
Statutory rape	20	5.2
Aggravated assault	7	1.8
Indecent assault	6	1.6
Robbery	6	1.6
Contributing to the delinquency of a minor	5	1.3
Other sex offenses	4	1.0
Offenses against public justice	4	1.0
Burglary	2	0.5
Manslaughter	1	0.3
Minor assault	1	0.3
Weapons offenses	1	0.3
Blackmail/Extortion	1	0.3

Table 19–3
Dispositions for 383 Defendants
(*percent*)

Charge	Found Guilty	Guilty as Charged	Guilty Plea	Guilty in Jury Trial	Guilty in Nonjury Trial	Guilty Dispositions That Result in a Prison Sentence
Rape	51.7	29.1	19.5	45.5	45.3	62.2
Sexual Assault/ attempted rape	65.3	39.1	21.7	50.0	80.0	66.7
Statutory rape	30.0	20.0	15.0	50.0	22.2	16.7
Aggravated assault	100.0	71.4	28.6	100.0	100.0	28.6
Indecent assault	50.0	50.0	33.3	—	33.3	33.3
Total (including other charges)	50.7	29.9	19.2	50.0	44.4	59.1

3. Over one-half of all cases that entered Common Pleas Court resulted in a guilty disposition, with one case in four resulting in at least one defendant being sentenced to state prison for a period of 2 years or more. Another one case in ten resulted in at least one defendant being sentenced to county jail for a period of less than 2 years.

Table 19–4
Defendant Dispositions for Selected Offenses: Common Pleas Court [1976]
(*percent*)

Offense Category	Guilty	Guilty as Charged	Guilty Plea	Guilty in Jury Trial	Guilty in Nonjury Trial	Guilty Dispositions That Result in Prison Sentences
Rape (N = 331)	55.0	36.6	19.9	74.1	40.9	91.0
Burglary (N = 2,167)	58.4	43.6	44.7	80.0	52.4	39.7
Robbery (N = 1,930)	66.7	51.2	43.0	76.0	55.8	76.7

Source: 1976 *Annual Report* of the Philadelphia Common Pleas and Municipal Courts.

Table 19–4 compares rape case dispositions with those for robbery and burglary cases for 1976. Because the Philadelphia Police Department does not publish findings that permit an audit trial from complaint through arrest and charging, the authors used the annual summary statistics of the Philadelphia Court of Common Pleas.[3] On the basis of those statistics, the following conclusions can be drawn:

1. A case of rape is less likely to involve a guilty plea than is a case of either robbery or burglary.

2. A finding of guilty in a rape case is more likely to result in a prison sentence than is the same finding in a robbery or burglary case.

3. The defendant in a rape case is more likely to be acquitted than is the defendant in a robbery or burglary case.

It appears that rape cases that make it to the trial stage fare nearly as well (from the complainant's standpoint) as robbery or burglary cases (although not as well as homicide cases, which have a 78.9% probability of resulting in a conviction, and a 93.7% probability of that conviction resulting in a prison sentence).[4] For Philadelphia, in particular, the situation is likely to improve; the district attorney has instituted a rape prosecution unit within his office. Other cities have already made similar investments with some success.

The most important requirement for improved handling of rape cases, however, is that these cases are not screened out at the station house. It must be noted that rape cases are likely to be disposed of at an earlier stage than cases of robbery, burglary, or homicide. The authors have described the possible ways in which the police sometimes usurp the courtroom function, discarding rape cases that include several unlikely circumstances, and, in effect, declaring the offender not-guilty without a trial. Police utilization of an extralegal, victim precipitation logic contributes significantly to the number of cases marked unfounded and prematurely removed from the criminal justice system.

In view of the rigorous screening process at the station house level, one may well inquire why more rape cases that do proceed to trial do not result in convictions and prison sentences. Less than one-quarter of all reported rape cases proceed to trial in the Court of Common Pleas. Certainly a selection process that is this arduous ought to yield a significantly greater number of convictions.

The myths supporting the notion that women are likely to make false accusations of rape, that rape is a charge easily made but difficult to defend against, that women say no but mean yes, and so forth, seem to be tacitly acknowledged in the standards of proof required by fact finders. Even in a bench trial, the factor most strongly associated with case disposition is the presence of a weapon. While corroborating evidence is not a requirement of Pennsylvania rape law, it is often necessary, in fact, to obtain a conviction. A weapon provides corroboration of the element of force, but nearly one-half of all rapes do not involve a weapon. Certainly other means of force can be, and are, used by defendants to overcome the resistance of their victims, and certainly most judges would agree that this is so. Yet over and over again, the absence of a weapon results in acquittal. Similarly, a victim who testifies before a jury that the rape was painful, yet offers no supporting medical evidence, is less likely to see her attacker convicted then if she claims that the rape caused no physical pain.

These findings substantiate a great reluctance on the part of judges and juries to convict defendants in rape cases. Victims' uncorroborated claims of brutal beatings, choking, the presence of multiple attackers, and repeated intercourse, for example, are seldom found to be significantly related to case outcome. When any of these factors does emerge as significant, it is always overshadowed by consideration of victim precipitation, victim characteristics, and/or the lack of corroborating evidence. This occurs, in spite of the existing facts that (1) the use of victim precipitation logic is purely subjective and not recognized in either the statutes or any departmental guidelines, (2) rape is a brutal and devastating experience for the victim, regardless of race or socioeconomic status, and (3) corroboration is not required by statute.

There appear to be two reasons why these inappropriate standards are so intricately bound up with case outcome. First is the notion that victims who are poor and uneducated or adolescent are viewed by fact finders as legitimate victims. That is, they either precipitated the crime ("asked for it") or are not worthy of the system's protection anyway. Secondly, it has been suggested that these victims may have little access to, or understanding of, the prosecutorial mechanisms of the criminal justice system. They are unfamiliar with the law and the courts. They have difficulty testifying and do not make strong enough demands for system response. These two explanations may really represent only one basic premise: Full access to the system may be granted only to those rape victims who are viewed as worthy of the system's protection.

The same factors appear to be applicable to the sentencing decision. The weight of the evidence and severity of the incident have less impact on the sentencing decision than do the victim characteristics and victim–offender relationship. And, whereas part II of this book illustrates the importance of victim characteristics and victim–offender relationship in assessing the prognosis for postrape adjustment, it is clear that the criminal justice system misinterprets these variables in meting out punishment to convicted offenders. For example, if a black man rapes a white woman, he is more than twice as likely to be incarcerated than if he rapes a black woman, in spite of the fact that victims of intraracial rape are likely to have a more difficult adjustment process than victims of interracial rape.

Certainly the goals of sentencing are not clearly defined and, therefore, cannot be evaluated on the basis of the findings reported here. Punishment, deterrence, incapacitation, rehabilitation, and retribution may all, in varying degrees, motivate the sentencing judge. However, none of these goals seems to be realized in the sentencing policies used by judges in this study. Whereas there has been some movement toward increased uniformity in sentencing and the meting out of more sentences for serious crimes,[5] the Philadelphia research indicates that sentencing for the crime of rape has been neither uniform nor appropriately severe in serious cases. It is doubtful that legislation alone would be sufficient to achieve these goals.

Attitudes about men, women, and rape appear to be the major determinants in rape case disposition and sentencing. If the police response to rape is improved—if more suspects are apprehended and more cases screened into the courts—will court outcomes more accurately reflect the real issues surrounding rape? The authors believe that this is doubtful. Increased case volume is not likely to effect any attitudinal change among criminal justice system decision makers and may serve primarily to create further problems for already overburdened court management.

Given the police and court figures cited in this study, we come to a reconsideration of the issue raised at the beginning of this chapter: Should a rape victim report the incident to the police? The authors say yes, for several reasons. In a very real sense, the criminal justice system is the only viable and legitimate avenue for redress. Civil remedies can rarely be sought, and no alternative legal remedy offers the prospect of punishment for the offender and the means of ensuring that he will not rape the victim or someone else again. Personal revenge or local vigilantism can effect these ends, but both reactions risk a criminal justice response. In addition, public attitudes may be changed by the vigilance of victims and organizations designed to press for change.

The situation for rape victims who do report has been improving. Both nationally, and in Philadelphia, the criminal justice response to the victim is better than when this study began, and procedures at that time were better than they had been in years before. Once rape emerged as a core issue of the rising feminist movement of the sixties, it quickly became the focus of a great deal of media attention. As a result, most of the criminal justice problems associated with rape cases became widely known.

In many cities the system responded. Often, police departments changed their procedures for handling rape complaints. In Multnomah County, Oregon, a rape investigation model was developed, including a rape investigative checklist detailing the procedures to be followed from the point of initial telephone contact, and a "standard rape kit" for the collection of all required evidence. Standardized procedures for interviewing both the victim and the suspect, as well as for case investigation, processing of physical evidence, arrest, and participation in judicial proceedings, are followed by the sex crimes detail in all rape investigations. The clearance rate in rape cases was over 80% during the first 2.5 years of model utilization, and the conviction rate in these cleared cases was 100%.[6] Many prosecutor's offices, including Philadelphia's, also devoted new, special attention to rape. Judges' pronouncements are now more carefully monitored, and prejudicial attitudes expressed toward rape victims may be tantamount to political suicide.[7]

In addition, increasing services are now being offered to victims of, and witnesses to, crime, specifically to victims of sexual assault. In Philadelphia, two programs are well established: Women Organized Against Rape and the Center for Rape Concern.

In sum, although overall figures may be depressing, the criminal justice environment for rape victims is improving and a system of supportive services has developed. These innovations may be of limited comfort to a victim who has been turned away and called a liar by the police, or who has been threatened by the defendant's father at the first court appearance, or whose case has been overturned on appeal requiring the whole trial process to begin anew. But, because there are no real alternatives and because there are concerned people now built into the process, the authors advocate that victims report to the police in the event of a sexual assault.

This new investment in the handling of rape cases is becoming problematic, however, to the extent that it requires competition for limited funds and resources at a time of increased public awareness of a variety of serious crimes. Physical and sexual attacks against children within the home are more frequent perhaps than rapes of adult women. Also, the extent of physical abuse of women by their husbands and boyfriends is becoming evident. The elderly, particularly in the inner city, have become prey to the young. Burglary and robbery are still widespread, and there are more and more reports detailing the cost of "white collar" crime and the extent of government corruption.

Ought police to create new specialized units for each of these problems? Ought prosecutors to similarly specialize? If so, the aim, in each case, would be similar to that of LEAA's career criminal program, which is designed to impact on serious criminal repeaters. This program provides "small town" attention to "big city" cases, not permitting them to get lost in the parade of cases through the courts each day.

This kind of effort, however, is expensive, and although the crime of rape has received some attention, more and more needs are being championed. Perhaps we may not be able to afford a fair criminal justice response to rape. There may be too many important cases for each rape case to receive "small town" treatment.

Another issue mostly neglected in the new movement toward buttressing the victims of rape involves redefining an ultimate goal of the movement. Most writings on rape, this study included, share a bias. The factors that prevent rape victims from seeing their attackers sent to prison are discussed and recommendations made that might increase the flow of offenders into our system of corrections. Punishment and deterrence are the motives, and the convicted rapist, once jailed, is ignored. Seemingly forgotten is the wealth of literature that describes our corrections system as an abysmal failure. The punishment fails to deter, and rehabilitation is not affected. Once new procedures are in place, and rape victims receive the support that they deserve, efforts must be made once again to resolve the issue of what ought to be done with all these rapists for whom imprisonment has so far been sought. There is still much to be accomplished, then, on many fronts.

Notes

1. For example, the rape incident occurred in another jurisdiction, the victim did not wish to file a formal complaint, the complaint could not be located because it was filed under the name of the complainant's parent or guardian.

2. Frank Cannavale, *Improving Witness Cooperation* (Washington, D.C.: L.E.A.A., 1976), p. 38.

3. Philadelphia Common Pleas and Municipal Courts, *Annual Report of the Philadelphia Common Pleas and Municipal Courts,* 1976.

4. Ibid.

5. See, for example, James Q. Wilson, *Thinking about Crime* (New York: Basic Books, 1975), and Leslie T. Wilkins et al., *Sentencing Guidelines, Structuring Judicial Discretion* (Washington, D.C.: National Institute of Law Enforcement and Criminal Justice, February 1978).

6. Harold T. Amidon and Terry A. Wagner, "Successful Investigation and Prosecution of the Crime of Rape: A Descriptive Model," *Journal of Police Science and Administration* 2 (June 1978): 141–156.

7. Louis Harris, "Judges Blasted on Rape Rulings," *Philadelphia Evening Bulletin,* Nov. 12, 1977.

20 Summary

The findings presented in the foregoing pages are derived from the most extensive study of rape victims undertaken to date. A total of 1,401 rape cases were included in the research; in 790 cases, an assigned social worker successfully completed at least one home-visit interview with the victim. Most of the raw data are provided the basis for analysis were collected during these interviews.

Several other sources of data were utilized in the preparation of this study. Examination of actual police files in selected cases provided the authors with added insight into police procedures in rape cases, including the nature of police-victim interactions. An eyewitness account of twenty-five rape cases at the trial stage described the rape victim within our court system. Finally, comparison of the study's findings with those of national studies and other research in the area of sexual assault enabled the authors to evaluate their findings within a much broader context than would have otherwise been possible.

The considerable scope of this study is, in part, a reflection of the interdisciplinary nature of its methodology. Social workers, psychiatrists, criminologists, and lawyers all participated in the data collection and analysis, contributing their own, often differing, perspectives in evaluating the practical and theoretical significance of the various findings. What follows is a brief summary of those findings:

The Victim's Readjustment to Living

1. Adult rape victims (aged 18 or older) are most likely to face serious short-term adjustment problems, adolescent victims (aged 12-17) are less likely, and child victims (aged 0-11) are least likely. However, both adolescent and child victims are likely to "catch up" with adult victims as they, themselves, become adults and pass through critical points in their psychosexual development.

2. Living with nuclear family members is likely to facilitate the adjustment process; being married, however, has a negative impact on most areas of adjustment.

3. Employment adversely affects postrape adjustment.

237

4. A history of truancy or police trouble hinders the adjustment process.

5. A history of sexual or nonsexual assaults makes adjustment more difficult.

6. Prior psychiatric assistance is related to increased adjustment problems.

7. A high school education has an adverse impact on most areas of adjustment.

8. A rape incident characterized by extreme physical brutality will lead to serious adjustment problems. However, the absence of violence altogether also leads to serious problems, of a different character.

9. When elements of a rape incident can be reasonably construed as potentially life-endangering (for example, presence of a gun), their negative effects on adjustment are likely to increase over time.

10. Incidents that involve penile-vaginal intercourse or deviant sexual acts (for example, fellatio, rectal intercourse) usually lead to a number of adjustment problems. However, rapes that involve mock tenderness (for example, fondling and caressing of the victim), either instead of or in addition to other sex acts, also lead to postrape difficulties of a somewhat different nature.

11. A rape by a casual acquaintance or relative stranger leads to more serious adjustment difficulties than does a rape by a friend, family member, or total stranger.

12. The location of a rape may lead to specific adjustment problems associated with that location.

The Police

1. When a policewoman is present at the interrogation of a complainant, the complainant is less likely to be disbelieved, and her case is less likely to disappear from police files or receive a nonoffense charge. This is true even when a policewoman is present in only a secretarial capacity.

2. The police are most likely to mark as unfounded the cases of those victims who are obese, have received psychiatric assistance, are 12 or more years old, allege penile-vaginal intercourse, or receive welfare subsidies.

3. Complainants who are not believed are most likely to report unpleasant interactions with the police.

4. The police are likely to mark as unfounded cases where the circumstances of the victim-offender relationship are not wholly uncompromising, even where the victim's account of the incident is believed.

5. Many of the same factors correlated with marking the case

unfounded are correlated with the lodging of nonoffense charges for a case. This corroborates arguments that cases are given a nonoffense charge (for example, investigation of persons) to reduce the number of rape complaints and unfounded cases that appear in official statistics.

6. Cases that involve child victims (0–11 years old) often result in lesser sex offense charges, whereas cases involving older victims are so charged only under special circumstances (for example, if penile–vaginal intercourse is not alleged or if there is no weapon present).

7. Most cases that police solve, solve themselves. Very little detective work is used in the apprehension of suspects in rape cases.

8. The police are least likely to apprehend a suspect and solve a case where a stranger, acting along, forces entry into the victim's residence and completes a rape, or where an adult stranger, acting alone, completes a rape away from the victim's dwelling.

9. The police view a case as solved once a suspect is apprehended. Consequently, case preparation is best in those cases where no suspect is apprehended.

10. Cases involving black victims tend to be investigated somewhat less thoroughly than cases involving white victims.

11. Cases in which the victim and the offender knew one another prior to the rape and the offender denies the rape generally receive the least amount of police support. It is these cases that present the worst difficulties for the victim in court.

The Courts

1. If a victim is on welfare, her case is less likely to be held for trial and, if her assailant is convicted, less likely to result in a prison sentence of 2 years or more.

2. Case outcome depends largely on independently verifiable details of the rape incident—if the incident involved no roughness, no weapon, and some victim precipitation, then there is little possibility of a conviction. In cases where a weapon is used and there is no victim precipitation, a conviction will result in more than five out of six cases.

3. An accused rapist is more likely to be found guilty in a waiver trial than in a jury trial.

4. In waiver trials, a guilty verdict depends mostly on the presence of a weapon. However, cases in which no weapon is involved but other sex acts are committed are equally likely to result in a conviction.

5. Jurors are reluctant to return a guilty verdict in cases involving extreme brutality, unless there is also evidence of vaginal trauma.

6. A convicted rapist is less likely to be sentenced to 2 or more years in prison if it was an institution (for example, hospital, school) that reported the rape to the police, rather than an individual.

7. A convicted rapist is less likely to receive a prison sentence of 2 or more years if he is sentenced by a black judge or if he raped a victim of his own race.

The utilization of these findings in predicting the probable aftermath of a particular rape incident can be illustrated. The authors have constructed three rape scenarios and have applied the study's findings to each one. In each case, probabilities are determined by reference to terminal group categories for each set of variables.

Case A

The victim is white, 15 years old, and lives with her parents and brother. She attends school regularly and has always been a reasonably happy person. She is of average height and weight, and has never been assaulted before the present incident.

While the victim is home alone one evening, a 20–year-old black man whom she has not seen before gains entry to her home through an open window. He holds a gun to the victim's head and tells her to submit "or else." He completes penile–vaginal intercourse with her and quickly flees; the entire incident is of less than 20–minutes duration. The victim suffers some discomfort, but no physical pain or injuries.

The victim's mother arrives home a short time later and immediately calls the police when told what has happened. A policewoman is present at the police interrogation of the victim. A social worker evaluates the victim as credible, with no evidence of victim precipitation in the case.

Analysis: The victim is likely to experience an increased fear of being out on the street by herself. The presence of a gun during the incident makes her four times more likely than other victims to still suffer from a considerable fear of streets 1 year after the rape. She is also likely to have an increased fear of being home alone, but the intensity of any such fear will be diminished because she lives with her mother. She will probably harbor some negative feelings toward unknown men for a short while after the rape and, within a year, is likely to have curtailed her social activities to some extent.

There is only a 25% chance that the police will apprehend this rapist. If they do, however, the victim's complaint will almost surely be marked as founded and a charge of rape lodged.

If apprehended, the overall probability that the victim will see her attacker convicted of rape is 90.6%. He is unlikely to plead guilty, and is slightly more likely to let a jury decide the case than a judge. There is an 83.3% chance that a jury will convict him (a 77.4% chance in a waiver trial), and he is very likely to be sentenced to prison (78%). There is a possibility that he will be sentenced to a prison term of 2 years or more, but it is more likely that he will receive a lighter sentence.

Case B

The victim is black, 30 years old, and lives with her husband. She is a high school graduate and presently works in a large office. She is noticeably overweight, and has been sexually assaulted on one prior occasion.

One afternoon, as she is about to leave work, she is approached by a black male coworker whom she knows by name but whom she only sees on occasion when entering or leaving the office. He invites her to a small party for some of the office personnel, to be held at his apartment within the hour, and even offers her a ride there. Upon entering the apartment, the victim discovers that there is no one else there, and soon surmises that she has been tricked. When she resists her assailant's sexual advances, he begins to choke her. Unable to achieve penetration because of continued resistance, he finally manages to rape her anally. The entire assault lasts for more than 1 hour.

The victim flees from her attacker's apartment at the first opportunity and runs out onto the street. A passer-by notices her disheveled condition and offers to take her to a nearby hospital. A hospital staff member reports the incident to the police. There is a policewoman present at the police interrogation of the victim. A social worker evaluates the victim as credible, with no evidence of victim precipitation in the case.

Analysis: The victim is likely to experience disruptions in her normal eating and sleeping patterns. The fact that the rape involved rectal intercourse will increase the likelihood that she will suffer from more frequent nightmares. As she is employed, it is twice as likely that these nightmares will continue for at least a year following the rape. She will fear being home alone. She will probably curtail her social activities, but the fact that she is married will tend to normalize her social patterns over time. She will experience increased negative feelings toward known men, and such feelings will more likely persist as she does not live with her father. She will also harbor negative feelings toward unknown men, and her heterosexual relationships are likely to worsen. Her husband may demand to know what she was doing in the offender's apartment.

There is a 97.9% chance that the rapist will be apprehended. However, as the victim is obese, there is a 62.6% probability that the case will be marked as unfounded even though a policewoman is present at the victim's interrogation. If the case is marked as founded, there is nearly one chance in three that it will be given a lesser sex offense charge.

If the case does make it past the police screening, it will almost certainly be held for trial. There is a 90% chance that the victim will see her attacker convicted. There is about one chance in three that he will plead guilty. If he does not, he is likely to waive his right to a jury trial. Because rectal intercourse was involved, there is a 77.8% chance that a judge will find him guilty (only a 23.5% likelihood of conviction in a jury trial, since there is no evidence of vaginal trauma). If convicted, he may go to prison but is more likely to receive probation. There is virtually no possibility that he will be sentenced to 2 or more years in prison.

In comparing the above two cases, one sees that the criminal justice response to the rape victim is not always consonant with her needs. The victim in case A will face relatively few adjustment problems. However, because the criminal justice system responds to traditional notions as to the relative seriousness of certain incident factors (for example, interracial rape), the offender in this case, if caught, is likely to be punished severely. The authors do not mean to suggest that a prison sentence in this case is unreasonable, or that certain rapes are not serious matters. However, how does one reconcile the criminal justice treatment of this case with it's treatment of case B? In the latter case, the victim is likely to face more severe difficulties over a much broader range of interpersonal and intrapsychic functioning. Nonetheless, she will find a far less sympathetic criminal justice system then did the victim in case A, in spite of the fact that the assailant's apprehension is virtually assured. If her case gets to court, she may see a conviction and even a prison sentence for the offender, but chances are great that her complaint will never make it out of the police station. The extent to which she has been traumatized is irrelevant—other factors, many of which have no bearing upon the validity of her complaint, will be considered instead.

Case C

The victim is 10 years old and lives with her mother, who is on welfare. Her mother is called away suddenly one evening, and asks an 18–year–old male neighbor to keep an eye on the victim for a few hours. He agrees and is subsequently joined at the victim's home by three other male neighbors, all of whom are known to the victim.

After becoming fairly intoxicated, the offenders attempt to rape the victim, threatening her with violence if she refuses to submit. When she continues to resist, she is brutally beaten by the offenders. She is forced to perform fellatio on her attackers and, over the course of 2 hours, is raped by all of them. She suffers vaginal trauma, as well as intense physical pain from the beating she receives.

Upon arriving home, her mother immediately calls the police. There is no policewoman present at the police interrogation of the victim. A social worker evaluates the account of the rape as credible, with no evidence of victim precipitation.

Analysis: Because the victim is only 10 years old, most adjustment problems are not likely to surface right away. There is almost a 50% chance that she will experience increased nightmares, but living with mother will lessen the extent of any such increase. Any increased fear of being home alone will also be mitigated by her mother's presence in the home. She is likely to experience an increased fear of being out on the street alone, and any increased negative feelings toward known men may be aggravated over time because she does not live with her father.

The police will apprehend the offenders and will almost certainly mark the case as founded. There is almost one chance in four that the case will result in a nonoffense charge. Because of the victim's socioeconomic status, it is unlikely that a lesser sex offense charge will be given.

There is a 90% chance that the offenders will be convicted if the case comes to trial. However, as the victim's mother is on welfare, there is about one chance in three that the case will not make it past the preliminary hearing. The offenders are not likely to plead guilty and, because of the victim's age, will almost certainly waive their right to jury trial. If they do so, there is a 77.8% chance that a judge will find them guilty, and a 64.3% chance that they will be sentenced to prison, although probably for less than 2 years.

This last case illustrates the difficulty in attempting to apply the research findings to a case involving a child victim. Although the hypothetical circumstances would have caused an enormous range of problems in an adult victim, a child victim appears to be almost immune to most short-term adjustment problems, even in the most extreme situations. The difficulties confronted by the clinician in treating child victims are obvious. Potential problem areas cannot be as readily identified as in the case of an adult victim. There are, however, two possibilities for utilizing the findings of this study in the treatment of child victims. One possibility is to examine the problems likely to confront a given victim if she were an adult and to proceed on the assumption that these are the problems most likely to confront the child victim when she eventually reaches adutlhood. However, the perspective from which the child victim views certain aspects of the rape (for example, sexual aspects) is likely to continue to color her reactions to it even as her perspective changes. Projected correlations may therefore prove to be somewhat inaccurate. A second possibility is to view any small increase in a particular problem over time as the tip of an iceberg that is yet to be fully revealed. Seemingly insignificant problems emerging over a year's time may be interpreted as the first signs of long–term adjustment patterns. This approach, however, fails to consider the likelihood of repression of the rape incident by the child victim with a consequent decrease in most adjustment problems 1 year after the rape. Clearly, much further study is needed to test the validity of these and other approaches to the treatment of child rape victims.

The authors hypothesize that adjustment problems and the criminal justice system's treatment of rape cases may be causally connected. Furthermore, this connection may exist in either direction. For example, a victim who finds herself accused by the police of precipitating the rape incident will probably have greater difficulty readjusting to living. Emotional support has been withheld from one likely source—can it be counted on from other sources? Accusations of victim precipitation coming from the victim's husband or family may have an especially devastating effect in combination with such insinuations from the police or the courts. On the other hand, a victim who finds that even people who know and love her have doubts as to the credibility of her rape account is likely to have second thoughts about seeking redress in a less partial forum. Any resulting lack of confidence in the strength of her case will probably have an adverse effect on her interactions with the criminal justice system (that is, police, judges, and juries may be less inclined to believe her).

The recurrence of certain findings throughout the analysis suggests the existence of several general principles regarding the aftermath of rape. The authors have identified four such themes:

1. It is the police who are most likely to determine the manner in which rape victims and cases are treated by the criminal justice system. The police are largely in control of whether a victim is believed, whether a case is sufficiently investigated and the offender apprehended, and whether the quality of the courtroom presentation is adequate to insure a reasonable possibility of conviction. The victim who is not believed by the police, or who does not otherwise receive their full cooperation for any number of reasons, is not likely to see her case brought to a successful outcome. If money is to be invested in the criminal justice system for the benefit of victims of rape, it should be focused first on the police's handling of rape complaints.

2. Rape hurts everyone. Traditional notions that the black and the poor are less affected by rape are simply not valid. In the adjustment correlations, variables relating to the race and socioeconomic status of the victim are conspicuous by their absence. However, the criminal justice handling of rape cases involving such victims is still likely to be characterized by less efficiency and less compassion than is found with white,

middle-class victims. Interviews taken by a representative of the Center for Rape Concern indicate that police personnel, as well as some judges, believe that poor, black women are less affected by sexual assault because they normally live in a violent environment. New legislation is unlikely to help the rape victim while such attitudes still permeate the criminal justice system.

3. Traditional notions as to the relative seriousness of certain types of rape have no basis in fact. Both the criminal justice system and the media appear to equate seriousness with brutal rapes, interracial rapes, and rapes with more than one offender. None of these generalizations is, in fact, correct. On the basis of the research findings, one could reasonably conjecture that certain types of so-called nonbrutal rapes will cause even more serious problems than some brutal rapes. Similarly, interracial rapes do not characteristically result in more serious adjustment problems, nor do group rapes. The amount of violence in a rape incident is only one factor to be considered in assessing the difficulties likely to confront the victim. From the standpoint of postrape adjustment, a victim who is unable to mentally segregate the rape from her everyday world will have serious, often long-term, problems. And, this inability is most likely to result from cases in which the degree of rape violence or brutality involved is relatively low.

4. Victims are blamed for their victimization. They are blamed by the police, who may unilaterally decide that particular cases ought not even to be heard by a judge or jury; they are blamed by the courts, which consider victim precipitation to be a more reliable indicator of guilt or innocence than is victim credibility; and they are blamed by their husbands, boyfriends, and families, who seize on ambiguous elements of the rape to relieve their own feelings of guilt. Adjustment problems associated with relatively nonbrutal rapes, marking the rape complaints as unfounded or other difficulties experienced by the victim in her interactions with the police, poor treatment by the courts, and the unfavorable outcome of cases lacking clear evidence of physical brutality—all can be traced, to a large extent, to the issue of victim blame.

Conclusion

The study undertaken by the Center for Rape Concern was not intended to be used solely in the preparation of this book. The identification of significant correlations between victim and incident factors, on the one hand, and adjustment problems and the criminal justice system response, on the other, was envisioned as the basis for a new, more individualized approach to the counseling of rape victims. In fact, social workers and psychiatrists at the Center for Rape Concern have already incorporated the findings of this study into their own counseling techniques. Detailed profiles of the victim and the incident can provide a starting point for the exploration of specific rape–related difficulties in each case. Problems that are likely to emerge can be discussed with the victim, who is then assured that such reactions to rape are natural and have been exhibited by other victims under similar circumstances. It is hoped that accelerated awareness and treatment of adjustment problems will, in turn, accelerate the process by which normal activities and interactions are reestablished following a rape. Whereas it is still too soon to assess the actual impact of using these findings in a clinical setting, the authors suggest that this possibility ought to be carefully considered by others.

Index

Index

About the Authors

Thomas W. McCahill received the M.A. degree from the University of Edinburgh, Scotland. He is president of the ECTA Corporation, a Philadelphia-based consulting firm specializing in evaluation, computer support, and technical assistance to criminal justice and health services agencies. He is also a lecturer for Temple University's Center for the Administration of Justice, where he teaches courses in sex crimes and the law; crisis intervention: rape; and drug abuse. Mr. McCahill is currently a core team member of a national evaluation of probation, project director of a number of technical assistance and evaluation projects, and research associate for a 10-year follow-up study of probationed sex offenders.

Linda C. Meyer received the Ph.D. from the University of Pennsylvania, Center for Studies in Criminology and Criminal Law, Philadelphia, Pennsylvania, where she studied under an NIMH traineeship. She is associate director of research and evaluation at the Joseph J. Peters Institute (formerly the Center for Rape Concern), where she is responsible for the research, training, and educational programs. Dr. Meyer was the research director for the "Philadelphia Assault Victim Study." She has evaluated the effectiveness of correctional programs and is currently project director of a 10-year follow-up study of sex offender recidivism.

Arthur M. Fischman is a member of the Pennsylvania Bar, having received the Juris Doctor degree from the Temple University School of Law. He is general counsel for the ECTA Corporation, and has been a core team member of most of that firm's evaluation and technical assistance projects, including a follow-up study of probationed sex offenders and a feasibility study of outpatient group psychotherapy for probationed juvenile sex offenders. He is part of a team that is currently conducting a national probation evaluation.